Edgar Degas
Masterpieces of Art

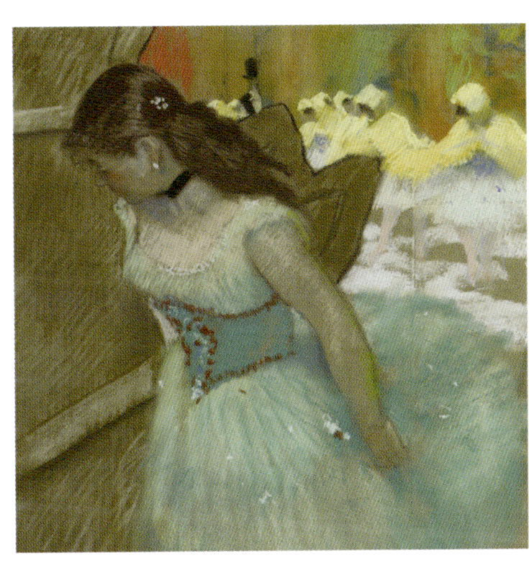

Publisher and Creative Director: Nick Wells
Commissioning Editor: Polly Prior
Senior Project Editors: Catherine Taylor and Laura Bulbeck
Picture Research: Gillian Whitaker
Art Director: Mike Spender
Layout Design: Jane Ashley
Digital Design and Production: Chris Herbert

FLAME TREE PUBLISHING
6 Melbray Mews
Fulham, London SW6 3NS
United Kingdom

www.flametreepublishing.com

First published 2016

18 20 19 17
3 5 7 9 10 8 6 4 2

A CIP record for this book is available from the British Library upon request.

Image Credits: © **Artothek:** 35 and the following: 40 Fine Art Images. Courtesy **Bridgeman Images** and the following: 1 & 46, 25t & 48 Sterling and Francine Clark Art Institute, Williamstown, Massachusetts, USA; 3 & 122, 4 & 110, 6t & 100, 9t & 102, 13t & 68–69, 16 & 84–85, 18 & 31, 19b & 37, 26 & 78, 30, 33, 34, 38, 39, 83, 89, 98–99 & 118, 113, 121, 124 Musee d'Orsay, Paris, France; 6 b & 63, 65, 116 Private Collection/Photo © Lefevre Fine Art Ltd., London; 7 b & 94 Burrell Collection, Glasgow, Scotland/© Culture and Sport Glasgow (Museums); 7 t & 72–73, 10b & 107, 44–45, 86 National Gallery of Art, Washington DC, USA; 8 & 101 Birmingham Museums and Art Gallery; 9 b & 103, 12 & 49, 80–81 National Gallery, London, UK; 11 & 66–67 & 70 Philadelphia Museum of Art, Pennsylvania, PA, USA/The Henry P. McIlhenny Collection in Memory of Frances/P. McIlhenny, 1986; 13 b & 108 Musee Marmottan Monet, Paris, France; 14 & 111 Musee des Beaux-Arts, Pau, France; 15 & 32, 42, 47 Metropolitan Museum of Art, New York, USA; 17 b & 57 Philadelphia Museum of Art, Pennsylvania, PA, USA/John G. Johnson Collection, 1917; 17 t & 41, 23t & 125, 23b & 112, 36, 50, 60, 74, 117, 119, 120 Private Collection; 19 t & 82 Musee des Beaux-Arts, Lyon, France; 20 b & 95 The Art Institute of Chicago, IL, USA; 20 t & 75, 22 & 90, 51, 53, 56, 59, 76, 79, 88 Private Collection/Photo © Christie's Images; 21 & 115, 25b & 52 Private Collection/Peter Willi; 24 & 61 Art Gallery and Museum, Kelvingrove, Glasgow, Scotland; 27 & 93 Museo Thyssen-Bornemisza, Madrid, Spain/De Agostini Picture Library/G. Nimatallah; 28 –29 & 54–55 Private Collection/De Agostini Picture Library; 43 © Samuel Courtauld Trust, The Courtauld Gallery, London, UK; 62 The Phillips Collection, Washington, D.C., USA/Acquired 1944; 64 Louvre, Paris, France; 77 State Hermitage Museum, St. Petersburg, Russia; 87 Fogg Art Museum, Harvard Art Museums, USA/Bequest from the Collection of Maurice Wertheim, Class 1906; 91 Art Gallery of Ontario, Toronto, Canada/Gift of R.W. Finlayson, 1969; Donated by the Ontario Heritage Foundation, 1988; 92 Yale University Art Gallery, New Haven, CT, USA; 97 National Gallery, London, UK/De Agostini Picture Library; 105 Metropolitan Museum of Art, New York, USA/De Agostini Picture Library; 106 Municipal Museum of Art, Kitakyushu, Japan; 109 Minneapolis Institute of Arts, MN, USA/The John R. Van Derlip Fund; 114 Glasgow Art Gallery and Museum, Scotland/ De Agostini Picture Library; 123 Private Collection/Photo © Peter Nahum at The Leicester Galleries, London. Courtesy **SuperStock** and the following: 10t & 104 ACME Imagery; 58 Buyenlarge; 71 Photoservice Electa/Universal Images Group; 96 Peter Willi.

ISBN 978-1-78361-994-8

Printed in China | Created, Developed & Produced in the United Kingdom

Edgar Degas
Masterpieces of Art

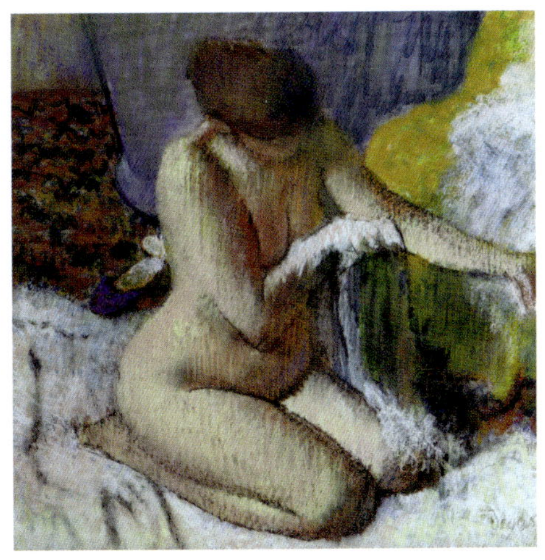

Michael Robinson

FLAME TREE
PUBLISHING

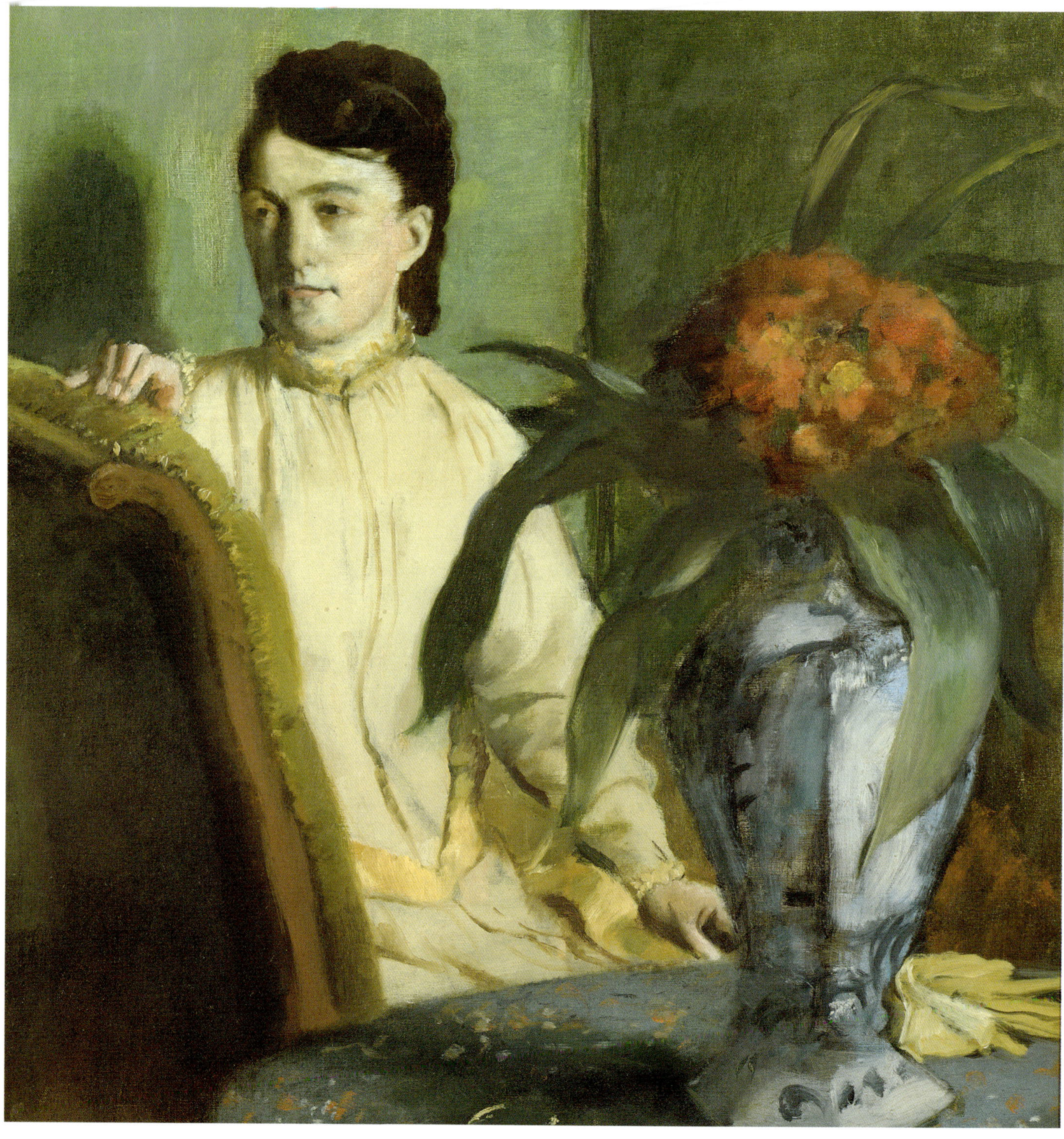

Contents

Edgar Degas: An Alternative Realist

Edgar Degas (1834–1917) does not easily conform to a particular movement in art. Although he participated in all but one of the so-called French Impressionist exhibitions between 1874 and 1886, he cannot be readily placed in that group. His style, choice of medium and subject matter were rather more diverse. Degas actually despised the term Impressionist, due to its somewhat pejorative origins, seeing himself as a 'Realist painter'. Like his near contemporary Edouard Manet (1833–83), Degas should be seen as one of the founders of a modernist tradition, bridging the gap between traditional Salon (academic) art and the early radical movement of the late nineteenth century.

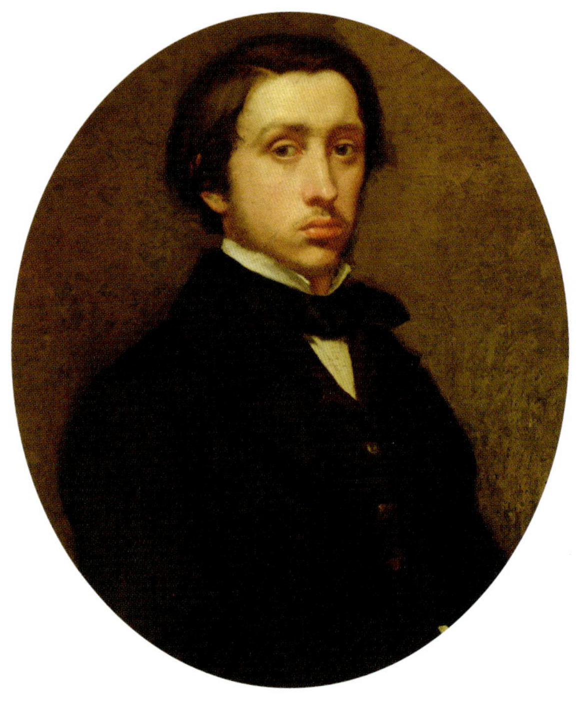

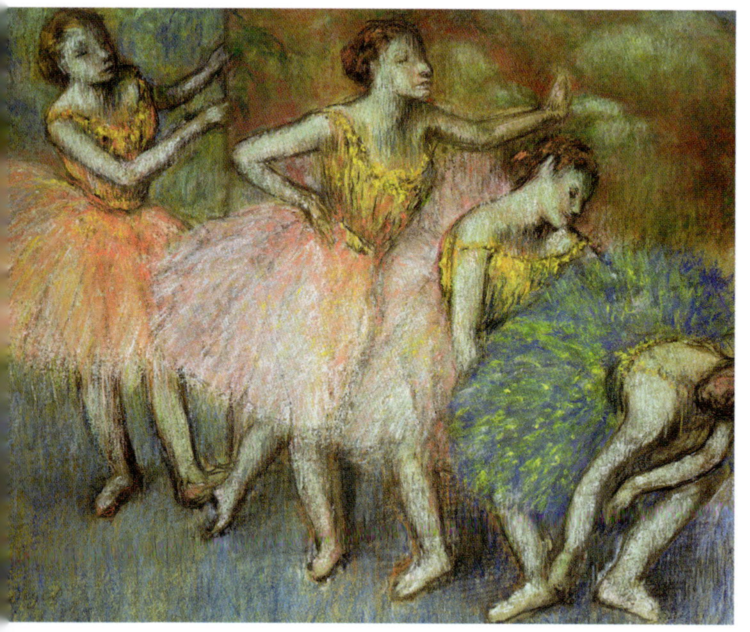

Historical Context

France underwent many political and social changes during the nineteenth century. Louis Philippe (1773–1850), a liberal constitutional monarch, was ruling France at the time of Degas' birth in 1834. He was styled as 'King of the French' rather than king of France, in order to avoid the fate of the *Ancien Régime* of 40 years earlier. Louis Philippe was a popular ruler among the bourgeoisie, but became increasingly disconnected from ordinary working-class people, which eventually led to a revolution and his abdication in 1848.

Between 1848 and 1870, France was ruled by Louis-Napoléon Bonaparte (1808–73), the first elected president of the French Republic. However, three years later he proclaimed himself Emperor Napoleon III, as his more famous uncle Napoleon Bonaparte had

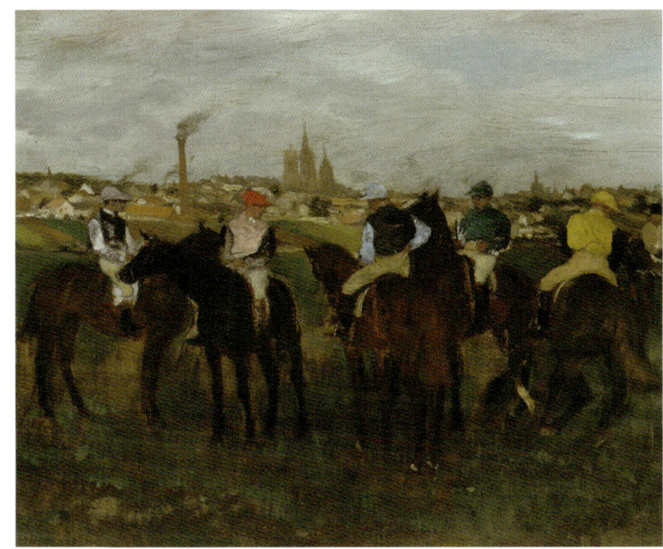

The Salon was an annual government-sponsored art exhibition in Paris, which effectively maintained the prestige of the Académie des Beaux-Arts and its predominant academic style of painting and sculpture. To maintain this standard, the selection of works was determined by a jury made up of academic artists, who regularly rejected works that in their opinion did not meet such standards.

It was the discriminatory attitude of the Salon jury that caused writers such as Baudelaire to write disparagingly about the existing system. Despite this, several of the so-called Impressionist artists submitted work to the Salon early in their careers, since at the time it was their only available exhibiting option. Needless to say, the jury rejected most of their work.

done nearly 50 years earlier. It was during these years of the Second Empire that the modernization of Paris began, under the control of the city's prefect Baron Haussmann (1809–91).

Beginning in 1854, the following two decades saw the wholesale destruction of old buildings and narrow streets to make way for wide boulevards, shops, cafés and apartment blocks for the burgeoning bourgeoisie. The centre of Paris one sees today is largely the work of Baron Haussmann's imaginative transformation of a medieval city into a modern metropolis. Additionally, his designs were to incorporate the new railway termini that linked the city to the new suburbs, created as a result of the displacement of the old city's inhabitants. These same suburbs, mostly along the River Seine, such as Argenteuil, also provided the scene for leisure activities at the weekends.

These changes and their impact on Parisian society are well documented by the artists of the time, including Degas, who sought to capture the essence of a modern city at all levels of society. These artists were responding to essays by the writer and critic Charles Baudelaire (1821–67). His first reference to the need for artists to paint 'the heroism of modern life', instead of the outdated historical narratives endlessly portrayed by the Salon artists, was in 1846, and most notably in an essay called *The Painter of Modern Life*, published in 1863.

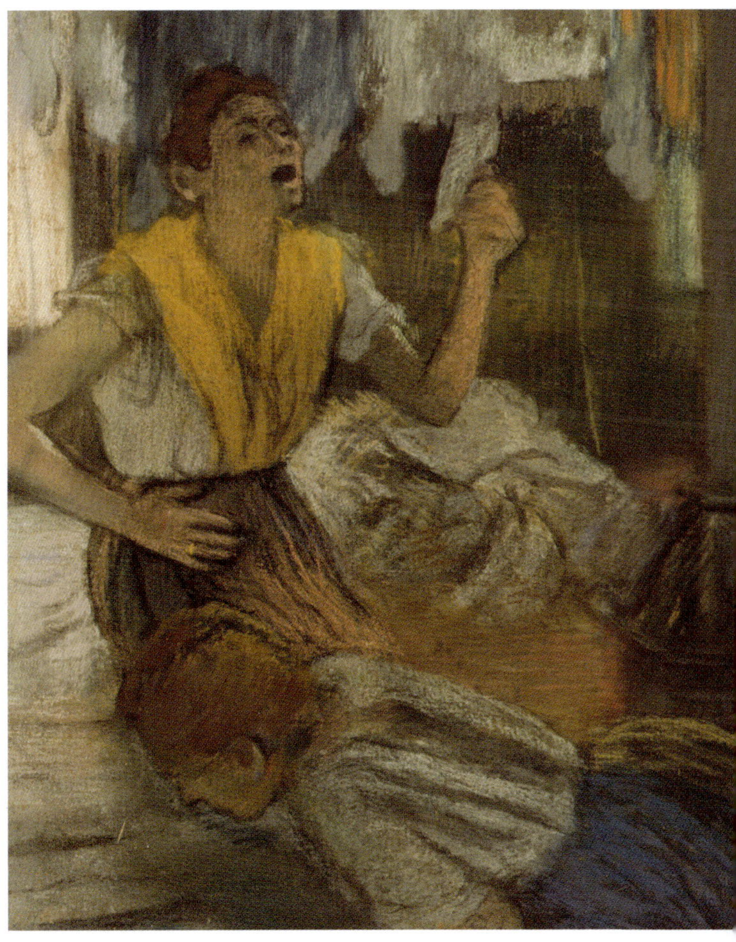

Early Life

Hilaire-Germain-Edgar de Gas (he changed his name to Degas later in his career) was born in Paris on 19 July 1834 into a wealthy French banking family. His father was the manager of a branch of the family's bank, and his mother was of French-Creole descent, her family coming from New Orleans. She died when Edgar was only 13 years old, a loss that was to affect him for many years to come. His father was a very cultured man, who enjoyed music and the theatre, actively encouraging his son to pursue his artistic interests, in particular portraiture.

Degas attended the Lyc 'ee Louis-le-Grand for his formal education between 1845 and 1852, before setting up his own studio in the family home under the tutelage of the academic artist Félix-Joseph Barrias (1822–1907). Much of this time was spent at the Louvre, copying the Old Masters, including Rembrandt and Goya as well as French artists of the Romantic period, such as Eugène Delacroix (1798–1863). By 1854 he had enrolled in the studio of the artist Louis Lamothe (1822–69), a disciple of the great Neoclassical painter Jean-Auguste-Dominique Ingres (1780–1867). From this period of study he learned a healthy respect for the Italian Renaissance Masters.

In 1855 Degas met the then aging Ingres, who advised him to 'draw lines, young man, many lines, from memory or from nature; it is in this way that you will become a good artist'. A brief period of study at the École des Beaux-Arts in the same year added nothing to his knowledge, and he decided instead to spend the next few years studying the Renaissance in its original setting, Italy.

Travels to Italy

In July 1856 Degas travelled to Italy, where he remained for the next three years. In Naples, where the family's banking firm was based, he stayed with his paternal grandfather, René Hilaire, and uncles. He also stayed with his aunt Rosa Morbilli. Naples was a thriving artistic hub at this time, not just for art but also music. Degas visited the Teatro di San Carlo, one of the greatest opera venues in Europe. (It is worth remembering that the Palais Garnier in Paris had not yet been built

after fire destroyed its predecessor Le Salle de Peletier in 1873.) He also of course visited museums and galleries, copying the Old Masters, following his father's advice and concentrating in particular on portraits.

The following year he travelled to Rome, where he met fellow artist Gustave Moreau (1826–98). Both artists visited the Villa Medici, which was part of the French Academy. Here artists were able to study the Old Masters, including the winners, such as Ingres, of the much-coveted Prix de Rome. An early surviving work by Degas from this period is *A Roman Beggar Woman* from 1857 (*see* below and page 101). The draughtsmanship is clearly indebted to Ingres, but unlike the Master, Degas has observed and portrayed the woman quite dispassionately, a key feature of the modern idiom in painting in the latter part of the nineteenth century.

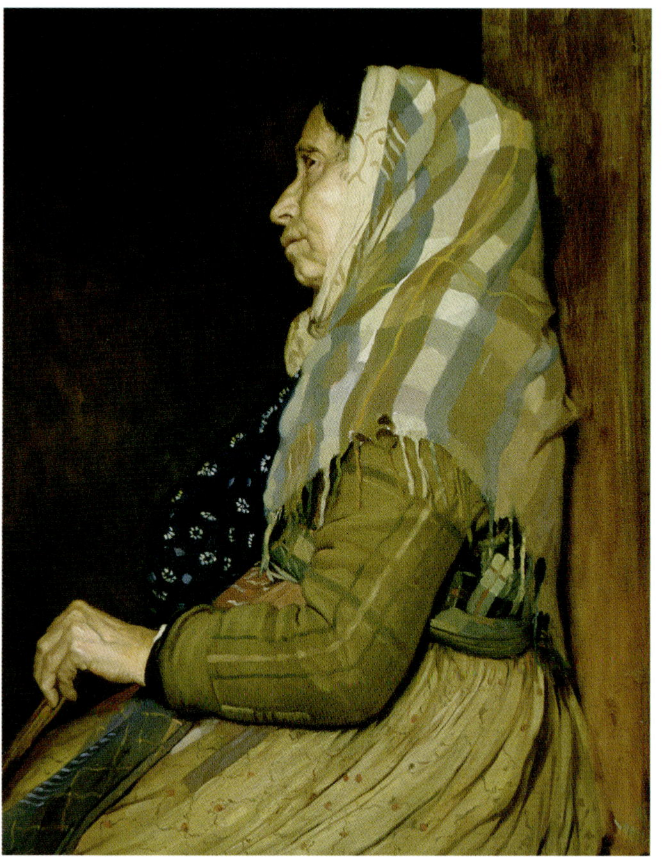

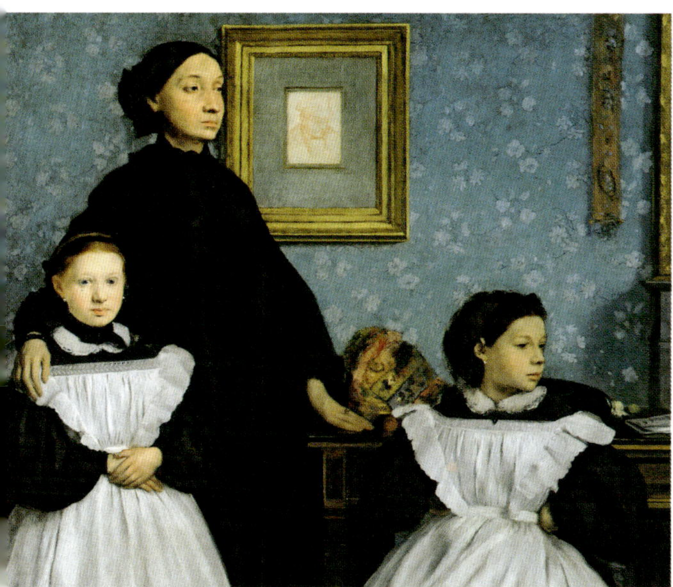

From Rome, Degas continued on to Florence via Assisi, where he encountered the works of Giotto (1266/67–1337), which made a lasting impression on him. In Florence he stayed with his aunt Laura, who was married to Baron Gennaro Bellelli (1812–64). It was during his stay here, as a first-hand witness to their unhappy marriage, that he made a series of preparatory sketches that would result in one of his most famous portraits, *The Bellelli Family* (1858–67) (*see* above and page 102). It is an immensely ambitious work that is both traditional and modern. There is a real sense of isolation and distance in the family grouping, particularly since the Baron has his back to the viewer and is separated physically from his wife and daughters. The Baroness is dressed in black, possibly in mourning for her late father, whose portrait is on the wall behind her.

Her poise and that of her daughter on the left are redolent of the mannerist style of the Florentine artist Bronzino (1503–72). This is counterbalanced by the almost casual and indifferent look of her husband that creates a sense of tension in the group. The focus of the painting is the other daughter, who makes the link between the two, adopting the formality of the dress like her sister, but glancing towards her father while awkwardly sitting on one leg. Originally exhibited at the Salon of 1867 under the title *The Family*, it is a tour de force of the modern human condition in bourgeois society, and marks an

evolutionary moment in mid-nineteenth-century portraiture, despite the fact it made little impression on the Salon critics.

Return to Paris – History Paintings

Degas returned to Paris in 1859. At this time in his career, like his contemporary Manet, Degas began painting historical narratives for exhibition at the Salon, while continuing with portraiture. Some of these paintings were exhibited at the Salon, but garnered Degas no recognition.

An example of his historical-style narratives is *Young Spartans Exercising* from *c.* 1860 (*see* page 103), based on a Greco-Roman story by Plutarch (AD 46–120) called *Life of Lycurgus*, in which Spartan girls are challenging their male counterparts to a fight. In Ingres' hands these protagonists would have been idealized in a Classical academic tradition. Despite the obvious references to a historical narrative and composition, the figures as depicted by Degas are more in keeping with contemporary young Parisians, emphasizing the awkwardness of their youthful poses at such a tender and impressionable age. This may have been the reason the painting was not shown at the Salon and remained in the artist's studio until his death, although it was reworked during this period.

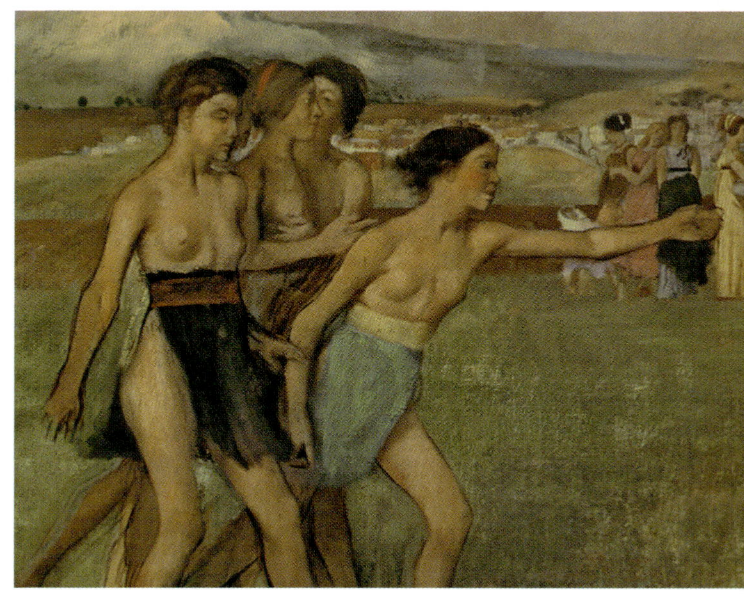

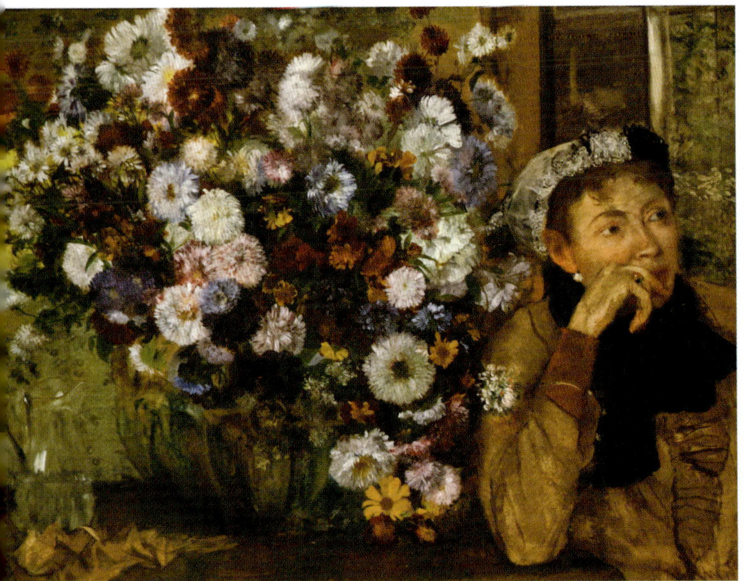

Return to Paris – Portraiture

Despite the lack of recognition by the critics at the Salon in the 1850s and early 1860s, Degas continued with portraiture. His own self-assured pose in *Self Portrait* from 1855 is a testimony to his confidence as a portrait artist. Combining aspects of the Old Masters with a contemporary theme, Degas began to assert his own style in much the same way he had with *The Bellelli Family* portrait.

A Woman Seated Beside a Vase of Flowers (1865, *see* above and page 104) is a portrait of Mme Valpinçon, with whose family Degas was staying in Normandy during 1860. It was the father of his lifelong friend Paul Valpinçon (1834–94) who had encouraged Degas to look at Ingres. The family owned Ingres' so-called *Valpinçon Bather* painting, a gift from the artist. Mme Valpinçon's pose is similar to that adopted by the subjects in Ingres' portraits, except that Degas has placed her at the edge of the picture plane. In this 'modern' take of a traditional pose, we, the viewers, are admitted into the artist's space to share this moment. The picture is almost totally dominated by the vase of flowers, which has all the hallmarks of a Delacroix painting, and yet our eyes are unable to rest and contemplate them because of the figure. Such is the modern condition espoused by contemporary writers such as Baudelaire, who suggested that art should be a fusion of the transient with the immutable.

Japonisme

Another influence on Degas and several other artists at this time was the introduction of *ukiyo-e* prints from Japan. These became very popular in the West following the reopening of trade barriers after a gap of over 200 years. Japanese motifs manifested themselves in a number of paintings and designed objects both in Paris and London. In the *c.* 1871 *Portrait of Mlle Hortense Valpinçon* (*see* page 109), these motifs are clearly seen on the lacquered cabinet in the foreground. Similarly, Degas' portrait of his fellow artist and friend James Tissot (1836–1902) also uses these motifs, most notably in the large picture at the top. Tissot was a client of the store La Porte Chinoise, which opened on the Rue de Rivoli, one of Paris's most fashionable streets, in 1862.

A more overt use of *Japonisme* appears in Degas' *Madame Camus* from 1869–70 (*see* below and page 107). She was a collector of Japanese objects and is seen in this picture holding one of her fans.

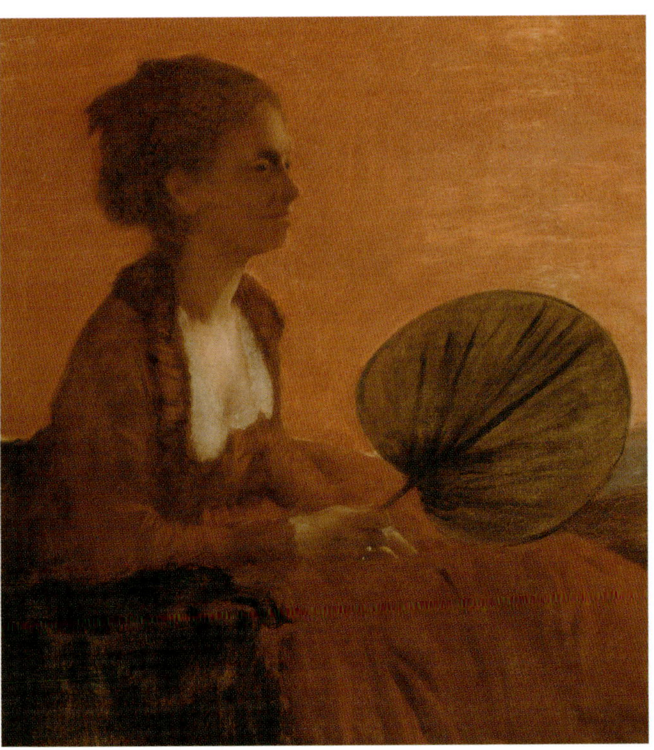

Degas as *Flâneur*

Based mainly on the writings of Charles Baudelaire in the 1860s, the *flâneur* was a 'gentleman stroller of city streets', a key figure in Paris, an observer of modern life, an anonymous man of the crowd, who revels in its 'immense reservoir of electrical energy'. In his 1863 essay *The Painter of Modern Life*, Baudelaire called upon artists to become *flâneurs* and record the modernity of Parisian life.

The best exemplars of this mode of pictorial representation were Manet and Degas, who met in 1862. Manet had gathered a small group of artists and writers, who usually met twice a week at the Café Guerbois. The Batignolles Group, as they became known, exchanged ideas and philosophies pertinent to their modern era.

One of the group was the writer and critic Louis Edmond Duranty (1833–80, *see* page 114), a passionate advocate of Realism in art who became a close friend of Degas. It was also here that he met the artists who would become known after 1874 as the Impressionists. The discussions at the café were to inform the art of this group regarding modern subjects.

A number of paintings from this time, and subsequently, demonstrate Degas as the *flâneur*, an observer of life, at all different levels of society. Perhaps the two most notable are *The Absinthe* from *c.* 1875–76 (*see* page 78) and *Place de la Concorde* of 1875 (*see* page 77). The latter very much sums up the role of the *flâneur*, seeking out the transience of modern life and recording it for posterity. The main protagonist is Baron Lepic (1839–89), strolling across the Place de la Concorde with his two daughters and dog. Lepic is indifferent to all around him, while the viewer on the left (perhaps a *flâneur* himself) observes. The emptiness of the square behind Lepic adds to the sense that this is a transitory moment.

Possibly the darkest of the images Degas produced as *flâneur* is *Interior* from 1868–69 (*see* above right and page 70). Much has been written about this mysterious painting, although Degas refused to discuss its meaning. There is a palpable tension in the room between the man and the woman, highlighted by the brooding atmosphere created by the fire

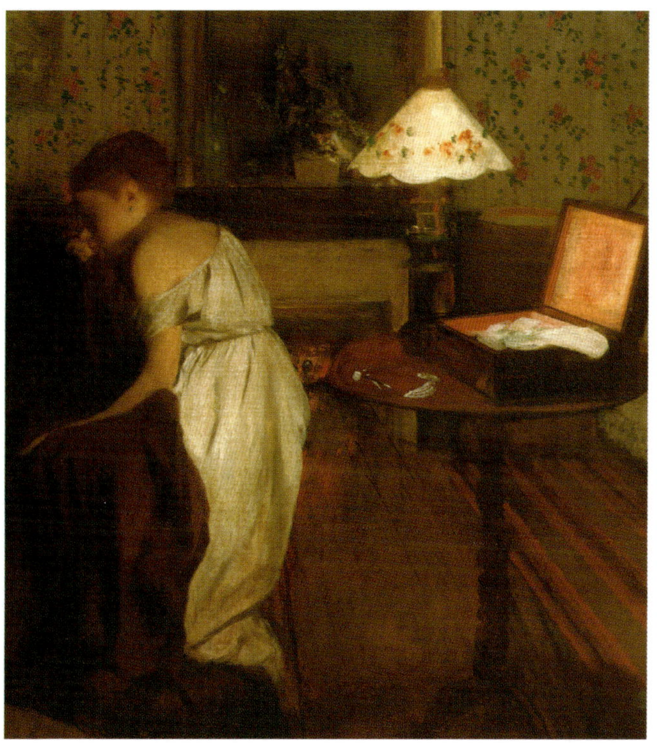

and lamp, and the unusual perspective. The painting is often also referred to as *The Rape*, mainly because of the presence of a corset on the floor and the woman's general demeanour. There have been several attempts by historians to fix the narrative of this painting to contemporary literature, but none is totally convincing.

Artistic Techniques and Styles

Unlike many of the Batignolles Group, Degas did not paint *en plein air* (meaning outdoors or 'in full air'), but made sketches to be used for paintings executed in his studio. Firstly, he was a traditionalist, allied more to the Realist mode of painting, and secondly, he was unable to tolerate being in direct sunlight for too long due to an eye condition.

His subject matter too was at odds with most of the Batignolles Group. Unlike Claude Monet (1840–1926) or Alfred Sisley (1839–99), he was not interested in capturing the fleeting transience of light in a landscape with a brush. His subject matter was urban life rather than the cityscapes rendered by Camille Pissarro (1830–1903). Despite the bold

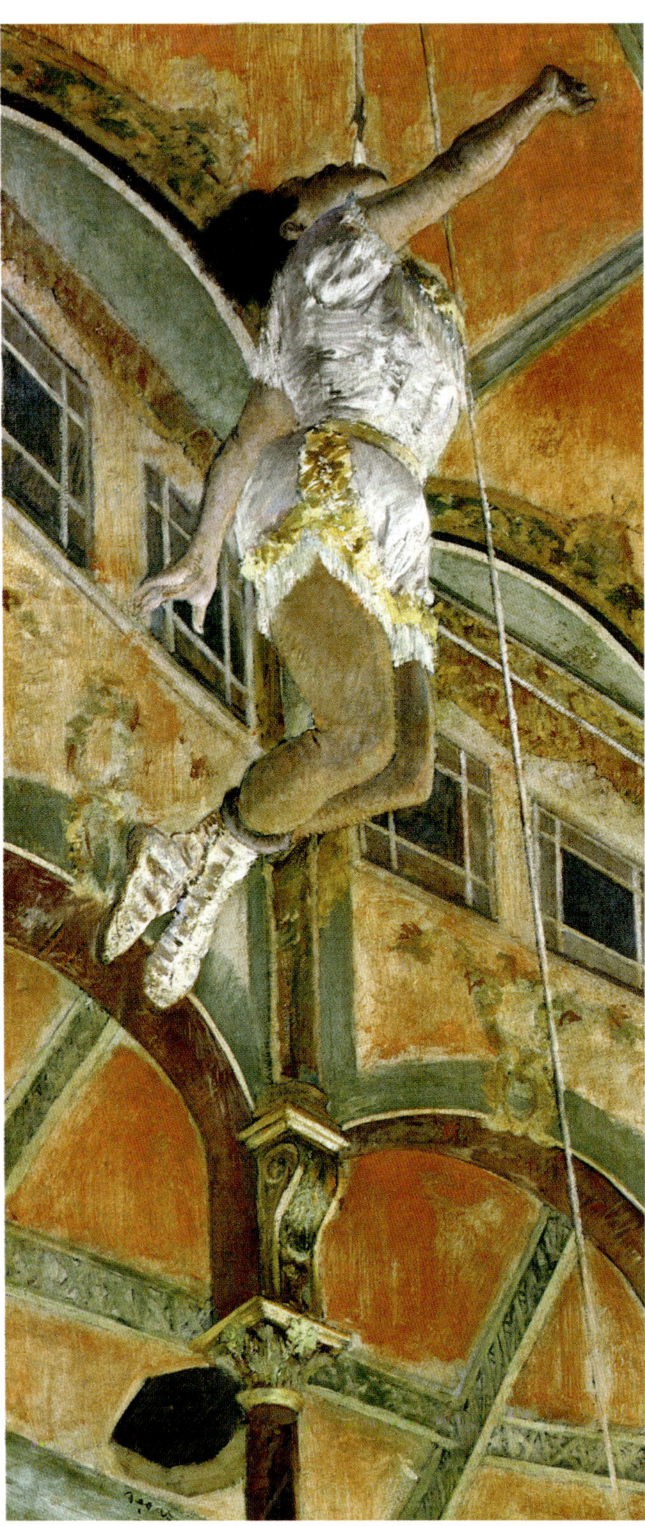

strokes used and the immediacy of the effect, Degas' paintings were well planned and executed indoors. He also explored a number of different techniques of painting, both in medium and background surface.

Up to this point Degas had worked exclusively in oil on canvas for his finished paintings, in keeping with academic tradition, in order that they could be submitted to the official Salon for exhibition. The preliminary drawings for these works were executed in pencil, charcoal and occasionally pastel. By the mid-1870s, although continuing to use oil for some paintings, Degas began using pastel and monotypes for finished works.

The monotype is a seventeenth-century technique that involves drawing an image on a smooth surface with paint (or ink) and transferring that image on to a sheet of paper, which can then be enhanced in a number of different ways, for example by over-painting in colour. *Café Concert at Les Ambassadeurs* from 1876–77 is a prime example of this technique (*see* page 82).

Degas also used photographic images as reference for his paintings. He became interested in the movement of horses and people after seeing the work of photographer Eadweard Muybridge (1830–1904), who had demonstrated the pioneering technique of photographing motion. Thereafter artists were able to accurately record the movement of horses, for example, in a more realistic manner.

Another aspect of Degas' *oeuvre* was his use of perspective and oblique angles for dramatic effect. An early example is *Portrait of Painter Tissot* executed in 1867–68 (*see* page 105). There is a carefree elegance to the artist's pose, the angle of the posture mirroring the easel and canvas on the right. Like Manet, Degas used the cut-off technique in many of his paintings, such as in *The Opera Orchestra* (*see* page 30), where the heads of the dancers have been severed so that the viewer is only looking at the orchestra. The use of a bar in the foreground separates the viewer from the orchestra, another device common to Degas' compositions. Perhaps the most awkward and yet alluring composition by Degas is *Miss La La at the Cirque Fernando* (*see* left and page 49), where the viewer is forced to look upwards in much the same way as the audience would have been.

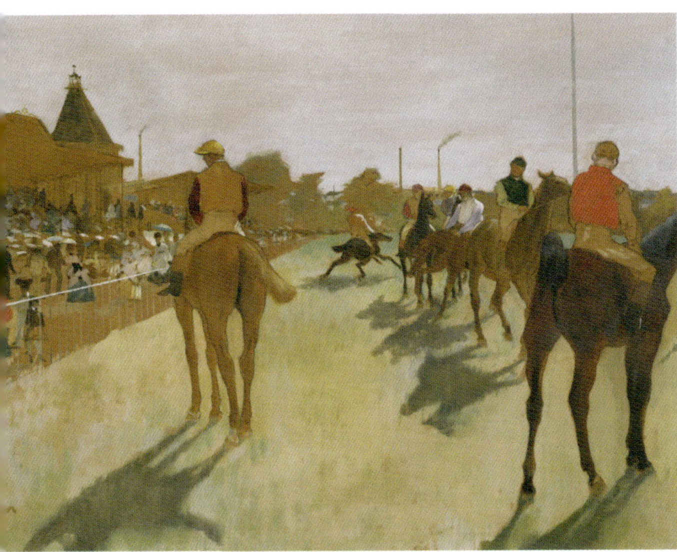

Horse Racing as a Subject

The Longchamp racecourse was opened in 1857 in the Bois de
Boulogne on the edge of Paris, becoming an instant attraction for the
French bourgeoisie and an ideal location for the *flâneur*. Unlike many
other artists, Degas preferred to paint off-guard scenes of the jockeys
and racehorses in preparation for the race rather than the race itself.
His aristocratic background and association with the haute-bourgeoisie
enabled him to gain access to restricted areas of the equine world both
on and off the course. He made copious notes in his sketchbooks of the
horses and jockeys, working them up later as full pictures in his studio.
It is probable that Degas' interest in horses began at the stud owned by
the Valpinçon family at Le Ménil-Hubert in Normandy where he used to
stay. It is known that he studied the horses there, since his sketchbooks
of the time are full of anatomical equine drawings. It is also known that
he studied equine forms at the studio of his friend Joseph Cuvelier
(1833–70), a sculptor who specialized in modelling horses.

In *Racehorses in Front of the Stands*, c. 1866–68, the tension before
the race is palpable in the picture, Degas emphasizing this by showing
one of the horses bolting in the mid-distance (*see* above and page 68).
Like those race-goers to the left of the picture, Degas is a 'man of the
crowd'. The artist reminds the viewer that this is a modern picture with
the inclusion of an industrial landscape in the background.

The Race Course – Amateur Jockeys Near a Carriage (*c*. 1876–87, *see*
page 83), is less about the races than a study of Parisian society. The
railway in the background provides a clue to the picture's modernity,
but we can fairly precisely date the image by the fashionably dressed
lady to the right, in the carriage. Using the techniques developed
by Muybridge on the photographic study of horses in motion, Degas
depicts more accurately the horse on the left being pulled up by the
jockey, after appearing to be racing against the train.

Franco-Prussian War and New Orleans

The French government declared war on Prussia in September 1870,
believing that they would defeat the Prussians in a dispute over territories.
In the event, it was the Prussians who were victorious, which led to
the resignation of Emperor Napoleon III, the beginning of the Third
Republic in France and the unification of the German states in 1871.
Degas volunteered to serve in the infantry, where it was first identified
that he had a problem with his eyesight. During his time in the army he
was under the command of his friend and fellow student Henri Rouart
(1833–1912, *see* below and page 108). Rouart was an industrialist, but
also a keen painter in the Impressionist style and an art collector. He was
the subject of a portrait by Degas in front of his factory after the war.

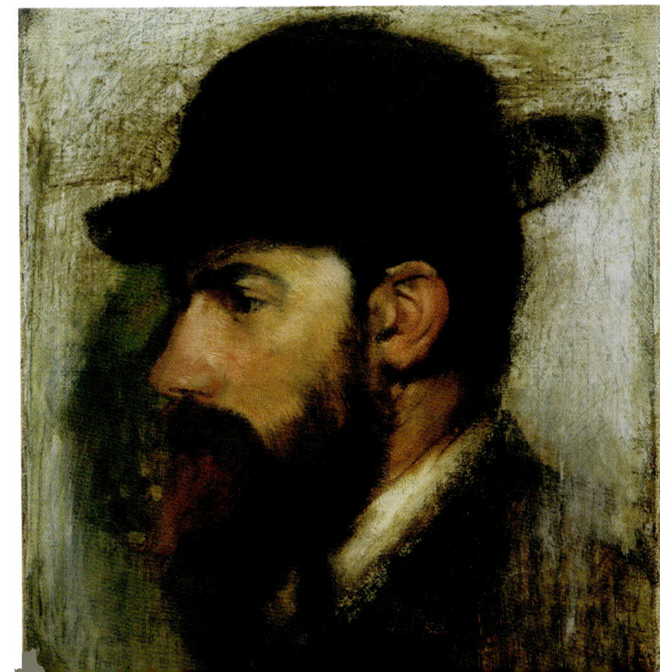

Following France's spectacular defeat and the collapse of the Second Empire, the city of Paris was under siege in the spring of 1871. Known as the Paris Commune, and lasting a little over two months, French forces were engaged in a battle with the so-called Communards, republicans who were fearful of a return to monarchical rule in the wake of the defeat. At this time Paris had a population of two million people and over 20,000 of them were killed by the French regular army, which also lost over 700 of its men. After the conflict ended, tens of thousands of arrests were made, with many of the main protagonists being deported. Another casualty of the Paris Commune was a number of key buildings destroyed by arsonists, including the Palais de Tuileries, a huge royal palace that had been in existence since the sixteenth century.

During this turbulent time, and for several months thereafter, many writers and artists sought refuge abroad. Claude Monet, Camille Pissarro and Alfred Sisley sought refuge in London, while Degas went to New Orleans.

He travelled with his brother René via London and New York, and stayed with his maternal uncle Michel Musson, a successful businessman in the cotton industry. Degas executed the painting *The Cotton Exchange, New Orleans* in 1873 (*see* below left and page 111) before leaving for Paris that year. In the picture, M. Musson is seen in the foreground inspecting the cotton quality and René is seen reading a newspaper. This picture became Degas' first work to be purchased for display in a museum.

Return to Paris and a New Venture

When Degas returned to Paris in 1873 the family's bank was failing and he learned that his brother René had amassed enormous business debts. In the following year their father died, and to save the family's reputation Degas sold his house and a large art collection to pay off his brother's debts. He was now, for the first time, dependent on the sale of his paintings for a living. Degas also found little had changed in the attitude of the Salon and the critics, who were still vociferously supporting the traditional academic style.

In December 1873 the Batignolles Group of artists that included Monet, Pissarro, Sisley and of course Degas, registered themselves as the Société Anonyme Coopérative des Artistes Peintres, Sculpteurs, Graveurs (Cooperative and Anonymous Association of Painters, Sculptors and Engravers) to facilitate the exhibition of their work, independent of the Salon. Their ranks were joined by Pierre-Auguste Renoir (1841–1919) and Berthe Morisot (1841–95).

Their first exhibition took place in April 1874 at the former studio of the society photographer Nadar (1820–1910), in the very fashionable Boulevard des Capucines. Noticeable by his absence was Manet, who, despite supporting their efforts, continued to seek recognition through the official Salon rather than the exhibitions organized by the Batignolles Group, a position that he maintained for the rest of his career.

Degas submitted 10 pictures to the exhibition, including *Ballet Rehearsal on Stage*, 1874 (*see* page 34). The critics were scathing about the exhibition, including Louis Leroy (1812–85), who castigated the group and in particular Monet, who had submitted a work entitled

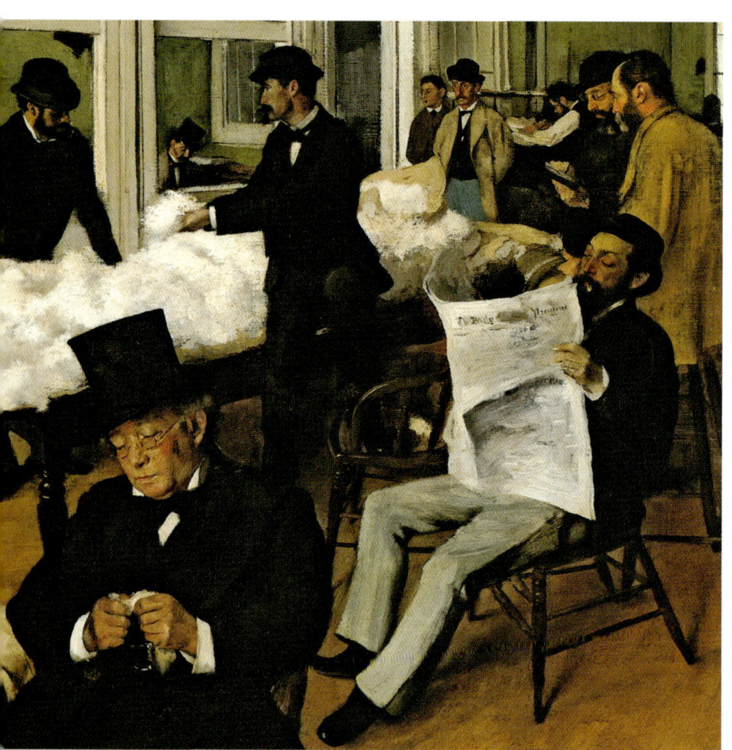

Impression, Sunrise, suggesting that the term 'Impression' should be used pejoratively, since it did not conform to academic standards. In so naming this style of painting, Leroy gave a tag to the group, which still survives today. Degas was not lambasted to the same degree and was the only one of the group to make a sale. He sold *The Dance Class* (1873–74, *see* right and page 32) to the musician Jean-Baptiste Faure (1830–1914).

In total there were eight Impressionist exhibitions between 1874 and 1886, Degas participating in all but one of them. 'Impressionist' was a term adopted by the group after 1877, although Degas refused to be accepted within that category, referring to himself as a 'Realist' painter.

Paul Durand-Ruel

During the 1870s, Degas began to lose interest in horse racing as a subject, preferring instead to cultivate a series of pictures of dancers. This may well have been a purely pragmatic decision, since his family's fortunes had waned and he was in need of money. He established a good working relationship with the art dealer Paul Durand Ruel (1831–1922), who was also actively supporting other artists within the Batignolles Group. Degas referred to his dancer pictures as 'my merchandise', suggesting that he thought of them in commercial terms, as did Durand-Ruel, who found a good market for them

It was during the Franco-Prussian War that Durand Ruel left Paris, opening a gallery in London to show the work of the Society of French Artists. It was there that he met Monet and Pissarro. On returning to Paris he began collecting and supporting the work of the Impressionists. Until that time he was a dealer in the works of the Barbizon School of paintings, which included Charles-François Daubigny (1817–78) and Jean-Baptiste-Camille Corot (1796–1875), often seen as the precursors to Impressionism.

Duranty and La Nouvelle Peinture

The second Impressionist exhibition in March and April 1876 took place in Durand-Ruel's own gallery at Rue le Peletier. There were now twice the number of pictures shown compared to the first

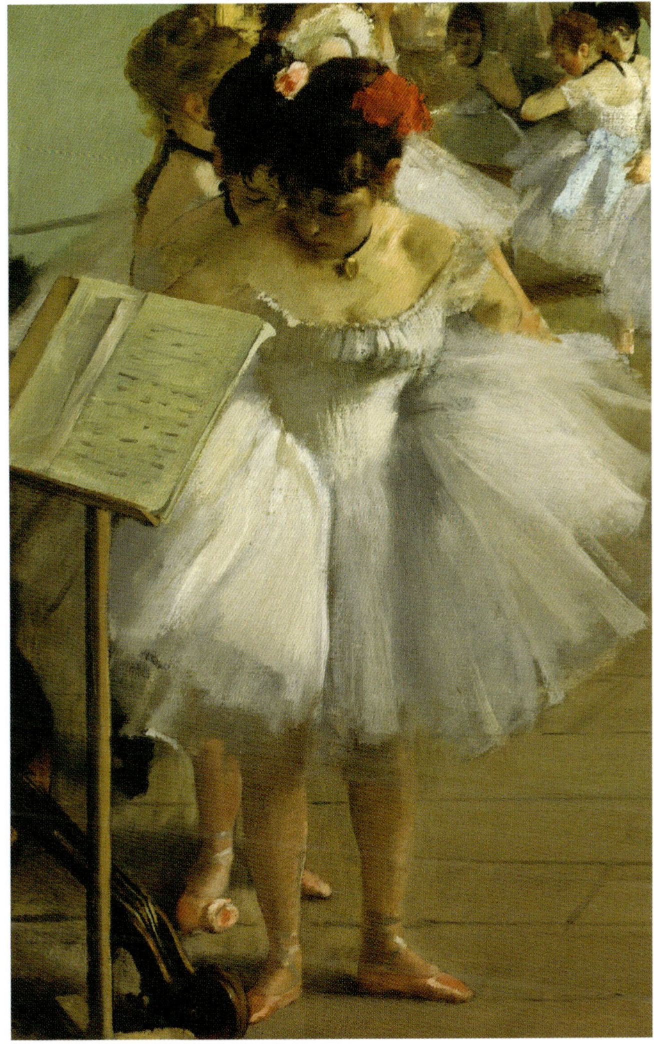

exhibition and new artists had joined the fold, such as Gustav Caillebotte (1848–94), who was an independently wealthy young man and became a collector of Impressionist paintings, subsequently donated to the state.

At this exhibition Degas showed *A Woman Ironing* (see page 74) and *The Cotton Exchange, New Orleans* (*see* left and page 111). Although included in the catalogue for this exhibition, *The Absinthe* (*see* page 78) was possibly not shown, as Durand-Ruel sold it through his London gallery to Captain Henry Hill, a veteran of the Battle of Waterloo, in 1815, who was living in Brighton.

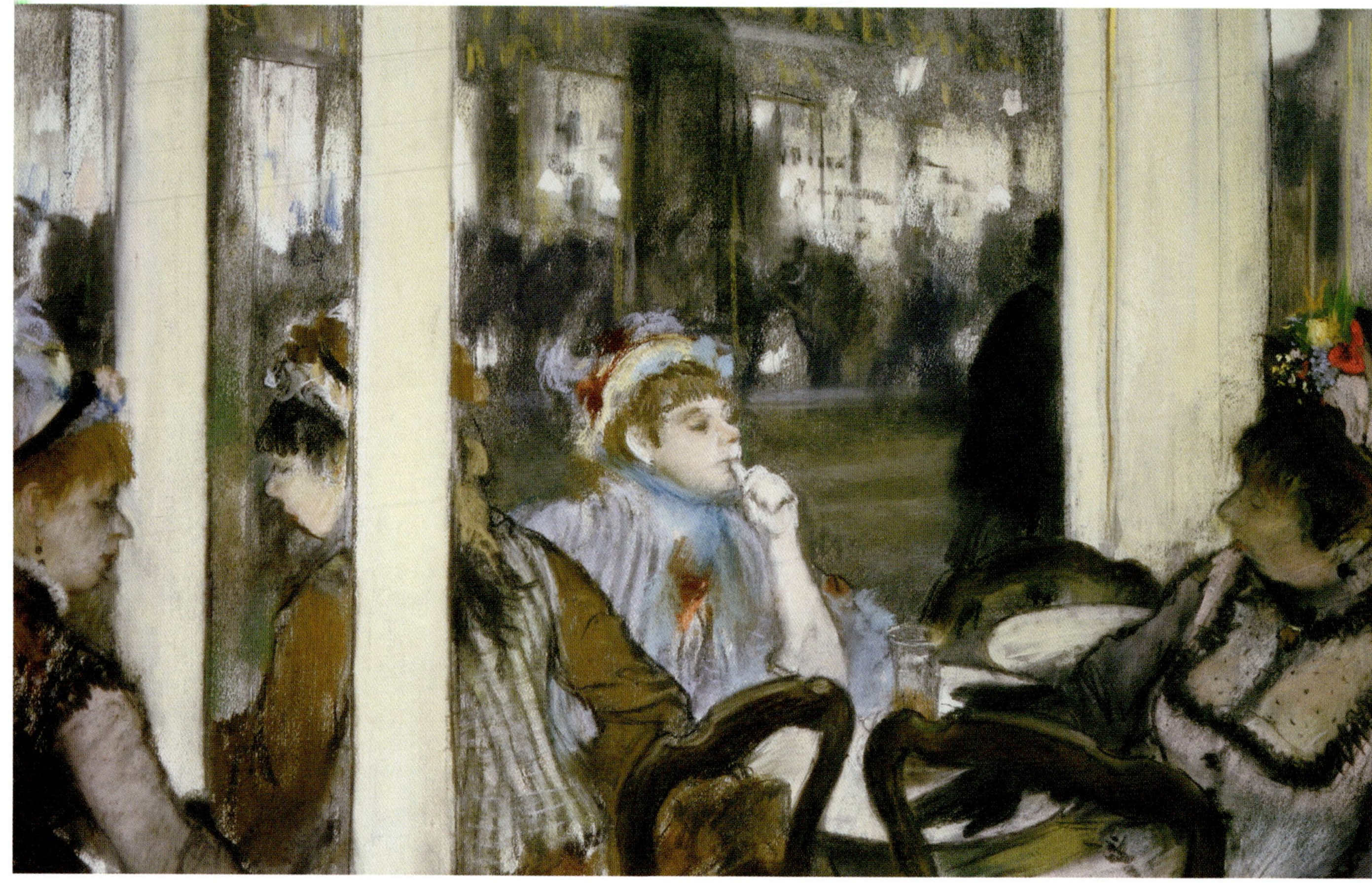

To coincide with the exhibition, the writer Louis Edmond Duranty published an article called 'La Nouvelle Peinture' ('The New Painting'), in which he was scathing about Salon art, suggesting that artists should say 'farewell to the human body treated as a vase from the point of view of the decorative curve', an obvious reference to Ingres. Instead he promulgated a theory suggesting that the new painting (Impressionism) was in effect a modern form of Realism. Although not referring to Degas by name, there are sufficient references to the artist's *oeuvre* to make this link.

Duranty was indifferent about landscape painting (the foremost subject of these exhibitions by artists such as Monet, Sisley and Pissarro), and was more inclined to the Baudelairian notions of depicting modern Paris as the *flâneur*, recommending that artists should depict 'the modern individual in the midst of his social habits, at home or in the streets'. For him it was not about the diffusive use of colour for effects (impressions),

but rather a focus on the pictorial world that is not composed in a contrived manner. He further suggested that the artist should be a 'street guide of human comedy', recording aspects of transitory moments in Parisian life. It is this aspect that, according to Duranty, separated Degas from the rest of the exhibiting group.

The link between Duranty and Degas in this regard is perhaps best demonstrated in the 1877 painting *Women on a Café Terrace, Evening* (*see* above and page 84), which is set very close to Durand-Ruel's gallery on Rue le Peletier. In this painting, the fantasy world of Ingres is completely destroyed, most notably in the notions of feminine beauty. The protagonists are prostitutes overtly plying their trade on the well-lit streets, the central figure tapping her teeth with impatience. The painting was shown at the third Impressionist exhibition in 1877, also on the Rue le Peletier, an example of Degas' sardonic wit.

The Ballet as a Subject

Although the Paris Opera Ballet had been in existence in Paris since the reign of Louis XIV (1636–1715), it was in the aftermath of the Franco-Prussian War and with the Palais Garnier theatre newly opened in 1875 that it blossomed into a key feature of Parisian life. It was this aspect that Renoir and Degas in particular chose as a motif for their paintings.

It was also a motif eagerly used by the American artist Mary Cassatt (1844–1926), who had moved to Paris in 1866 and was mentored by Degas. Whereas the depictions by Renoir and Cassatt are usually of the spectators watching the ballet or opera, Degas became the spectator giving us, the viewer, a privileged view of the stage not afforded by the other two. *Ballet from an Opera Box* (c. 1884, *see* below and page 57) is a prime example of this mode.

In much the same way as he had taken to studying the equine world to be able to paint more realistically, Degas began visiting the ballet to study the dancers in detail. Again, his social status in Parisian society provided him with access behind the scenes, enabling him to sketch dancers not just performing, but also in rehearsal and off-guard moments. His companion was the writer Ludovic Halévy (1834–1908), who was very well connected

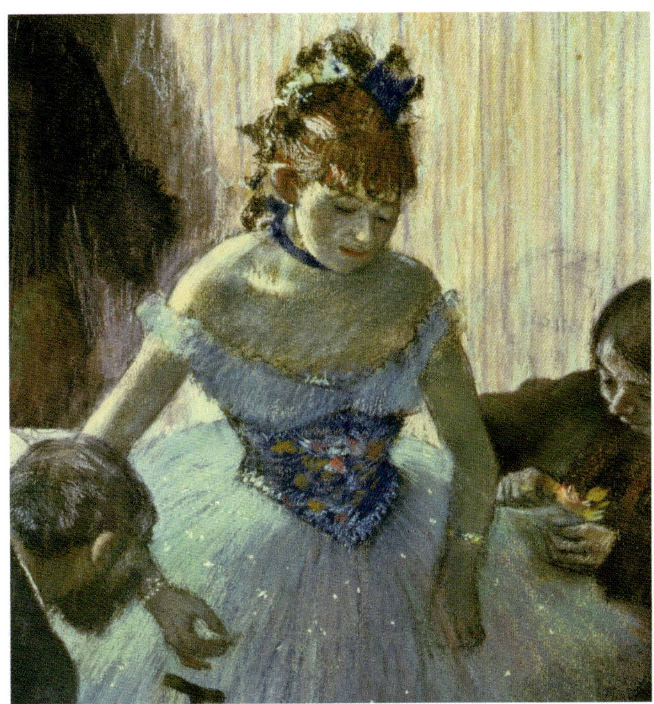

in haute-bourgeois circles. He had written libretti for several operas performed in Paris and was a frequent backstage visitor. Like Degas, Halévy was not averse to making sardonic observations of these encounters, often parodying French society and its polite mores. Both writer and artist were amused by the hypocrisy of their contemporaries in society. Degas depicted Halévy and a *flâneur* friend Albert Cavé backstage in *Friends at the Theatre*, from 1878–79 (*see* page 113).

The suggestion that these backstage visits had a sexual context is implicitly expressed in a number of Degas' behind-the-scenes pictures. An example of this is *Dancer in her Dressing Room* (1878, *see* above and page 41), in which we see the male voyeur watching the last-minute adjustments to the dancer's dress.

Dance Classes and Rehearsals

Jules Perrot (1810–92) was one of the foremost ballet dancers of the nineteenth century and went on to become a leading choreographer, before taking a position as ballet-master for the Imperial Ballet in St Petersburg, Russia. Degas paid homage to the man, including him

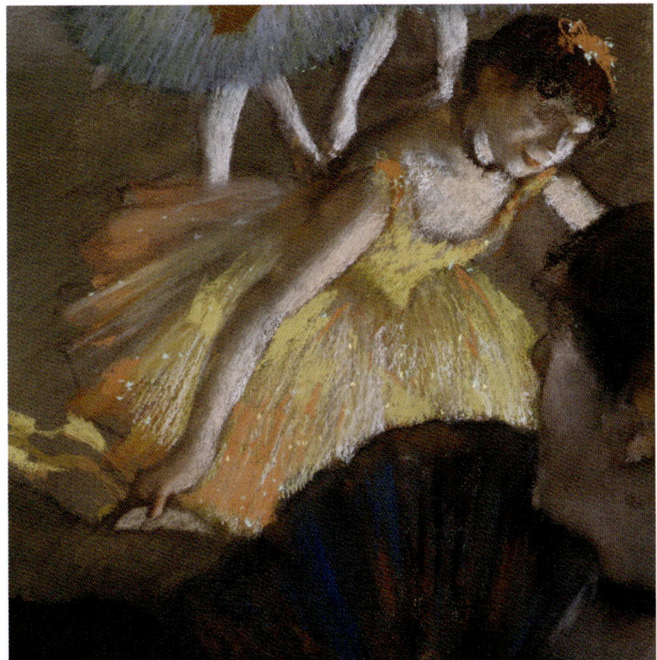

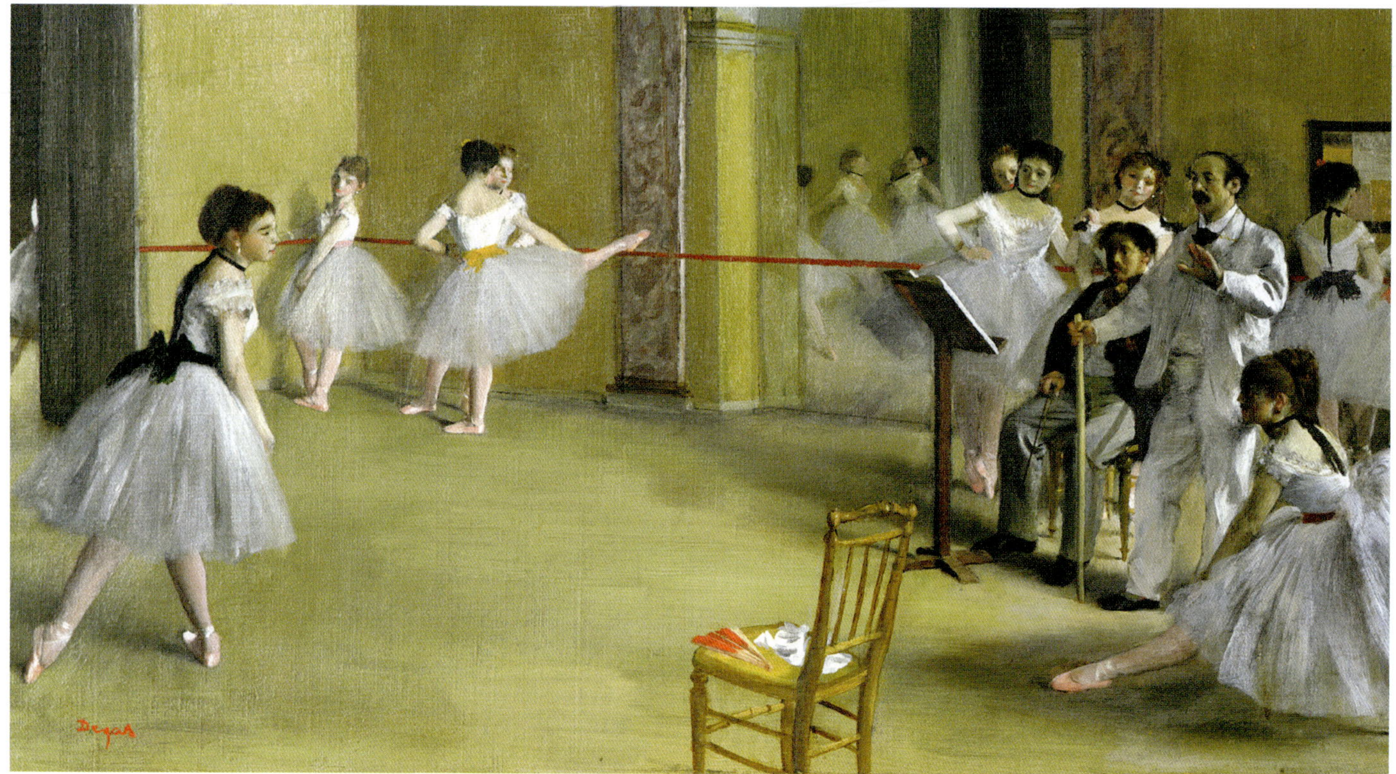

in several pictures as master of a ballet class in Paris, despite the fact Perrot did not take ballet classes in the city when he returned following his retirement in 1858. Originally *The Dancing Class* (*see* page 33) had an anonymous figure in place of Perrot, but the inclusion of the master gives the picture additional gravitas. The formality of his pose is countered by the informality of the dancer sitting on the piano scratching her back and the appearance of a small dog in the foreground.

Degas also knew other dance masters, including Louis Mérante (1828–87), who is immaculately dressed in a white suit in *The Dance Foyer at the Opera* (*see* above and page 31). He is seen with his white baton, used to beat on the floorboards to mark time. The room depicted is the Salle Le Peletier in the old opera house, which was destroyed by fire in 1873.

Spontaneous Moments

As a privileged backstage viewer, Degas was also able to see dancers in off-guard moments, when they were not being coached or rehearsing.

Dancer Putting on her Shoes (*c.* 1880–85, *see* page 53) and *Dancers in Red Skirts* (*c.* 1884, *see* page 58) are two such examples. One of the aspects that the artist became aware of was the sheer physical strength and stamina of these young women. Often they were pushed to physical exhaustion by the dance masters and even their mothers, eager to see their daughters progress. Many of these young women would begin their ballet coaching at seven or eight years of age, with the objective of passing examinations so that by about the age of 10 they would qualify for a stipend. These girls often came from working-class backgrounds and the stipend would make a useful contribution to the family's income. Should she reach the position of a leading dancer within the *corps de ballet*, her stipend may well exceed that of the main breadwinner in a household, hence the reason mothers are often present in Degas' pictures. In *Waiting* (*c.* 1882, *see* page 54), we see a tired young dancer accompanied by her mother, possibly anticipating her daughter's examination results; and in *The Dancing Class* (*see* page 33), a mother can be seen in the background consoling her daughter.

Dancers on Stage

The performances as depicted by Degas are always from the *loge*, or box, affording a privileged view. The dancer in *The Star, or Dancer on the Stage* (*c.* 1876–77, *see* below and page 37) is looking towards this privileged viewer as she demonstrates her elegance. The empty foreground adds to the sense that she is about to encroach further into the viewer's space, returning their gaze. In the 1877 *Dancer with Bouquet, Curtseying* (*see* page 38), the performance is complete and she is surveying the whole audience as she enjoys the applause. Her face, however, suggests exhaustion, an aspect echoed by one of the dancers behind her who is rubbing her own back.

Again the viewer is in a privileged position to see the dancer performing an arabesque movement in *End of an Arabesque* (*see* page 39), painted in the same year as the curtseying dancer. She is holding a bouquet, suggesting that either she is taking a curtain call, or Degas is employing a compositional ruse to balance the blue tutus of the background dancers.

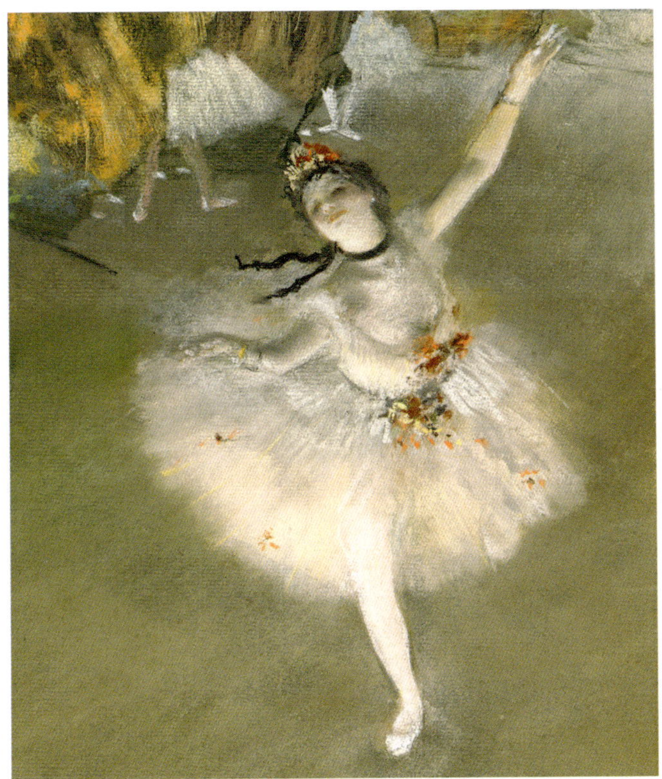

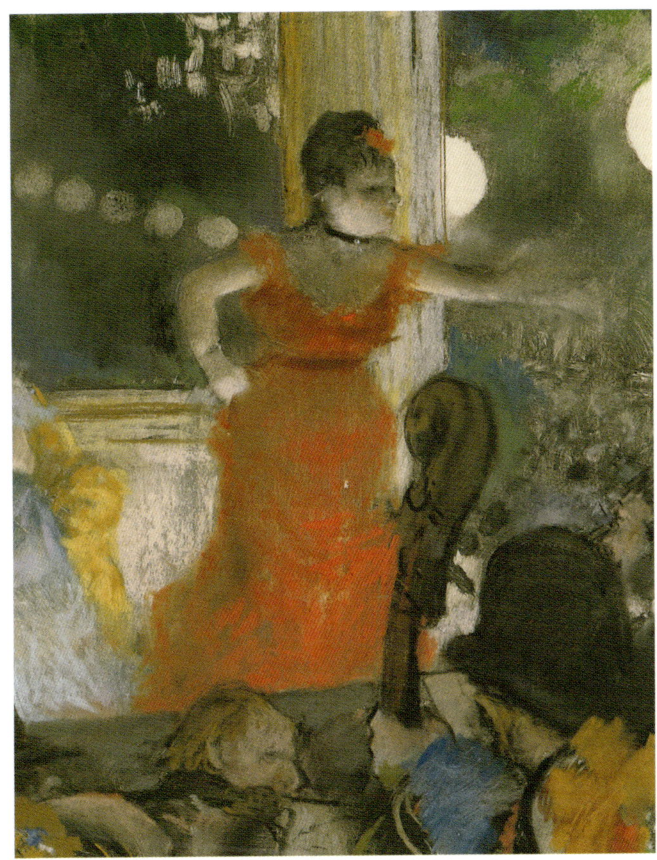

The Café Concert

Paris, as the entertainment capital of Europe, had much to offer in the last quarter of the nineteenth century. Apart from the opera and ballet, there were so-called café concerts. These were essentially bars that also provided entertainment, usually in the form of song. The number of café concerts expanded significantly in Paris at this time, since they were frequented as much by foreign visitors as locals. The café concert also became a favoured haunt of the *flâneur* artists, most notably Manet and Degas. The former tended to portray the staff and clientele of these establishments, while Degas focused on the performer, who was, almost exclusively, female. The favoured haunt of Degas was the Café des Ambassadeurs, located on the corner of the Place de la Concorde and the main thoroughfare of the Champs-Elysées. Like many others, it was an outdoor venue that had a particular appeal on summer evenings.

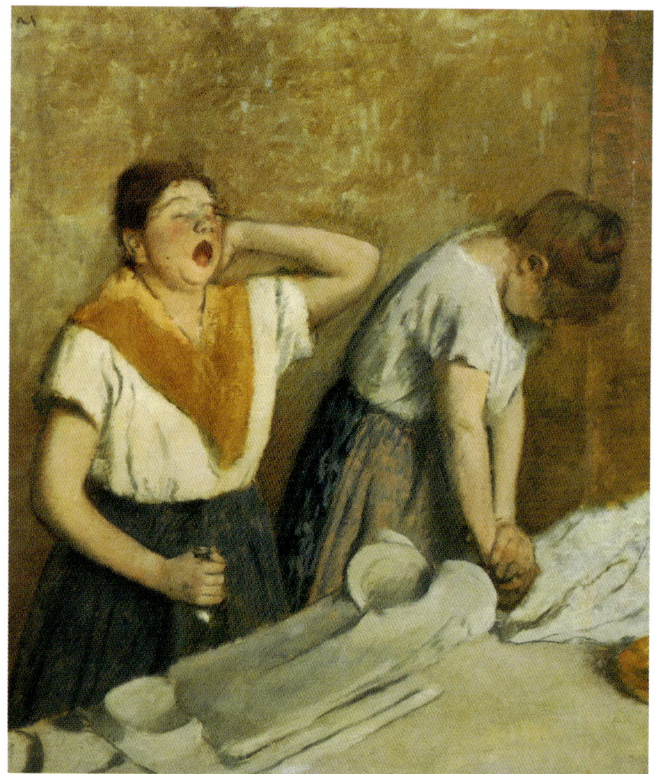

The Café des Ambassadeurs was considered by many as the leading café-concert venue, with a seating capacity of over 1,000 guests. It boasted an orchestra of about 18 musicians, and staged a dozen or so performers each evening, including singers, acrobats and comedians. In *Café Concert at Les Ambassadeurs* (1876–77, *see* page 82) Degas portrays the performer reaching out to this large audience. The composition invites the picture's viewer to be a part of the audience, behind the figures in the foreground, who, judging by their dress, are members of the *demi-monde* (the class of women considered to be of doubtful morality and social standing). That is not to say that these performers or the venue attracted the lower classes, by any means. The Café des Ambassadeurs attracted all social classes to these often lewd and bawdy entertainments, which were regularly scrutinized by official censors.

The performance area was also occupied by other women and was known as the *corbeille*, a reserved female-only enclosure for other entertainers (often unpaid beginners hoping for a break) waiting their

turn, or attractive women hired just for their looks. The impresarios of these establishments eagerly encouraged this sexual commercialism, although the women were forbidden from making overt suggestions as to their availability. Nevertheless, Degas alludes to his knowledge of the gestural signs used by the women to denote their intentions, for example the manner in which a fan is held. These so-called physiologies of human behaviour and manners were available in booklet form for all to purchase.

Working Women

Apart from depicting entertainment in Paris, Degas was also interested in other aspects of Parisian life, not least of which were ordinary working-class women at work. His first foray into this genre was *Woman Ironing*, executed in 1869 (*see* page 71). Unlike his subsequent pictures of this genre, Degas' sitter was a professional model, Emma Dobigny (1850–1925), who also posed for him in other pictures. Nevertheless, Degas has managed to authentically capture the tedium and weariness of the task.

His most famous picture on the subject is probably *The Laundresses (The Ironing)* of *c.* 1874–76 (*see* above left and page 75). It perfectly captures the mood, in essence the darker side of Parisian life,

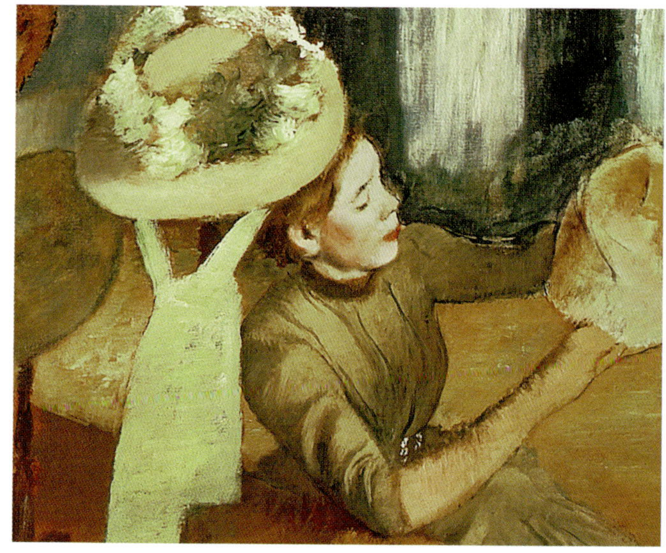

in which its society is becoming alienated from each other, as suggested by writers such as the contemporary sociologist Georg Simmel (1858–1918). This picture and others such as *Chanteuse de Café* (*see* page 87) also deal with another preoccupation of Simmel's, which is how the observer of the human condition can be close to the subject and yet simultaneously detached and remote from it, an aspect that Degas repeatedly and expertly examined.

Degas also depicted shop assistants. *The Millinery Shop* (*see* below left and page 95) depicts a shop assistant arranging hats for a window display. The unusual angle of view suggests that the girl is unaware of the artist's presence.

Friendship with Mary Cassatt

In the 1880s Degas completed a small series of scenes inside a millinery shop. As a painter of women he was of course interested in fashion, and Paris was its cultural epicentre. To facilitate this interest, Degas used to regularly shop with the American artist Mary Cassatt. In fact on some occasions Cassatt actually posed for Degas, trying the hats on.

Degas first visited Cassatt's Paris studio in 1877 and at once declared 'here is someone who thinks as I do'. Cassatt is often considered to be Degas' pupil, but in fact they were kindred spirits willing to learn from each other. Cassatt was, like Degas, from a wealthy background, well educated and an admirer of the Old Masters. Together they visited many of the galleries in Paris to discuss the work. Degas made several studies of Cassatt at the Louvre, attesting to her refined approach to art (*see* right and page 115). There is nothing to suggest that the relationship was anything other than platonic, since both would have been conditioned by the strict moral code of their class. It is interesting to note that neither artist ever married.

Both artists eschewed the tag of Impressionism in favour of Realism, but after their initial meeting, Degas persuaded Cassatt to participate in the Impressionist exhibition of 1879. Following on from this exhibition the two artists set up a print-making enterprise with Pissarro and the artist and printmaker Félix Bracquemond (1833–1914). Degas was always keen to explore new media for his work and in fact exhibited

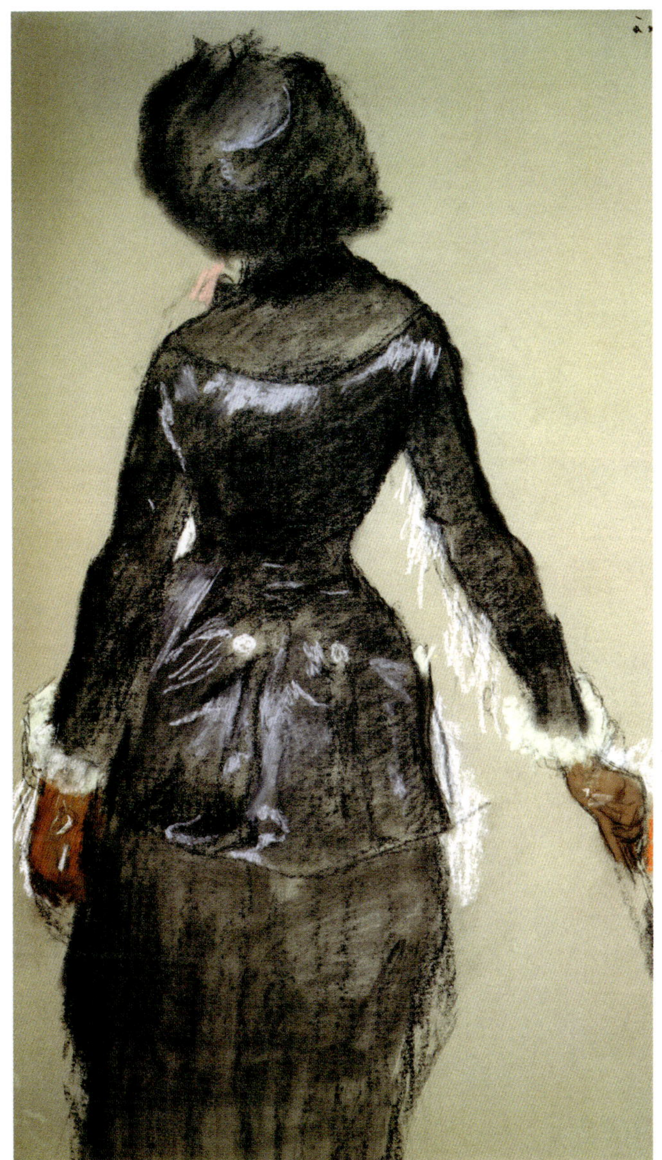

for the first and only time a number of his etchings at the fifth Impressionist exhibition in 1880.

The print-making enterprise never came to fruition for reasons that are still unclear, which led to a cooling of the working relationship between Degas and Cassatt. Their relationship became strained further when they disagreed over the Dreyfus Affair, but they remained friends until Degas' death in 1917.

The Dreyfus Affair

In 1894, a young Jewish French army officer named Alfred Dreyfus was convicted of high treason and sentenced to life imprisonment. The French authorities suppressed contrary evidence, highlighted in an article 'J'accuse' written by Emile Zola in 1898, which suggested a cover-up. The consequences of the so-called Dreyfus Affair deeply divided French society, along political as well as cultural lines. Degas was very outspoken as 'anti-Dreyfusard' and consequently labelled anti-Semitic.

Anti-Semitism was rife in Paris at this time, due to the prominent commercial activities of Jewish businessmen. Degas' own family's bank had failed and one of the largest European banks of the time was owned by the Jewish Rothschild family with branches in Naples and Paris, facts which may well have fuelled anti-Semitic feelings.

Prostitution and Brothels

Prostitution was a widespread phenomenon in Paris in the nineteenth century, becoming a feature of both contemporary art and literature. The most famous novels to feature prostitution at the time were

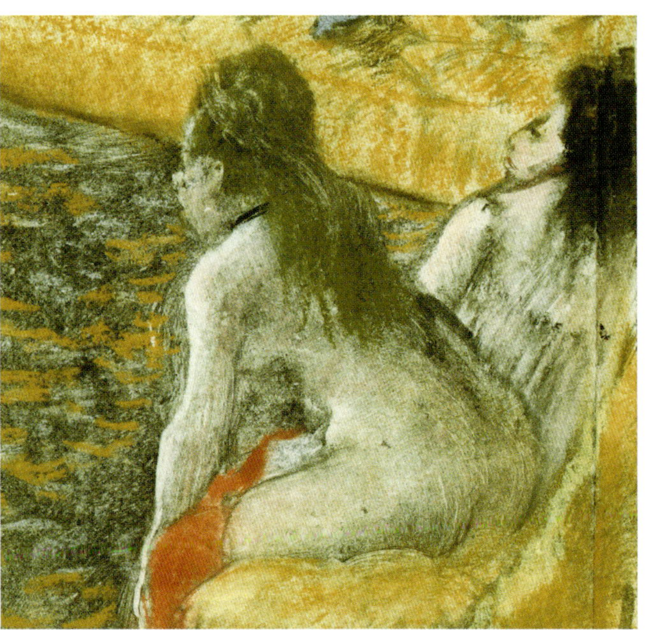

L'Assommoir (1877) and Nana (1880), both by Emile Zola (1840–1902). The main protagonist of the second novel featured in a famous portrait by Edouard Manet in 1877, a painting that was refused by the Salon jury because of its content.

In the late 1870s Degas began using the monotype as a medium. The technique was used in a number of brothel images created by Degas, including Waiting for a Client, executed c. 1879 (see below left and page 90). Degas' depictions are very far removed from the idealized bodies of Ingres' work, for example. Those conventions of nudity are completely subverted by Degas, who emphasizes the swollen bodies with their drooping breasts, together with the depiction of their pubic hair. He also adds a grotesque nature to the faces to underpin the sordid nature of commercial sex. Pablo Picasso (1881–1973) owned several of these monotypes, which served as reference and inspiration for much of his own work.

In many of these brothel scenes, a male client is seen on the fringes of the picture plane. In Waiting for a Client, his outline is shown on the extreme left of the image. The figure with the red stockings appears to be engaging with him using her whole body, exemplifying her availability. The same can be said of the figure wearing blue stockings, flagrantly displaying her genitals, while the body language of the other prostitute in the middle suggests indifference. All of the figures appear to be caricatures rather than resembling real people.

It has been noted by some art historians that the male figures in these scenes are caricatures of Jewish men, supporting the notion that Degas was anti-Semitic, since the protagonists would be implicated in the sordid world of prostitution, thus equating Jews with society's degenerates.

Female Nudes

In his series of nude bathing and toilet paintings, Degas subverts the conventions of display that dominated academic art of the same period. A case in point is to contrast The Birth of Venus by William Bouguereau (1825–1905), with Degas' Peasant Girls Bathing (c. 1875–76, see below right and page 112). The Birth of Venus ,which was exhibited at the Salon in 1879, is a full frontal idealized image that assumes a

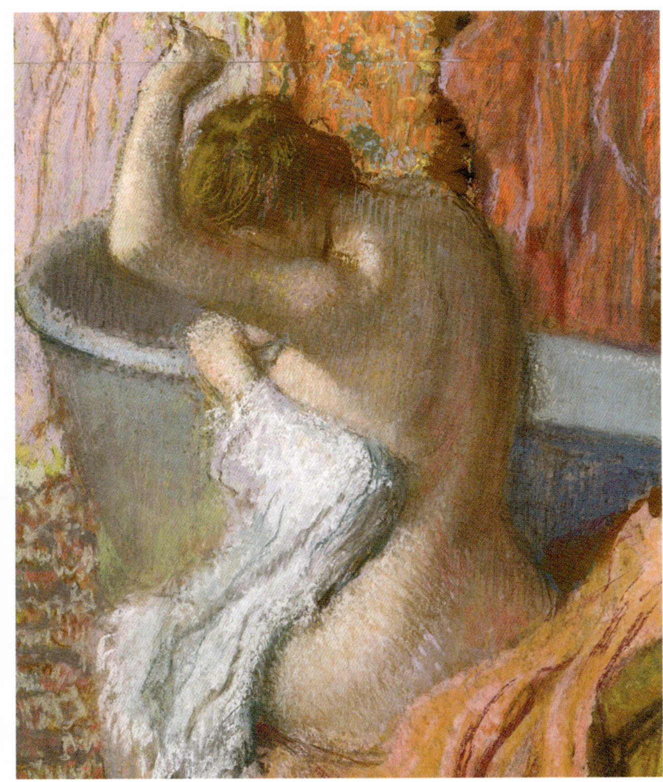

male spectator. Degas' *Peasant Girls Bathing* is a near-contemporary image, which disrupts this convention, since the spectacle becomes uneasy to the supposed male viewer, who is made to feel voyeuristic. The bodies are far from idealized and verge on abstracted forms.

In later pictures the images become more personal, the voyeurism more emphatic. In *The Toilet* (1883, *see* page 117), the space is more intimate, a theme that Degas continued in this genre. In all of these pictures the viewer is assumed to be a voyeur, and is treated only to back views with disjointed forms. To achieve this Degas includes, for example, a towel as in Seated *Bather* (1899, *see* above and page 125). For Degas the challenge is in the pictorial representation of these awkward poses and the often oblique angles, adding to the voyeurism, as though the viewer is watching through a keyhole. The intimacy of these pictures comes from the marks made by the artist, the sensuality of touch, not of the figures themselves but of the pastel. In this regard pastel is a very tactile medium and lends itself well to the sensuality of the female form, whether nudes or ballet dancers.

In 1886, at the eighth Impressionist exhibition, Degas showed a series of these female bathing scenes, making him one of the first artists to create a conceptual dimension to his work, something that we now take for granted. The critics attending this exhibition were particularly vitriolic about Degas' work. The novelist and critic Joris-Karl Huysmans (1848–1907) stated that Degas had 'brought to his study of nudes a careful cruelty, a patient hate'. For him, 'the enshrined idol' (woman) had been debased 'in the humiliating positions of her intimate ablutions'. This and other criticisms levelled at Degas' portraits of women have led many art historians to debate whether he was a misogynist.

Alleged Misogyny

Degas was first and foremost a painter of women in a predominantly female environment, within a patriarchal society. This was his speciality. He was dedicated to portraying Parisian life as a Realist painter. As such he was obliged to portray all aspects of the everyday in accordance with the Baudelaire creed, the 'heroism of modern life' rather than the idealization of women endlessly churned out for the titillation of visitors to the Salon. Accordingly Degas' art was never going to be 'pretty'. Sensuous, intelligent, engaging and sometimes witty, yes, but pretty and decorous, no.

In his lifetime Degas' sexuality was often called into question, because of his bachelor status and avowed celibacy. His sometime friend Manet

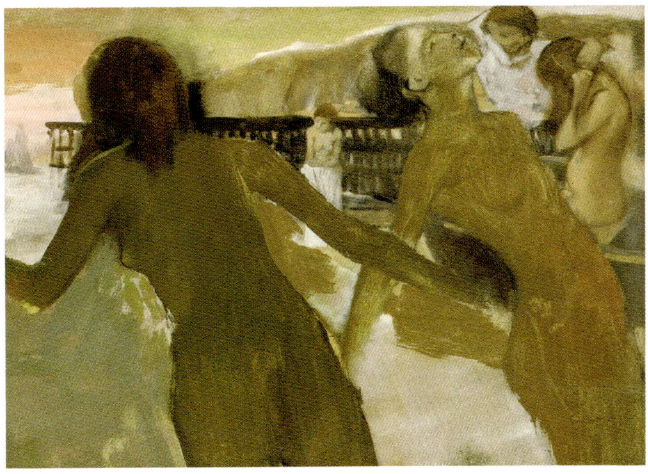

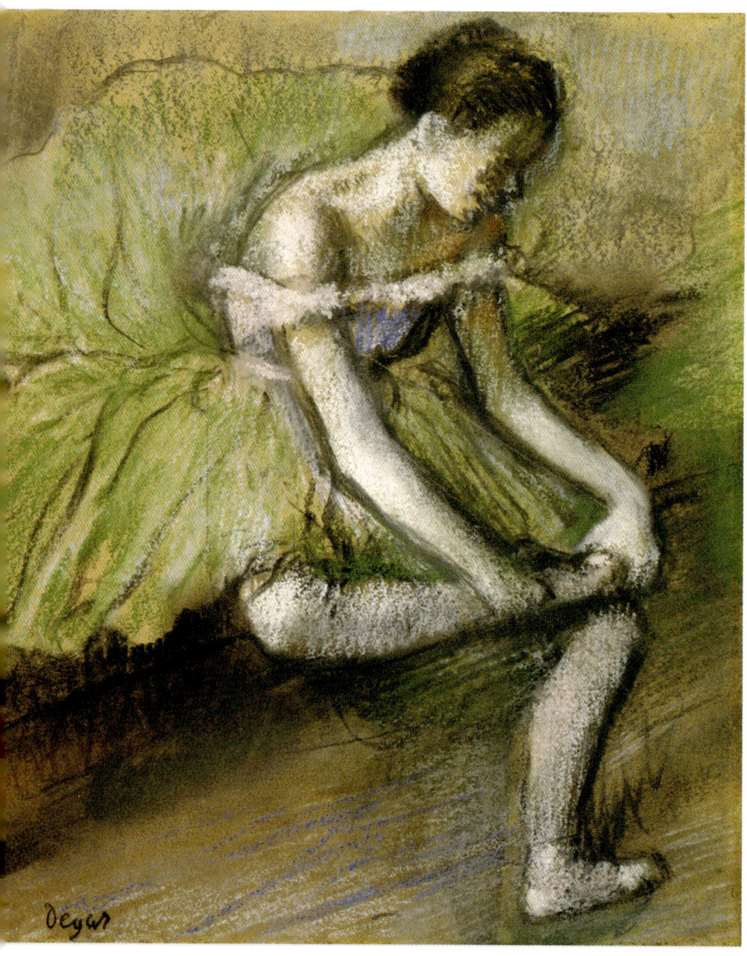

In the late twentieth century several feminist art historians have sought to unravel the complexities and ambiguities of Degas' *oeuvre*. The main problem for all art historians is the lack of correspondence left by Degas, relying instead on the pictures themselves to construct a somewhat ambivalent attitude to his alleged misogyny.

Failing Eyesight

By the 1890s Degas' sight was deteriorating and he was confined to paintings on a large scale and with broad strokes. He virtually abandoned painting in oils in favour of pastels, and in particular pastels over monotypes. Degas' eye condition was first diagnosed during the Franco-Prussian War of 1870 when he was enlisted in the army. He had a form of retinopathy, which gradually and progressively impaired his vision, to the point where he could no longer paint, after about 1908. During his painting career he was unable to bear continued exposure to bright sunlight or very cold weather. He was, however, able to work in artificial light in a controlled environment and he found the gas lighting at the café concerts conducive to his work.

As a result of this degenerative eye condition, Degas' work became more Impressionistic in its aesthetic. He was forced to use much broader strokes, and the colours used became less naturalistic and more vivid. A testament to this is *La Jupe Verte* executed in *c.* 1896 (*see* left and page 61). The title demands that we look at the diaphanous green skirt and forgive the poor draughtsmanship of the legs. At this time Degas had to ask his models to place the correct pastel in his hands, such was his inability to see colours clearly.

However, in spite of his failing eyesight, or perhaps because of it, Degas found another outlet for his creative talents in sculpture, since he was able to mould and create by touch.

Sculpture

Degas had begun sculpting probably as early as the mid-1860s using both clay and wax. Not surprisingly his subjects were ballet dancers, horses and the female nude. The first sculpture to be exhibited was

even joked that 'Degas is incapable of loving a woman, or even telling her he does'. Degas was a very private man and, apart from his café meetings, he spent most of the time away from his contemporaries, preferring the sanctuary of his studio, which was off limits to most people. This isolation, combined with his irascible nature and often acerbic wit, made him both a difficult companion and an easy target for the critics. Ultimately this led to Degas being labelled a misogynist.

Not all contemporary critics were incensed by Degas' 'bathers'. Gustave Geffroy (1855–1926), a supporter of Impressionism and in particular Monet, wrote that Degas was an observer of 'the arabesque of human form' in the context of a disinterested and detached party, almost as a man of science would undertake his studies.

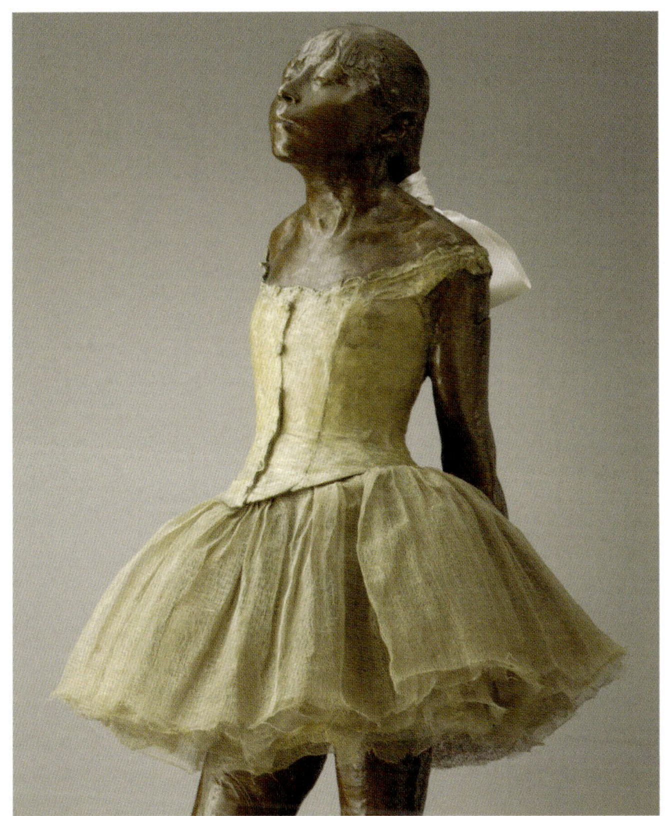

The End of the Impressionist Venture

In all there were eight Impressionist exhibitions, although it was not until the third exhibition in 1877 that the expression was used, much to the chagrin of Degas. In the following year disagreements in the group began to emerge. In part this was caused by various financial failures that led to a downturn in the Parisian economy.

For the fourth exhibition in 1879, Degas asserted his authority over the group and a more neutral title was chosen for the show: 'Exhibition of a Group of Independent Artists'.

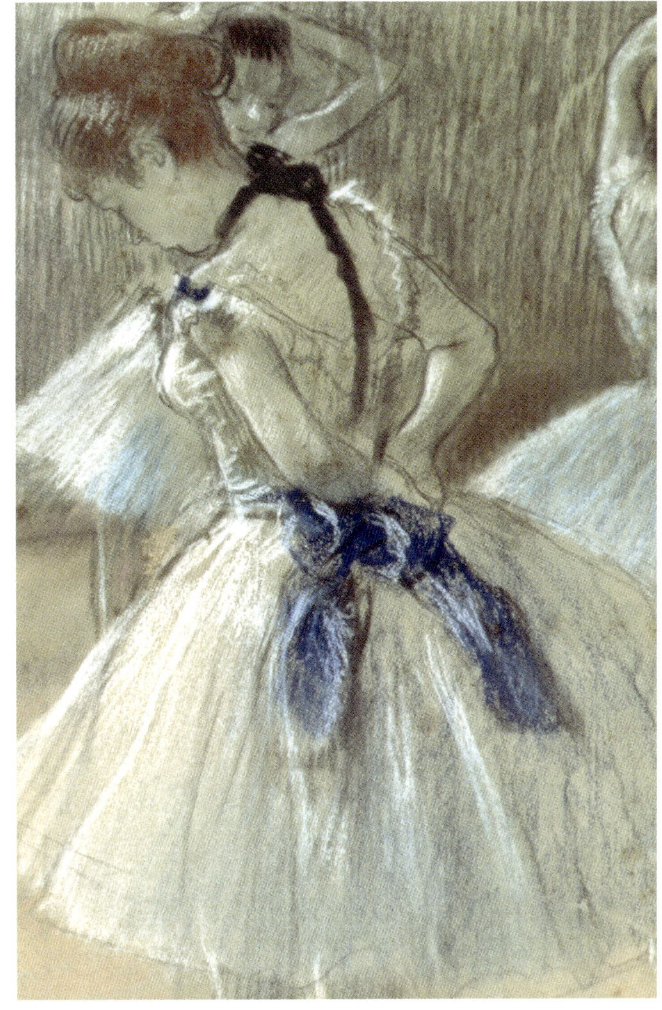

Little Dancer Aged Fourteen (*see* above and page 48) shown at the sixth Impressionist exhibition in 1881. The picture shown is of the bronze cast after Degas' death complete with a gauze tutu and satin bow. Degas also exhibited the wax model resplendent in the same accoutrements. The critic Huysmans, later so critical of Degas' nude bathers, was positively enamoured with this sculpture as part of a 'sculptural revolution'. Others were less complimentary, suggesting that the figure represented a monkey, or that it represented 'an ideal ugliness'.

Degas did not exhibit another sculpture in his lifetime and as his sight deteriorated he enlisted the help of his friend and fellow sculptor Albert Bartolomé (1848–1928). It was Bartolomé who was given the responsibility of repairing the various wax and clay models left behind in Degas' studio after his death, and subsequently having them cast in bronze. The sculptures left in his studio numbered over 150, but were clearly never intended for public exhibition as most of them were in a fragile state.

This exhibition was organized by Caillebotte, and most notable was the absence of both Monet and Sisley. Although Renoir exhibited, both he and Monet also submitted work to the Salon, which angered Degas, accusing them of abandoning their artistic principles.

At the time of the fifth exhibition, the only original members still showing work were Pissarro, Berthe Morisot (1841–95) and, of course, Degas. The others were still submitting work to the Salon, applauded by the writer Emile Zola, an original supporter of the Batignolles Group. Zola partly blamed Degas for this fracture in the Impressionist cause.

It was not until 1882 and the seventh exhibition that Monet, Renoir and Sisley returned to the fold. Ironically it was the only one of the eight exhibitions to which Degas did not submit work. Apart from this absence, it was the most homogenous of all the so-called Impressionist exhibitions, marking the end of Renoir's Parisian studies, in favour of more Classical nudes, and it saw Monet embarking on his 'series' paintings and moving to Giverny.

Apart from Degas' scandalous nudes in the eighth and final Impressionist exhibition in 1886, another emerging artist, Georges Seurat (1859–91), exhibited a similarly controversial picture, *La Grand Jatte*, which became a *cause célèbre*. The publication of a corresponding article by Félix Fénéon (1861–1944) called 'The Impressionists' actually spelt the death knell for Impressionism by suggesting that it was on the wane and that 'Neo-Impressionism' was its successor in Seurat and another artist, Paul Signac (1863–1935).

Final Years and Death

Following the last of the Impressionist exhibitions and the subsequent demise of the Batignolles Group, Degas relied instead on Durand-Ruel to sell his work. He had already shared an exhibition platform with other artists when the dealer showed his work at an exhibition of French artists' work in London in 1883. At the time when Degas abandoned working in oils, Durand-Ruel had the first of two solo exhibitions dedicated to the artist's work in Paris.

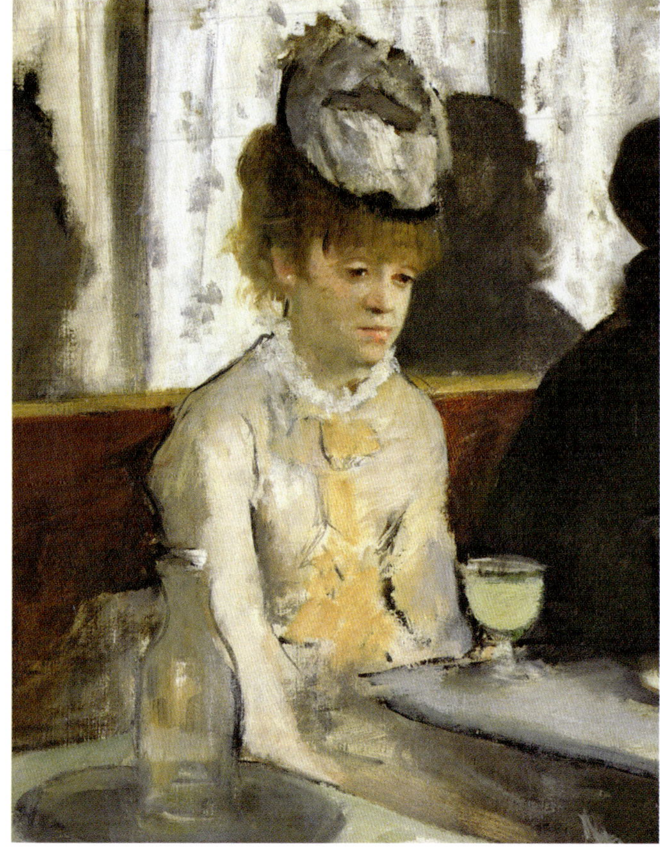

In 1900 Degas showed seven works at the Exposition Universelle in Paris, by which time he was almost blind and only able to work in large format. This expo was arguably the greatest of its kind before and since, with the possible exception of London's Great Exhibition of 1851. The Paris show attracted over fifty million visitors in its seven-month life, its main attractions being the Grand and Petit Palais that housed all the artworks and the new Metro system adorned in the Art Nouveau style that came to dominate much of Europe.

Between 1888 and 1910 Degas' work was shown on at least 12 occasions at separate exhibitions in London, including 'Painting and Sculpture by British and Foreign Artists' in 1893, which included his painting *The Absinthe* (*see* above and page 78). The novelist George Moore (1852–1933) also wrote an article in *The Magazine of Art* called 'Degas: The Painter of Modern Life', which further enhanced his reputation in Britain.

In 1911 Degas had a solo show at the Fogg Museum of Art in Cambridge, Massachusetts. In no small part the exposure of Degas was due to Durand-Ruel's efforts from 1886, aided by the American artist Mary Cassatt. At a time when Europe was buying very little Impressionist work, the American market was keen to avail itself of this 'new art'. As Durand-Ruel commented, 'The American public does not laugh, it buys.' The Fogg Museum now has the largest collection of Degas' work in the US.

At this time Degas was totally blind and spent the last decade of his life in relative isolation, with the exception of his live-in housekeeper. Despite his obvious successes, Degas felt that his life had been wasted, having not achieved the recognition he felt he deserved.

Degas died on 27 September 1917 and is buried in the family cemetery at Montmartre in Paris. His studio contained over 2,000 paintings and pastels, 150 sculptures and countless drawings, most of which were bound in sketchbooks.

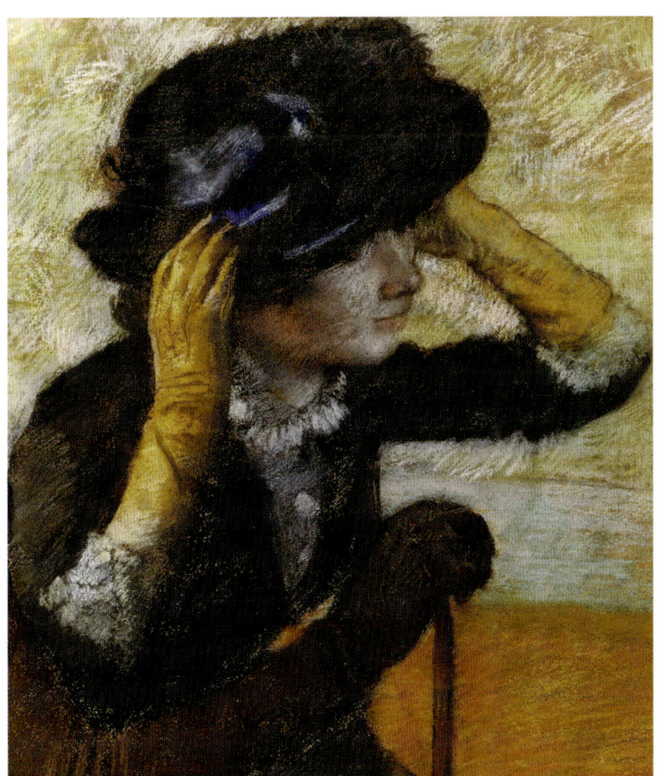

There was also a large quantity of etchings and other prints made by Degas. His collection of studio paintings was managed by Durand-Ruel's sons, George and Joseph, assisted by another dealer Ambroise Vollard (1866–1939), who prepared the inventory. The four sales amassed nearly half a million francs, with prices ranging from 3,000 to 20,000 francs. In addition, the French state purchased *The Bellelli Family* (*see* page 102) for 400,000 francs, which is now in the Musée d'Orsay.

At a time when France was still at war and Paris was being bombarded by German artillery, these sales figures are spectacular. Degas' reputation was now established in Europe and America.

Reputation and Legacy

Degas had no studio assistants or pupils, with the exception of Albert Bartolomé, to help him with his sculptures. He was also a close artistic mentor to Mary Cassatt and very influential to a number of other artists both in Paris and London.

Henri de Toulouse-Lautrec (1864–1901) was, like Degas, an astute observer of Parisian life. In his short career he managed to emulate much of Degas' *oeuvre*, including café concerts, women bathing and brothel scenes. His stylized caricatures at first appear quite similar to those of Degas, but are less mawkish and cruel. Degas' influence as a pastel artist can also be detected in the work of Édouard Vuillard (1868–1940) and others within the Nabis Group.

The first British artist to emulate Degas' vision of modernity was Walter Sickert (1860–1942). In March 1883 Sickert travelled to Paris and visited Degas' apartment and studio. Two years later he met with Degas again in Dieppe, this time posing for a pastel portrait with five of Degas' French friends. In 1898 Sickert moved to Dieppe and stayed in France for the next seven years. He took a studio in Paris and earned money teaching as well as establishing his reputation as an artist. He visited Degas on many occasions and on returning to London emulated his style mostly in oil paintings of music halls and nudes. It would be impossible to discuss Sickert without reference to his idol, Edgar Degas.

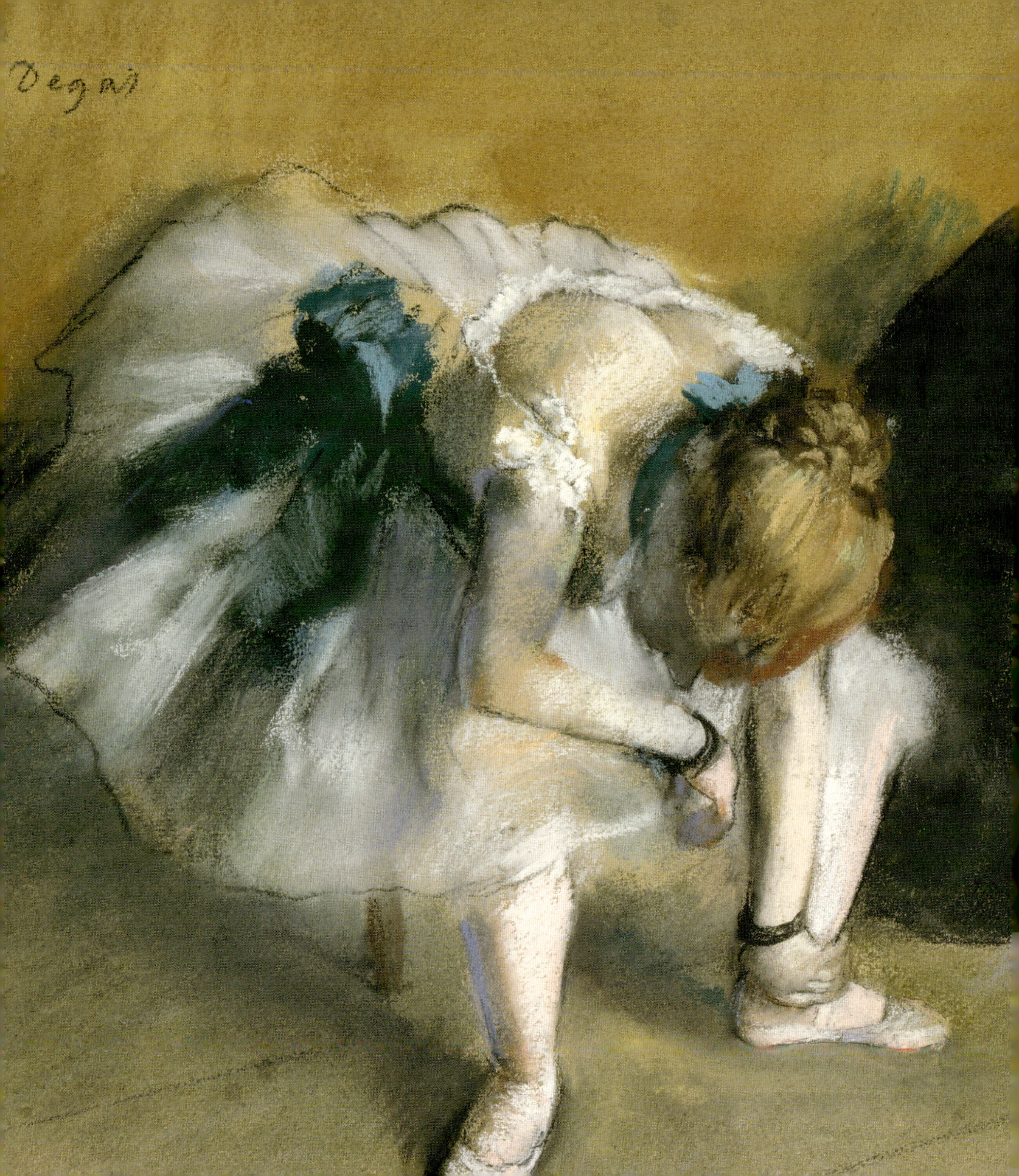
Degas

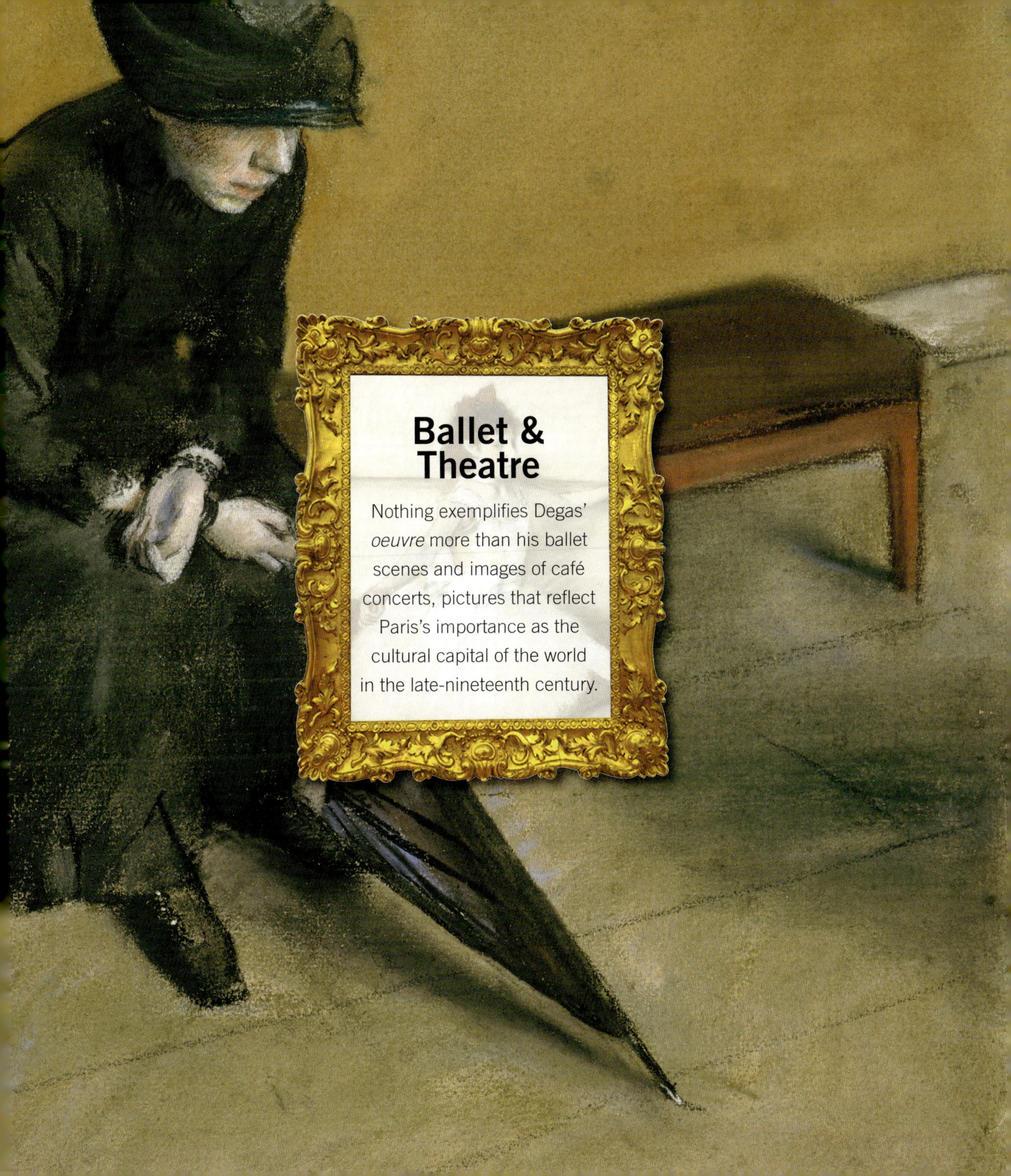

Ballet & Theatre

Nothing exemplifies Degas' *oeuvre* more than his ballet scenes and images of café concerts, pictures that reflect Paris's importance as the cultural capital of the world in the late-nineteenth century.

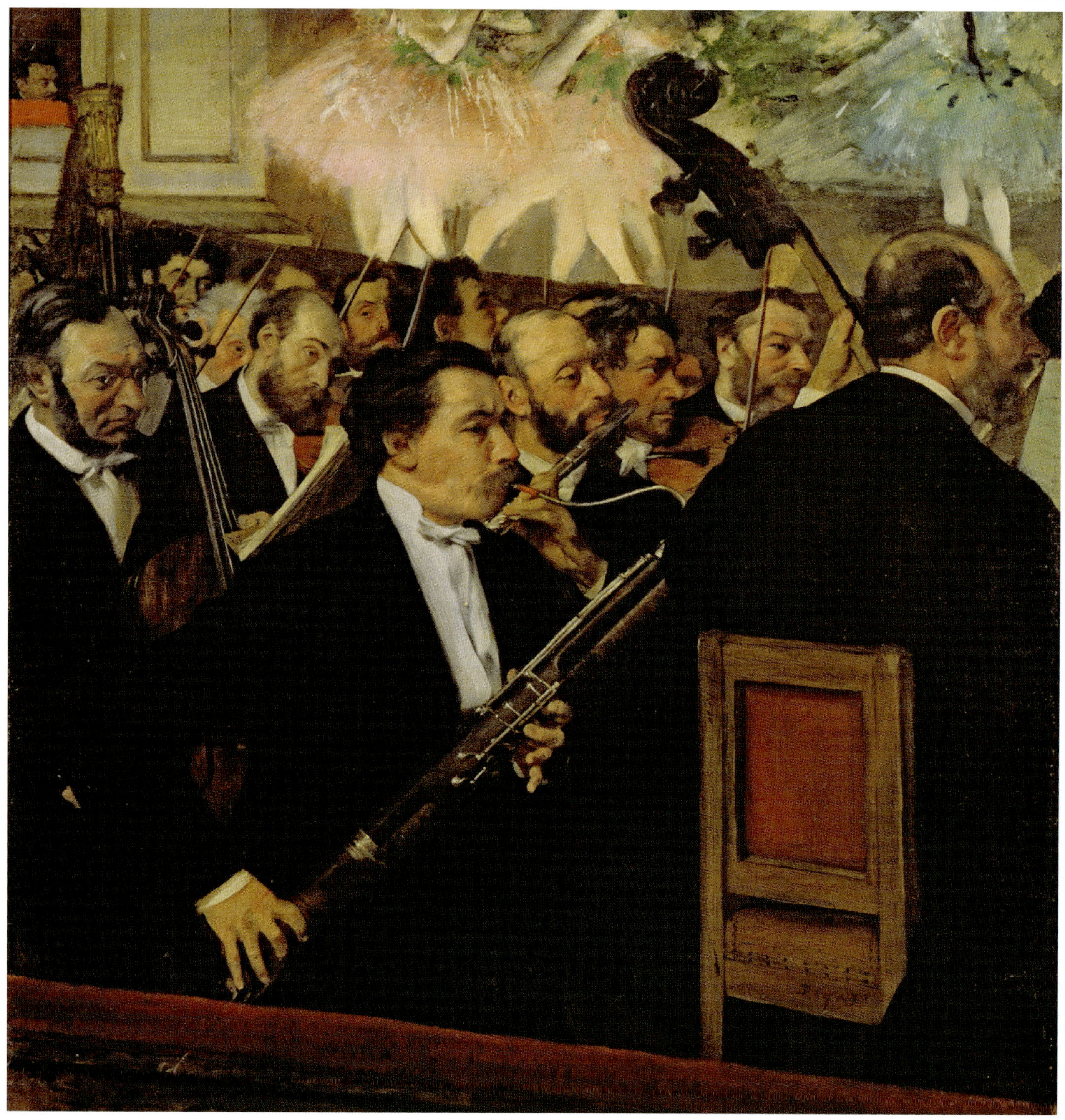

The Opera Orchestra, *c.* 1870
Oil on canvas, 56.5 x 46 cm (22$\frac{1}{4}$ x 18 in)
• Musée d'Orsay, Paris

The central figure in this composition is Degas' friend, the bassoonist Désiré Dihau.
However, he did not always use actual musicians in his compositions, preferring to
ask his friends to pose for him.

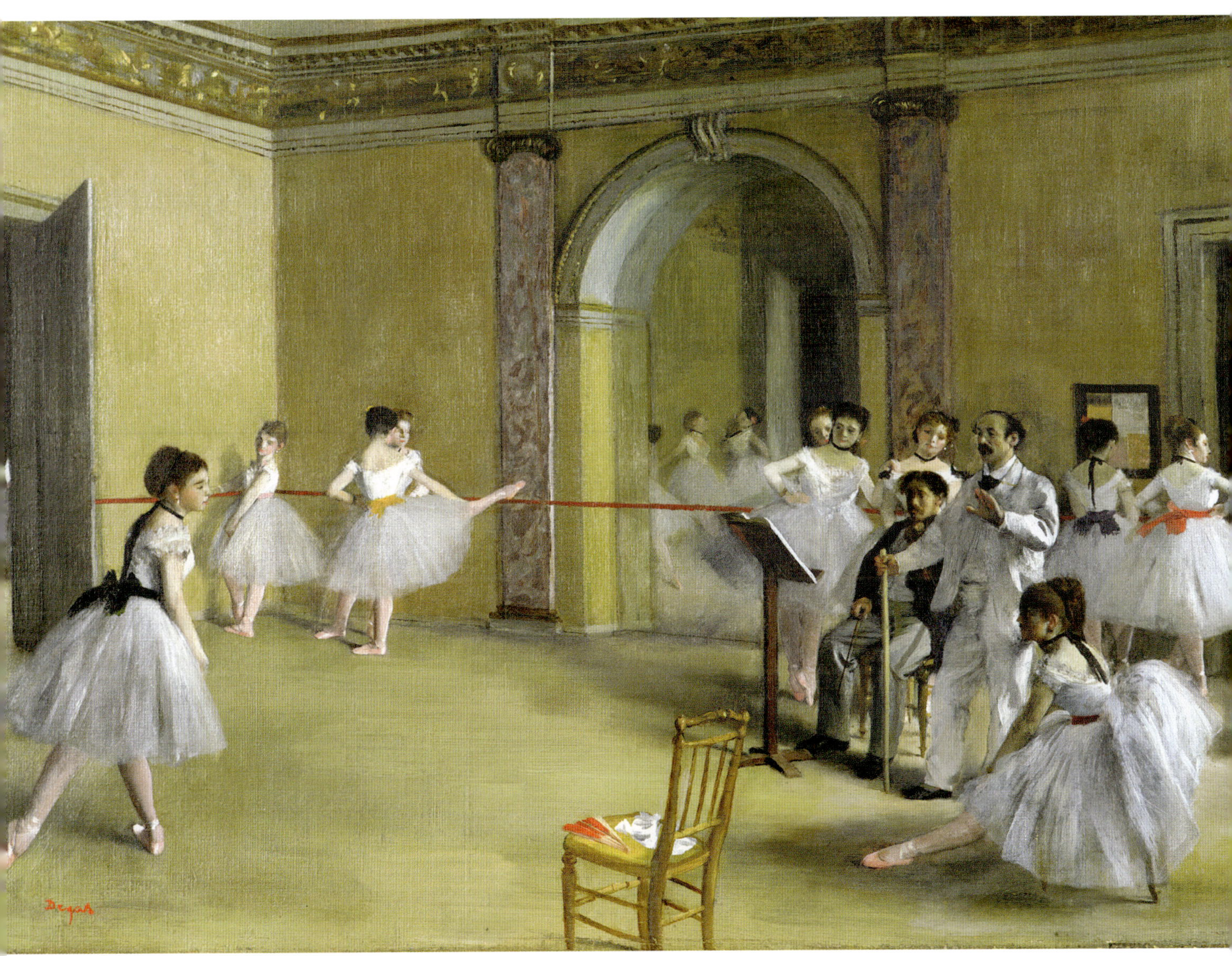

The Dance Foyer at the Opera, 1872
Oil on canvas, 32 x 46 cm (12½ x 18 in)
• Musée d'Orsay, Paris

This painting was exhibited at the fifth exhibition of the Society of French Artists in London by the art dealer Paul Durand-Ruel. He had opened a gallery in the city during the Franco-Prussian War.

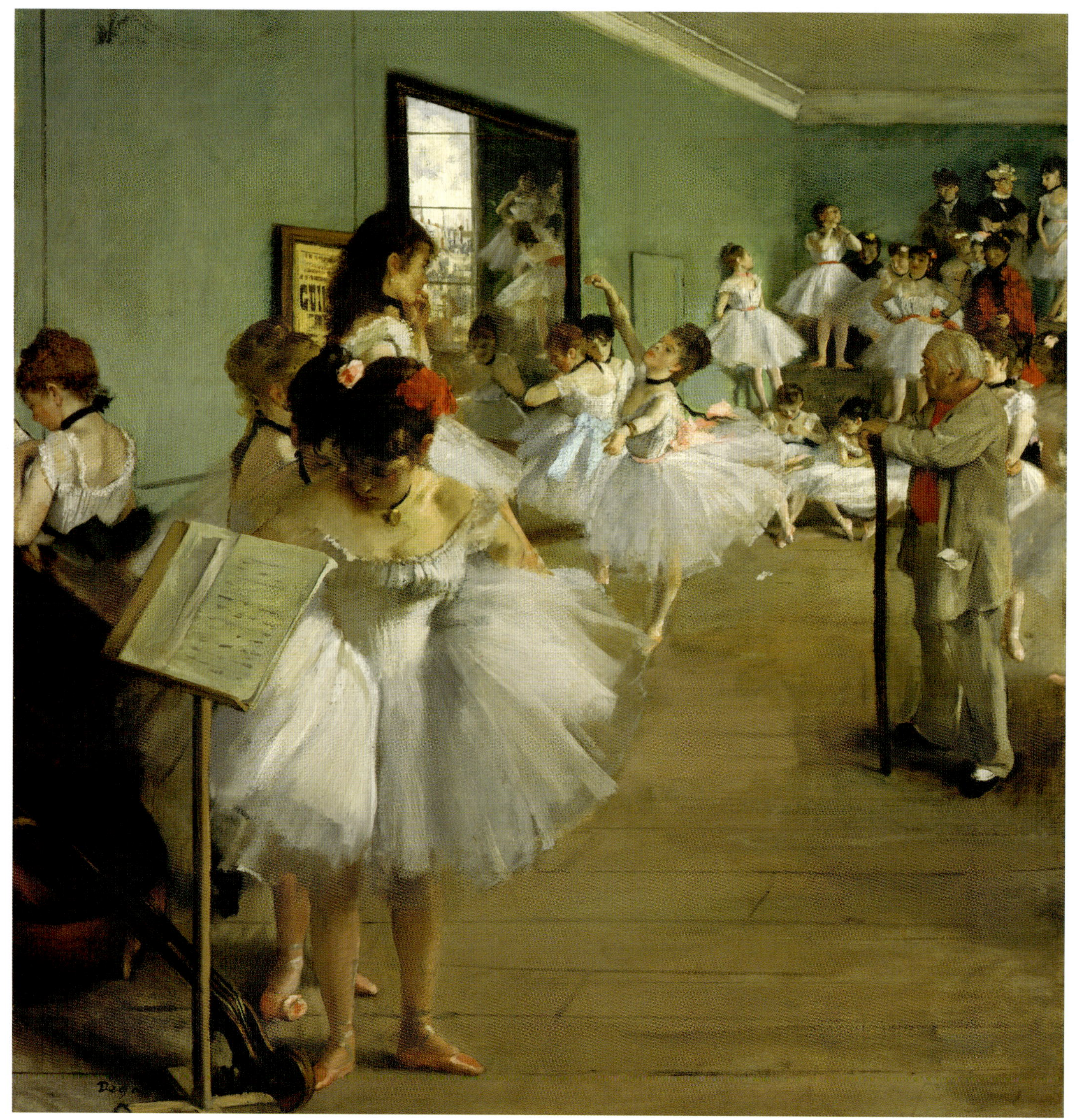

The Dance Class, 1873–74
Oil on canvas, 83.5 x 77.2 cm (33 x 30⅓ in)
• Metropolitan Museum of Art, New York

Although the interior can be identified as the old opera house, the scene is purely fictional, since the room was destroyed by fire in 1873, and M. Perrot (shown as the dance master) did not hold classes in Paris.

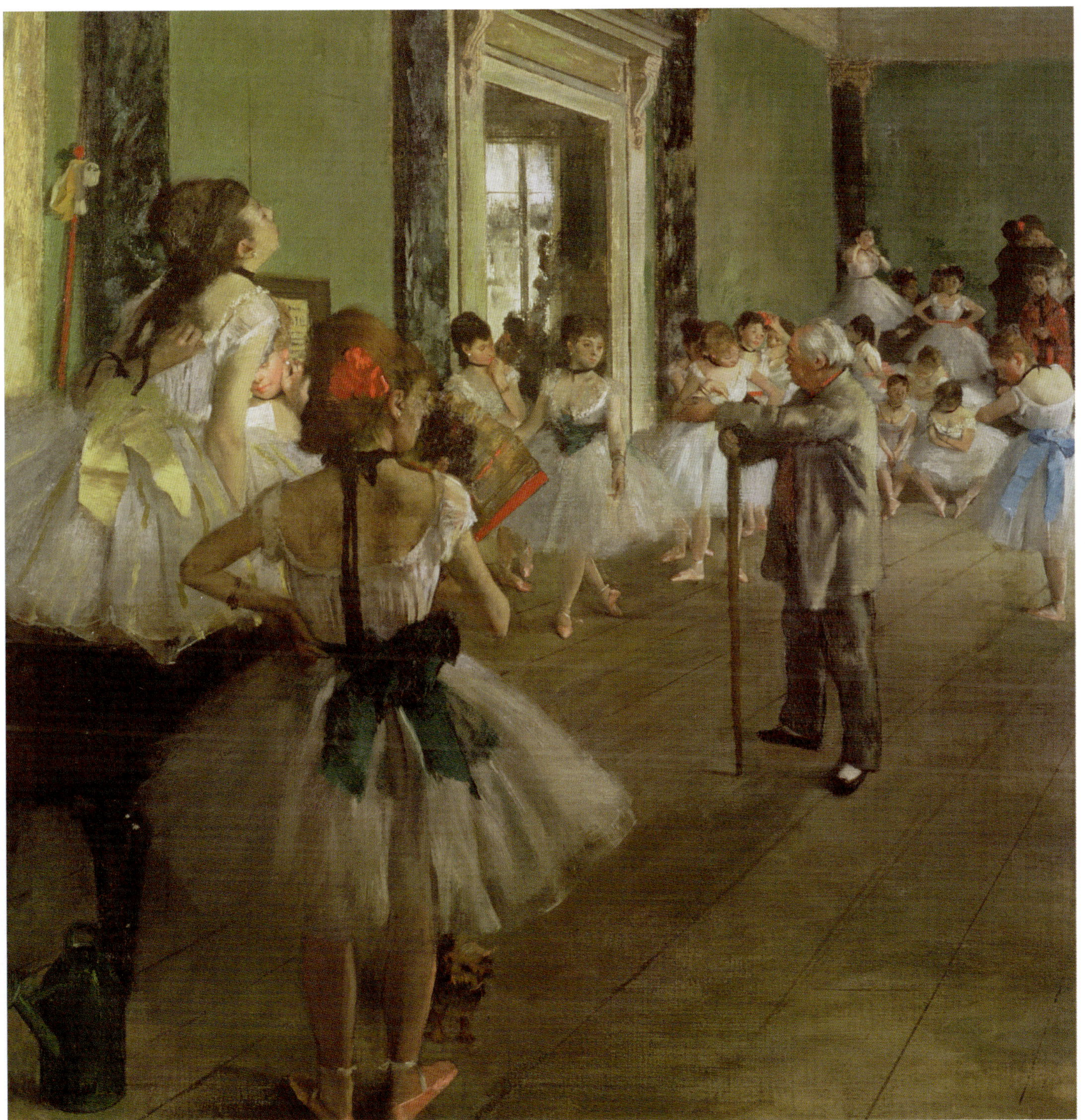

The Dancing Class, *c.* 1873–76
Oil on canvas, 85 x 75 cm (33$^1/_2$ x 29$^1/_2$ in)
• Musée D'Orsay, Paris

The viewer is guided along the picture's plane by the carefully constructed perspectives of the floorboards, from the two dancers in the foreground, past the figure of M. Perrot towards the group of dancers at the rear.

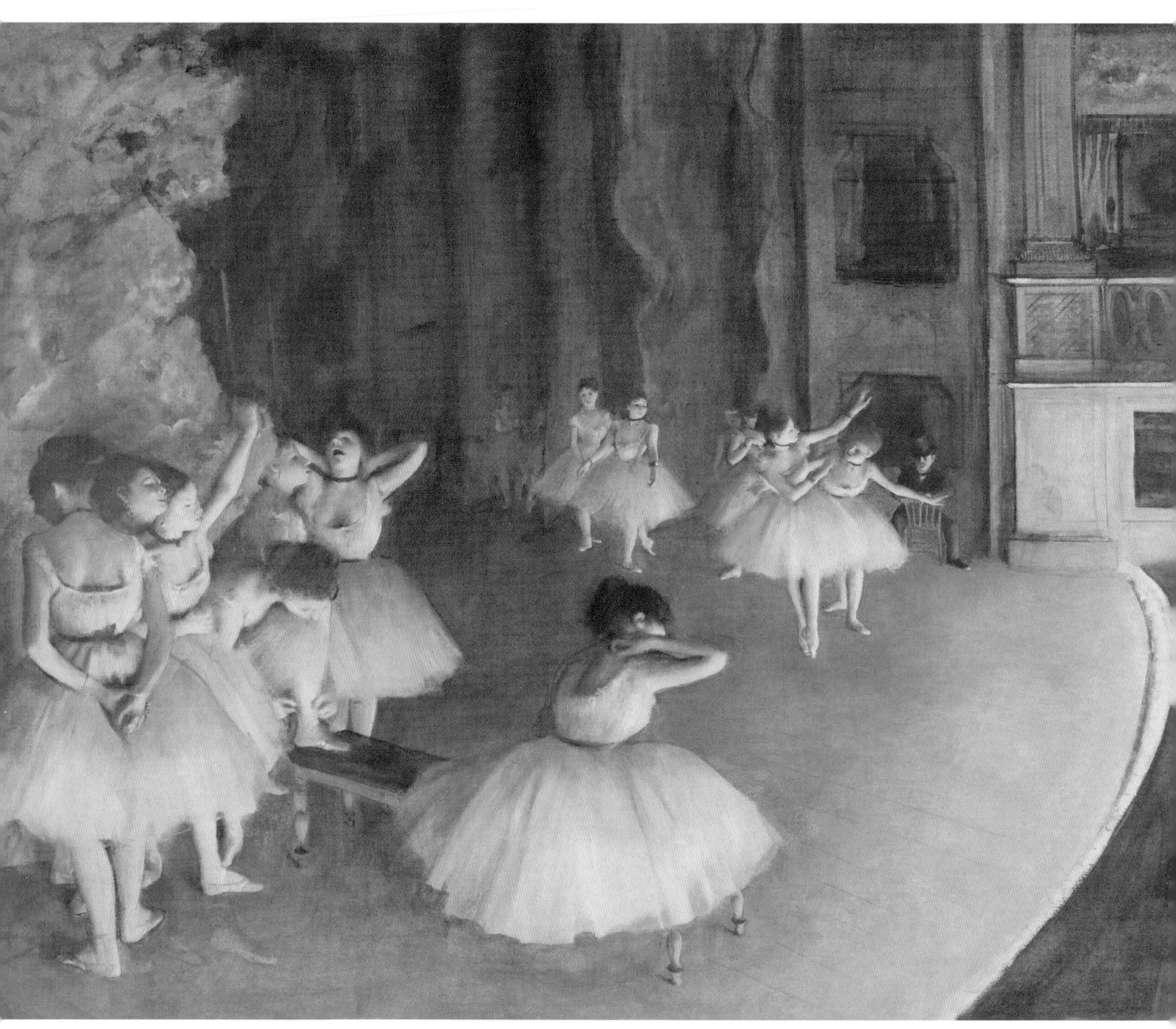

Ballet Rehearsal on the Stage, 1874
Oil on canvas, 65 x 81 cm (25^1/$_2$ x 32 in)
• Musée d'Orsay, Paris

One of three paintings that depict a rehearsal on stage, this wittily contrasts the
elegance of the dancers to the right with the more relaxed group on the left,
one of whom is yawning.

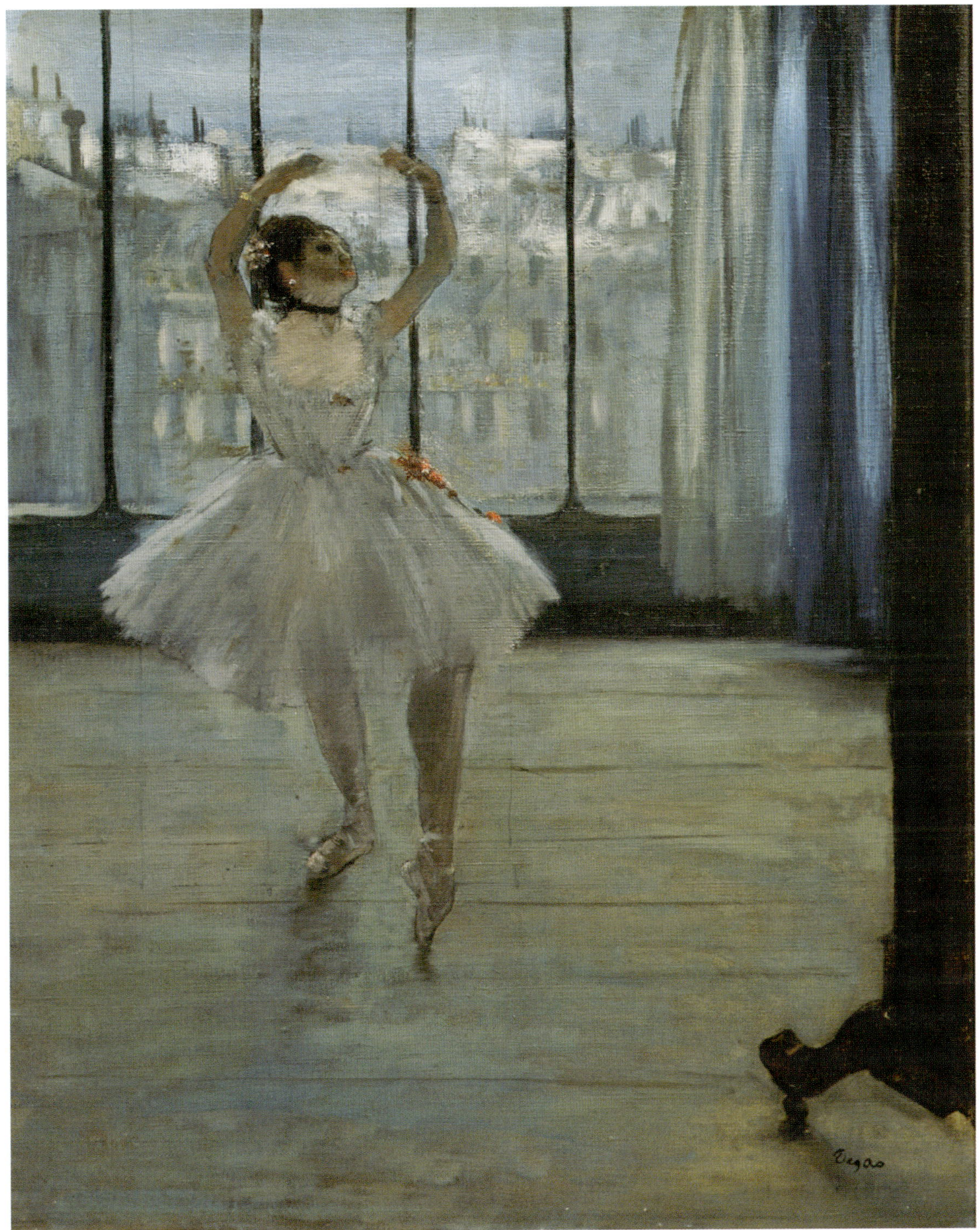

Dancer in Front of a Window (Dancer at the Photographer's Studio),
c. **1874–77** Oil on canvas, 65 x 50 cm (25$\frac{1}{2}$ x 19$\frac{2}{3}$ in)
• Pushkin Museum, Moscow

Posed in a photographic studio, the dancer's left leg looks awkward; perhaps a witty comment by Degas that she is having to hold this position while the photographer sets up his apparatus and takes the picture.

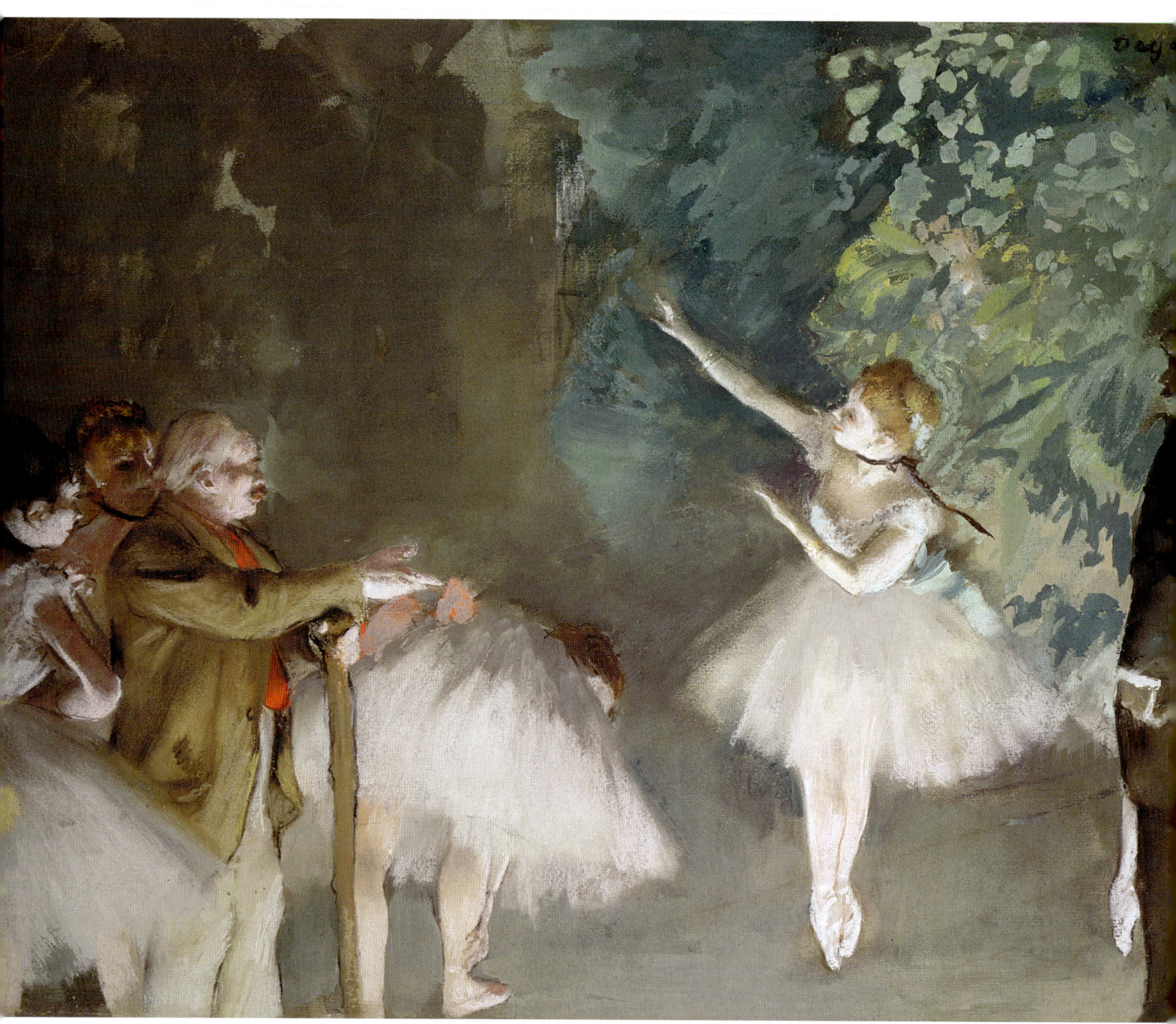

Ballet Rehearsal, 1875
Pastel and oil on paper, 55 x 68 cm (21^2/$_3$ x 26^4/$_5$ in)
• Nelson-Atkins Museum, Kansas

Another picture that features the flamboyant dance master Jules Perrot, in his signature red shirt and large cane. To the right is another man, possibly an impresario or a *flâneur*.

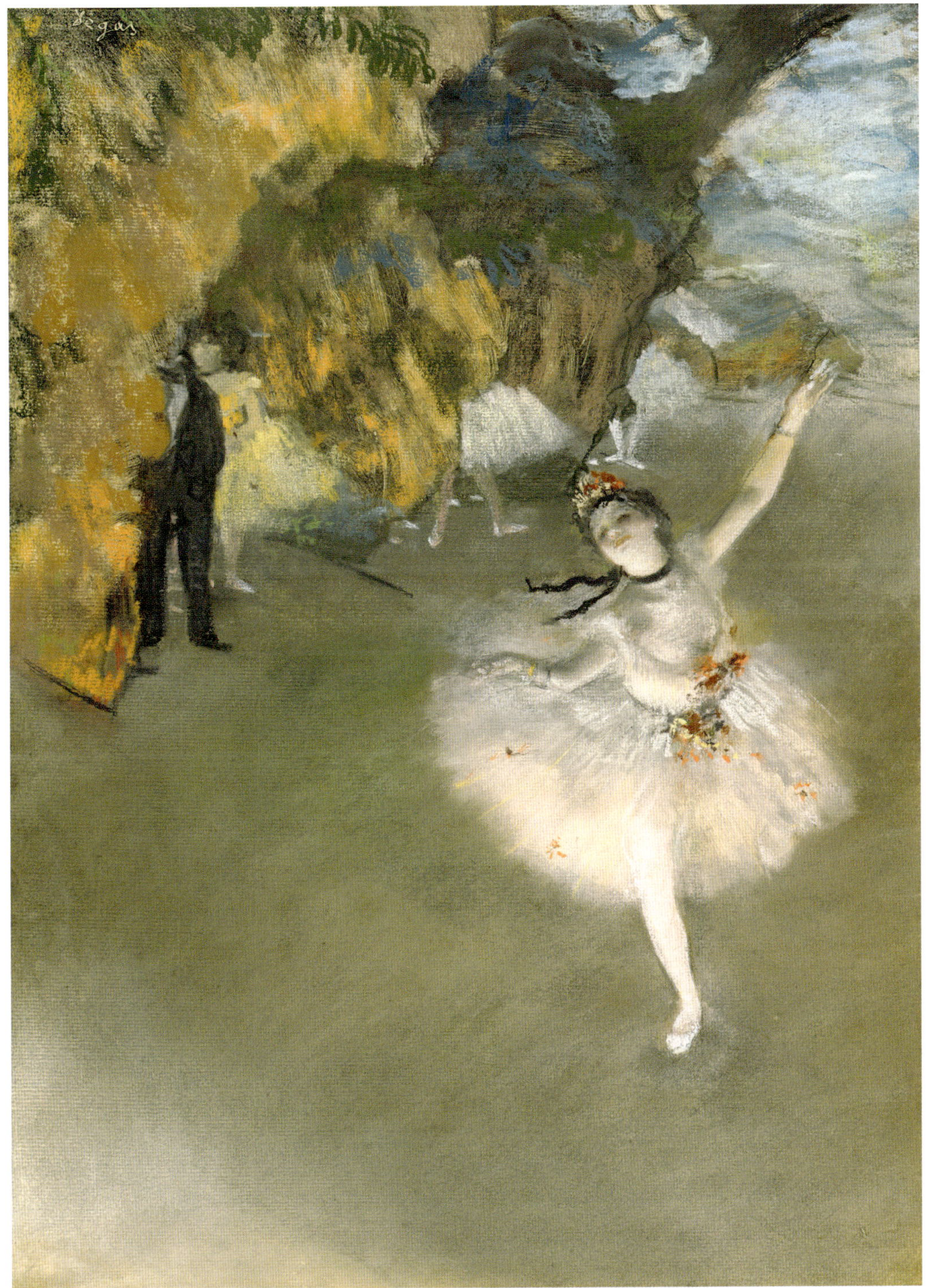

The Star, or Dancer on the Stage, _c._ 1876–77
Pastel on paper, 60 x 44 cm (23^2/$_3$ x 17^1/$_3$ in)
• Musée d'Orsay, Paris

The asymmetry of the composition reminds us that this is a transitory moment, as the viewer watches the dancer complete a difficult arabesque movement that Degas captures perfectly with her outstretched arms.

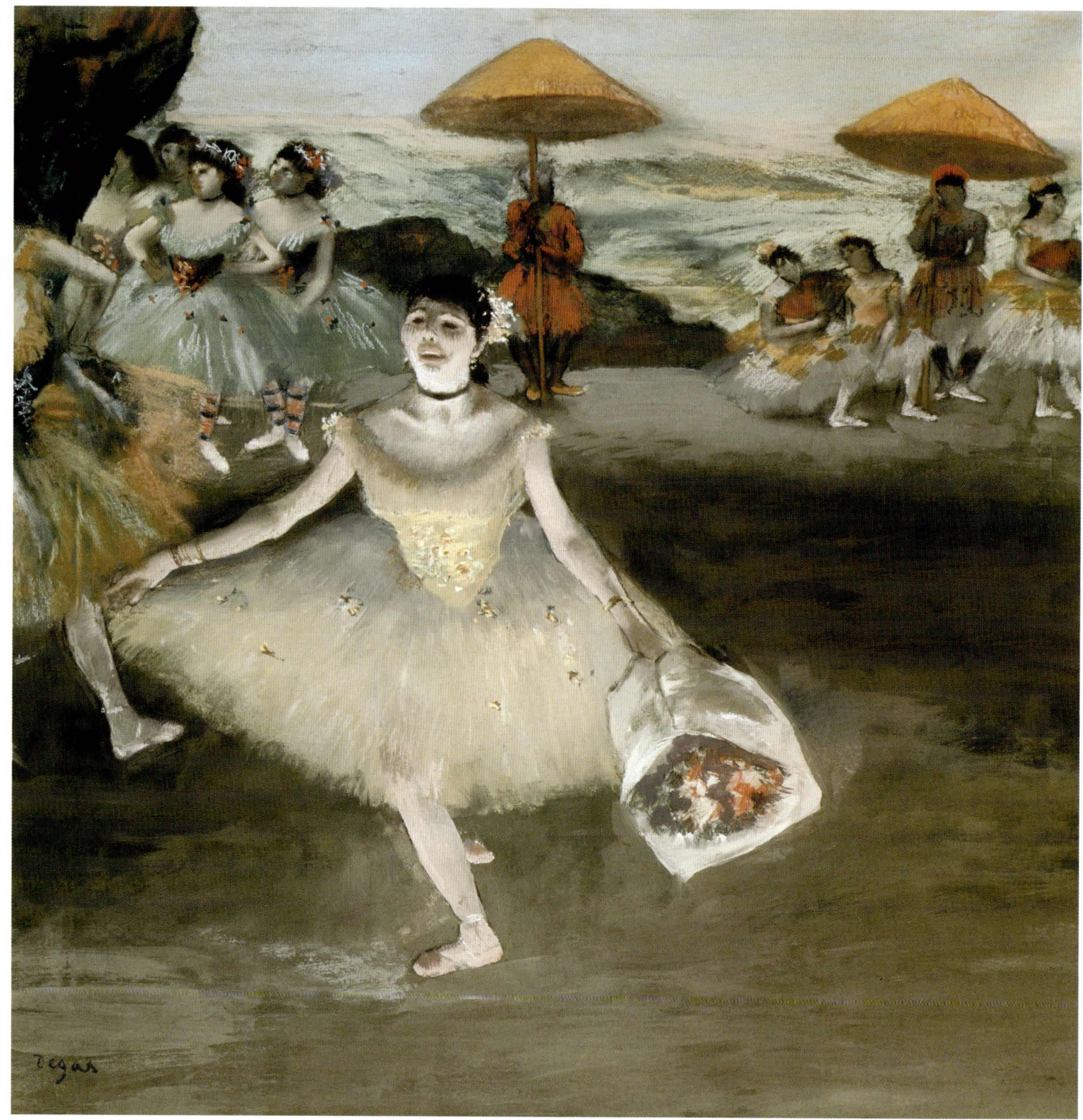

Dancer with Bouquet, Curtseying, 1877
Pastel on paper, 72 x 77.5 cm (28^1/$_3$ x 30^1/$_2$ in)
• Musée d'Orsay, Paris

The finale complete, the prima ballerina takes her bow, the *corps de ballet* assembled behind her. Her face is one of pure exhaustion and yet she retains a smile, acknowledging the unseen audience's adulation.

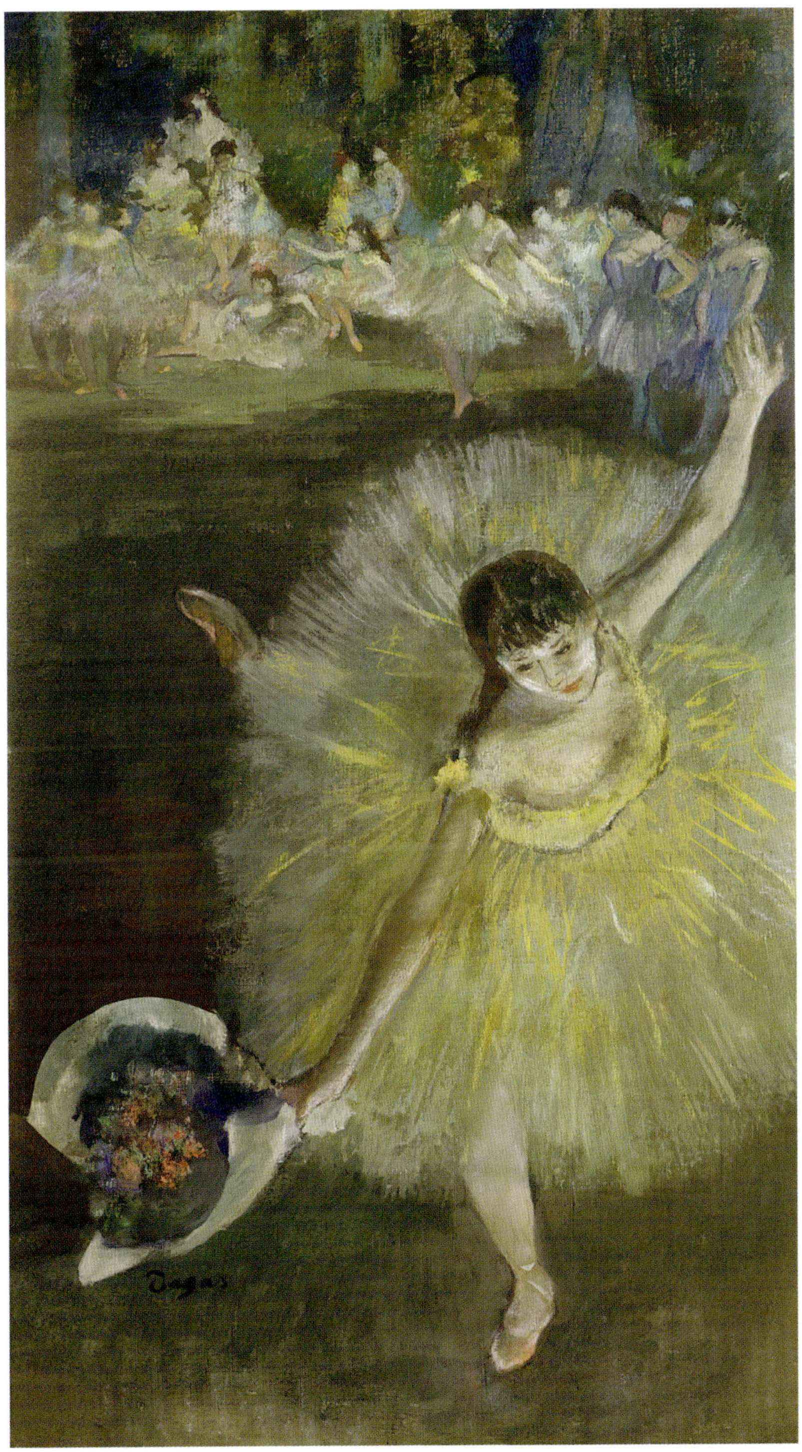

End of an Arabesque, 1877

Oil and pastel on canvas, 67.4 x 38 cm (26$\frac{1}{2}$ x 15 in)

• Musée d'Orsay, Paris

This is a difficult pose for a dancer to master and an equally difficult one for the artist to accurately render. Degas was not averse to mixing his media to create the right effect.

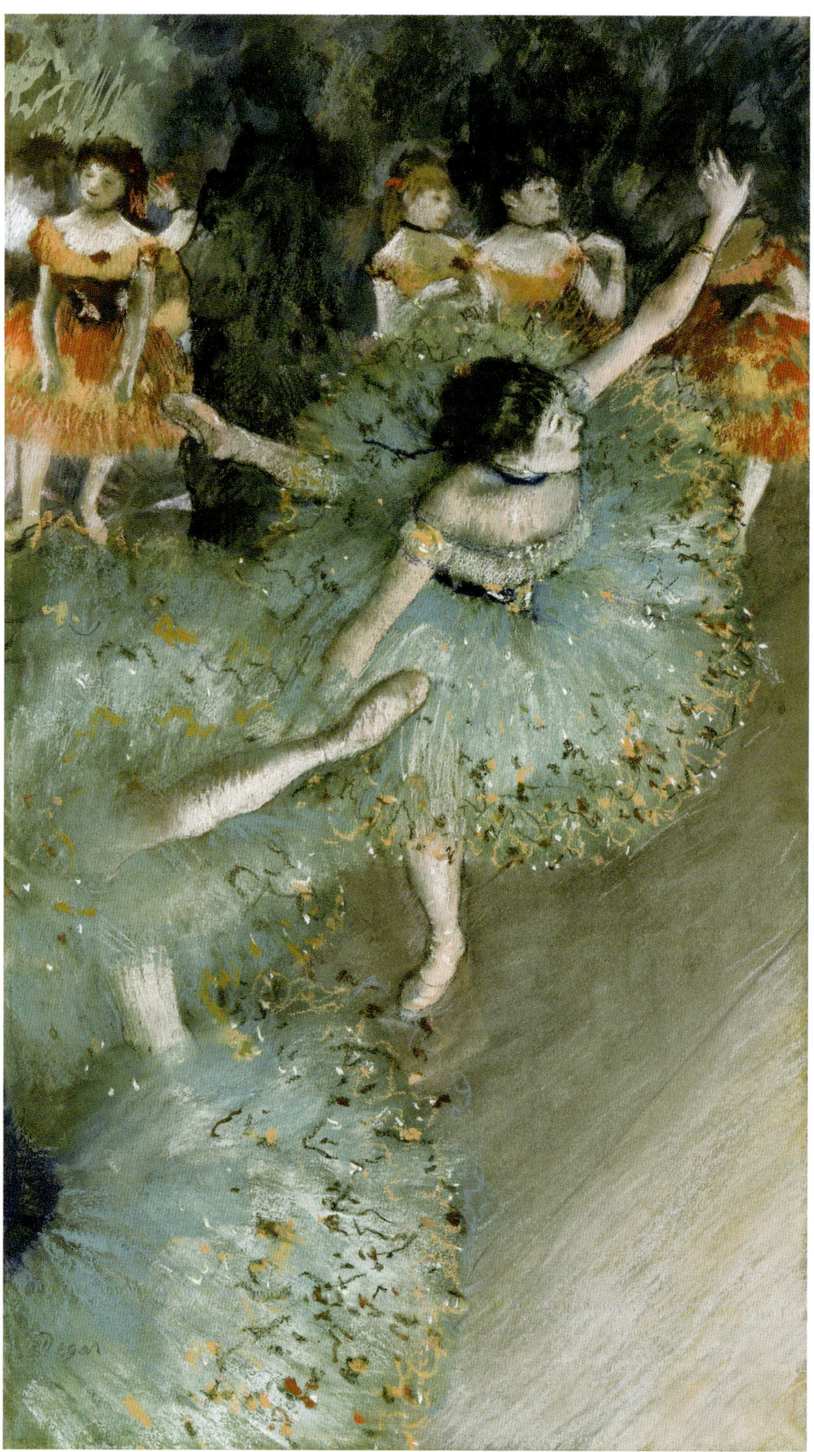

Ballerina on Pointe (Green Dancer), 1877–79
Pastel and watercolour on paper, 64 x 36 cm (25 x 14 in)
• Museo Thyssen-Bornemisza, Madrid

Walter Sickert and his wife Ellen purchased this picture in 1886. With Degas' permission, Sickert exhibited the work at the New English Art Club exhibition in 1888, founded two years earlier in London.

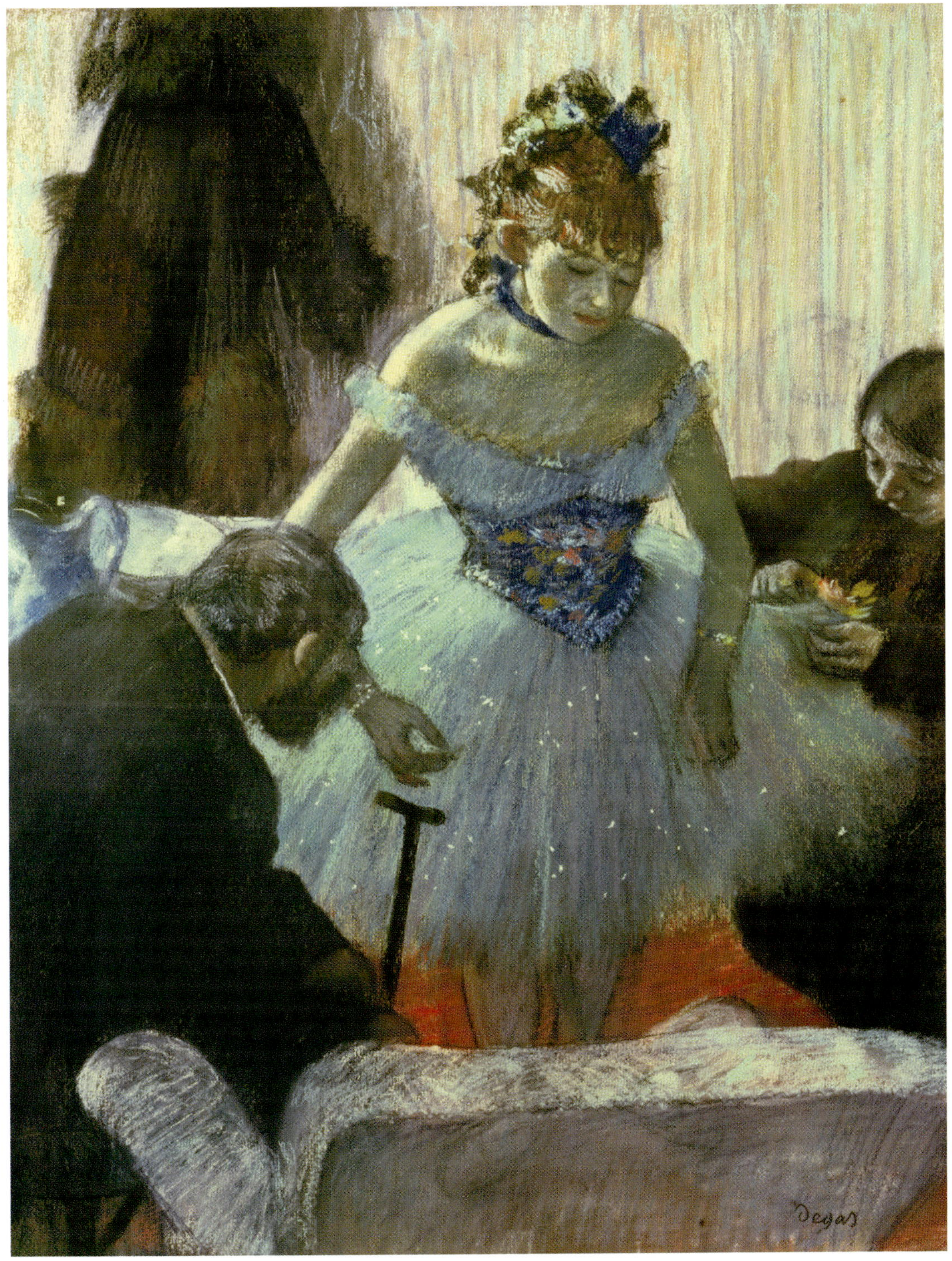

Dancer in her Dressing Room, 1878
Pastel on paper, 59 x 45 cm (23¼ x 17¾ in)
• Private Collection

Most young ballerinas at this time had 'protectors', who usually sponsored their careers and looked after their interests. The protector is seen closely monitoring his protégé, while last-minute adjustments are made to the dancer's costume.

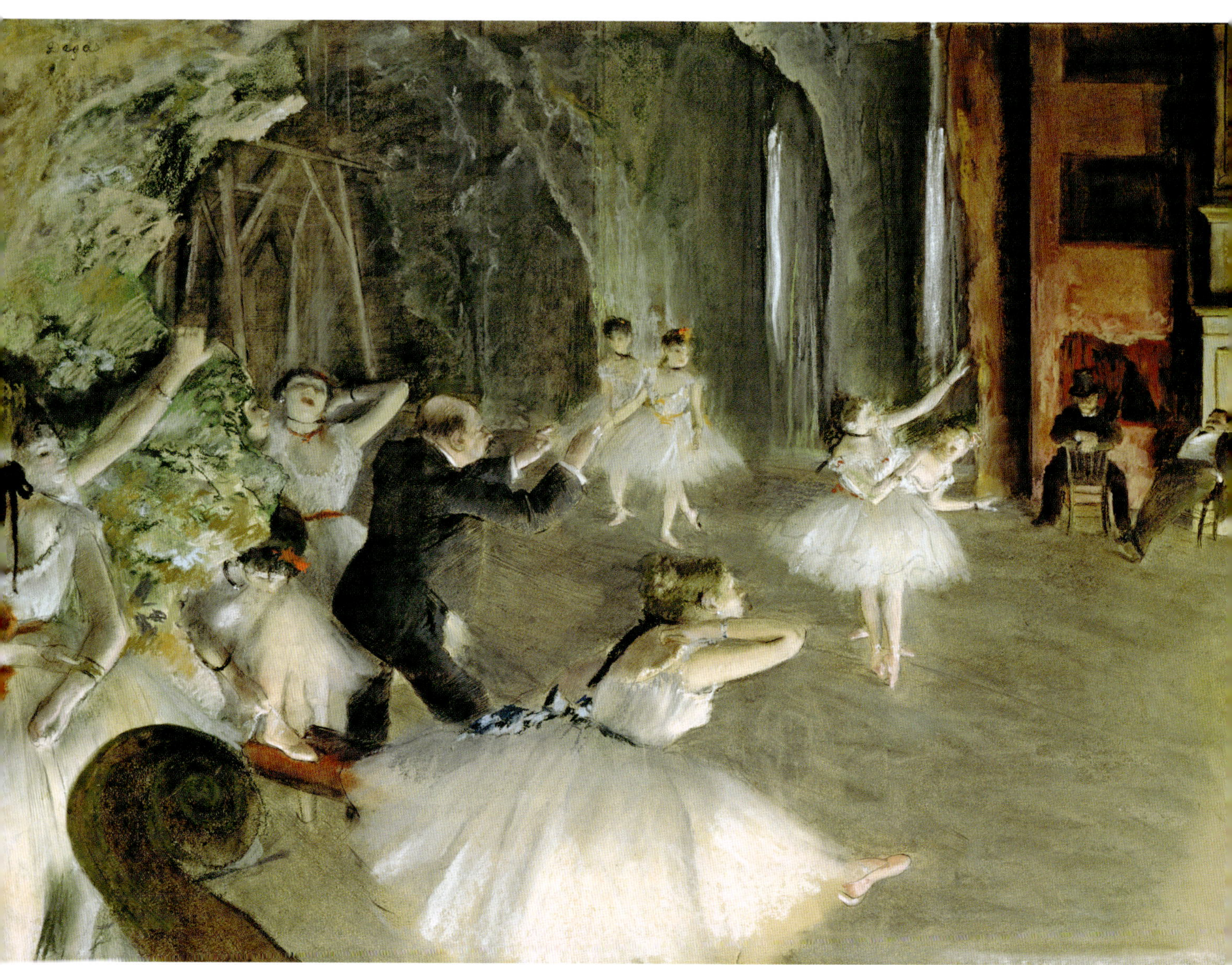

The Rehearsal of the Ballet on Stage, *c.* **1878–79**
Pastel on paper, 52.1 x 70.8 cm (20$\frac{1}{2}$ x 27$\frac{4}{5}$ in)
• Metropolitan Museum of Art, New York

The viewer appears to be in the orchestra pit, Degas having included the top of a double bass in the foreground. This is a compositional ruse intended to draw the viewer's eye towards the central dancer on the stage.

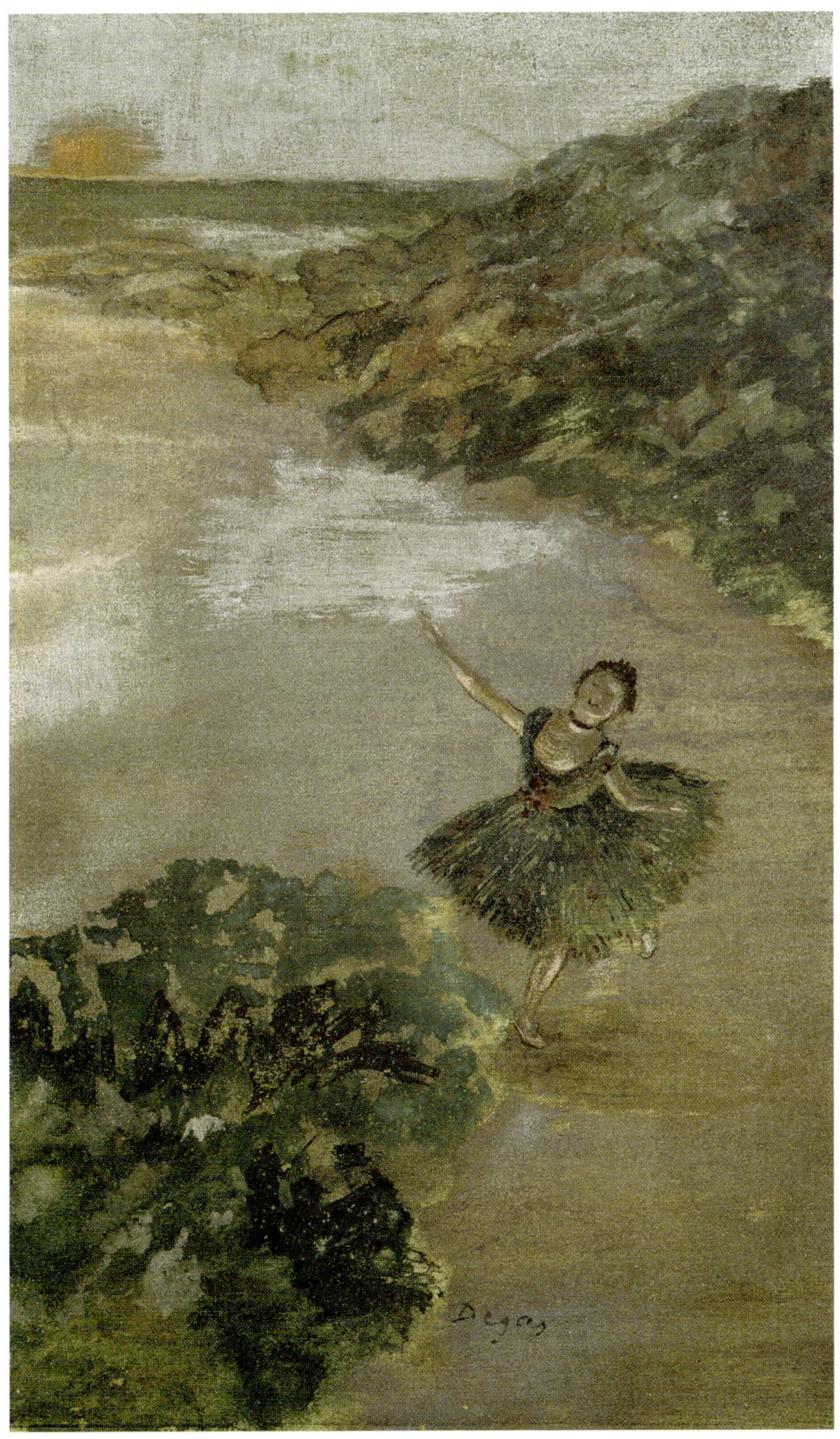

Dancer on a Stage, *c.* 1879
Gouache on silk, 24.1 x 14 cm (9¹/₂ x 5¹/₂ in)
• The Courtauld Collection, London

This section was originally part of a fan, decorated by Degas. It has elements of metallic paint, a device first used by the American artist Mary Cassatt, who became a friend of Degas and helped promote his work in the US.

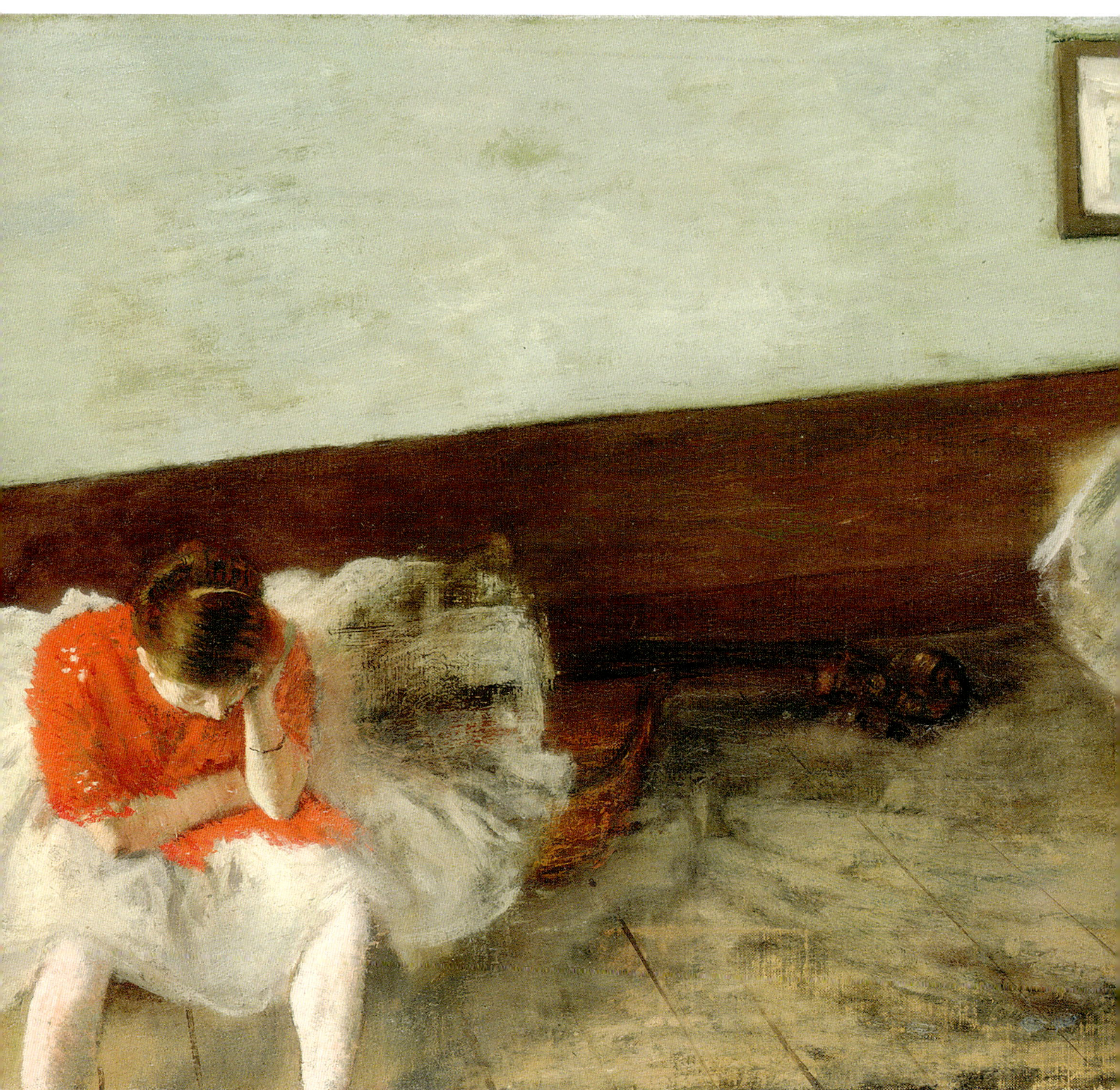

The Dance Lesson *c.* 1879
Oil on canvas, 38 x 88 cm (15 x 34^2/$_3$ in)
• National Gallery of Art, Washington D.C.

A panoramic view, the first of many dance pictures using the same format, which may have evolved from Degas' depictions of racecourses. It was shown at the fifth Impressionist exhibition in 1880.

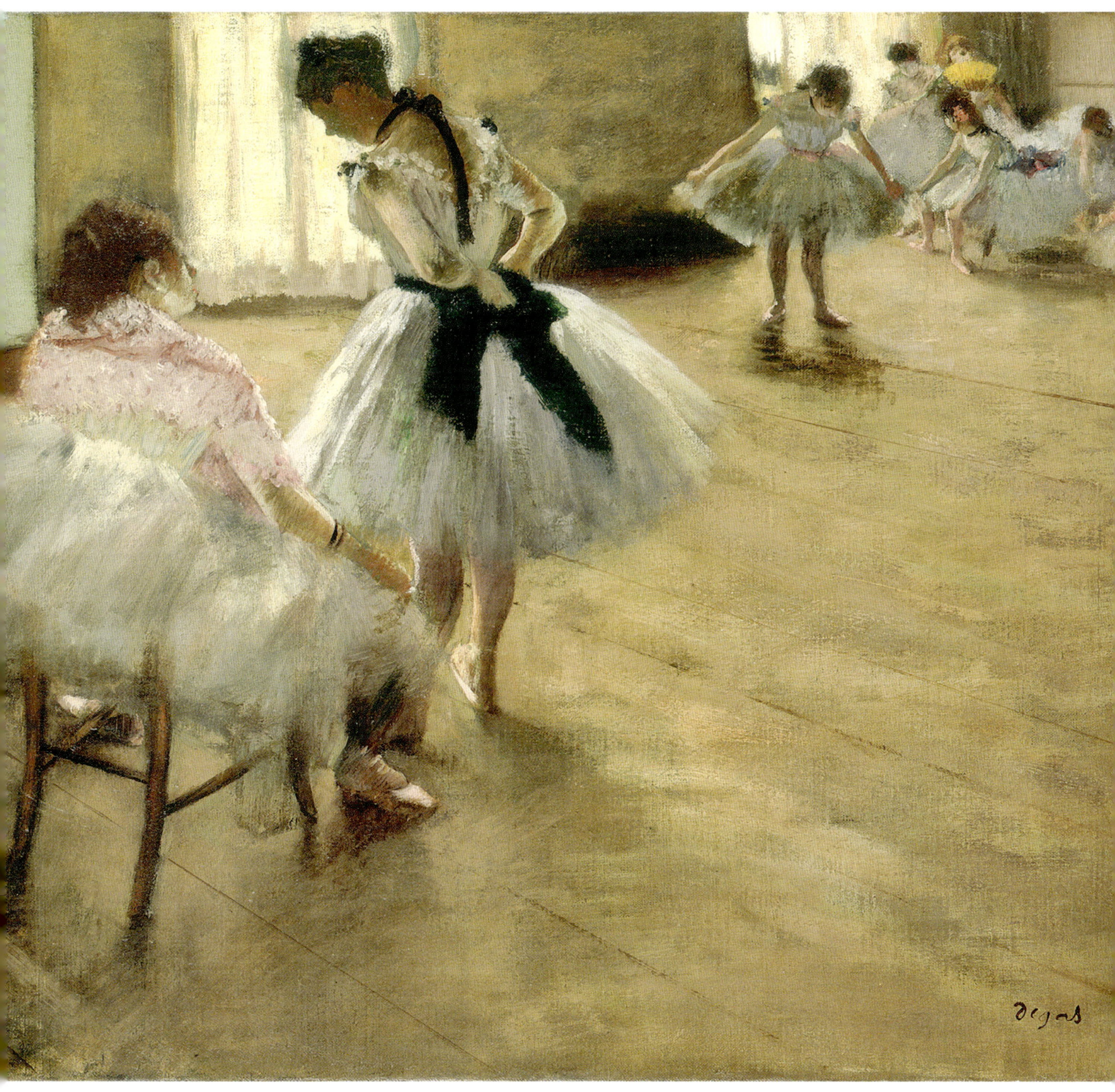

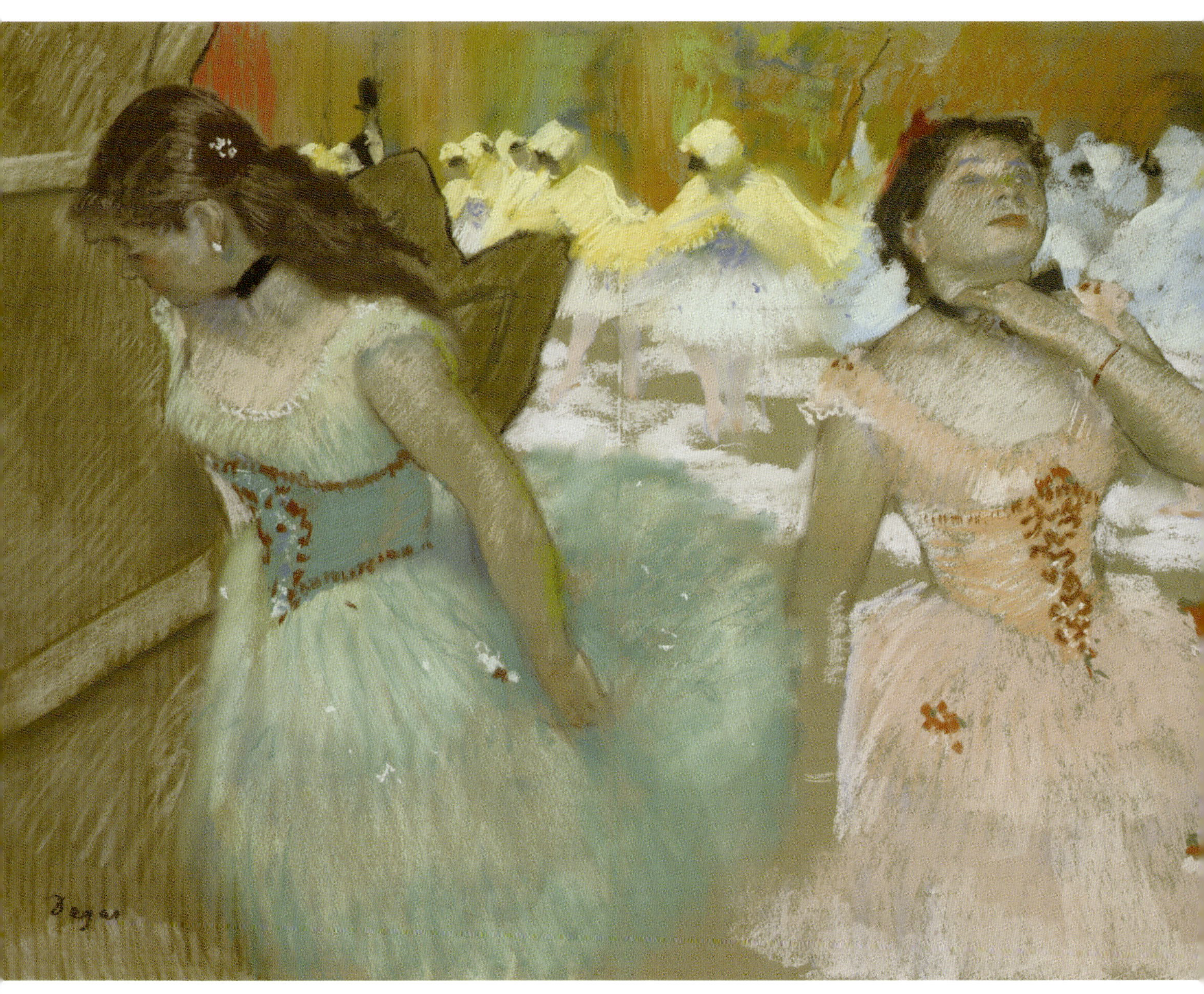

Entrance of the Masked Dancers, *c.* 1879
Pastel on paper, 49 x 64.8 cm (19^1/$_3$ x 25^1/$_2$ in)
• Clark Institute of Art, Williamstown, Massachusetts

This colourful picture is identifiable as a scene from the ballet *Don Juan*, or *Don Giovanni*. The viewer is in a prime spot, mirroring the gentleman on the other side of the stage, who has an equally privileged view of the dancers.

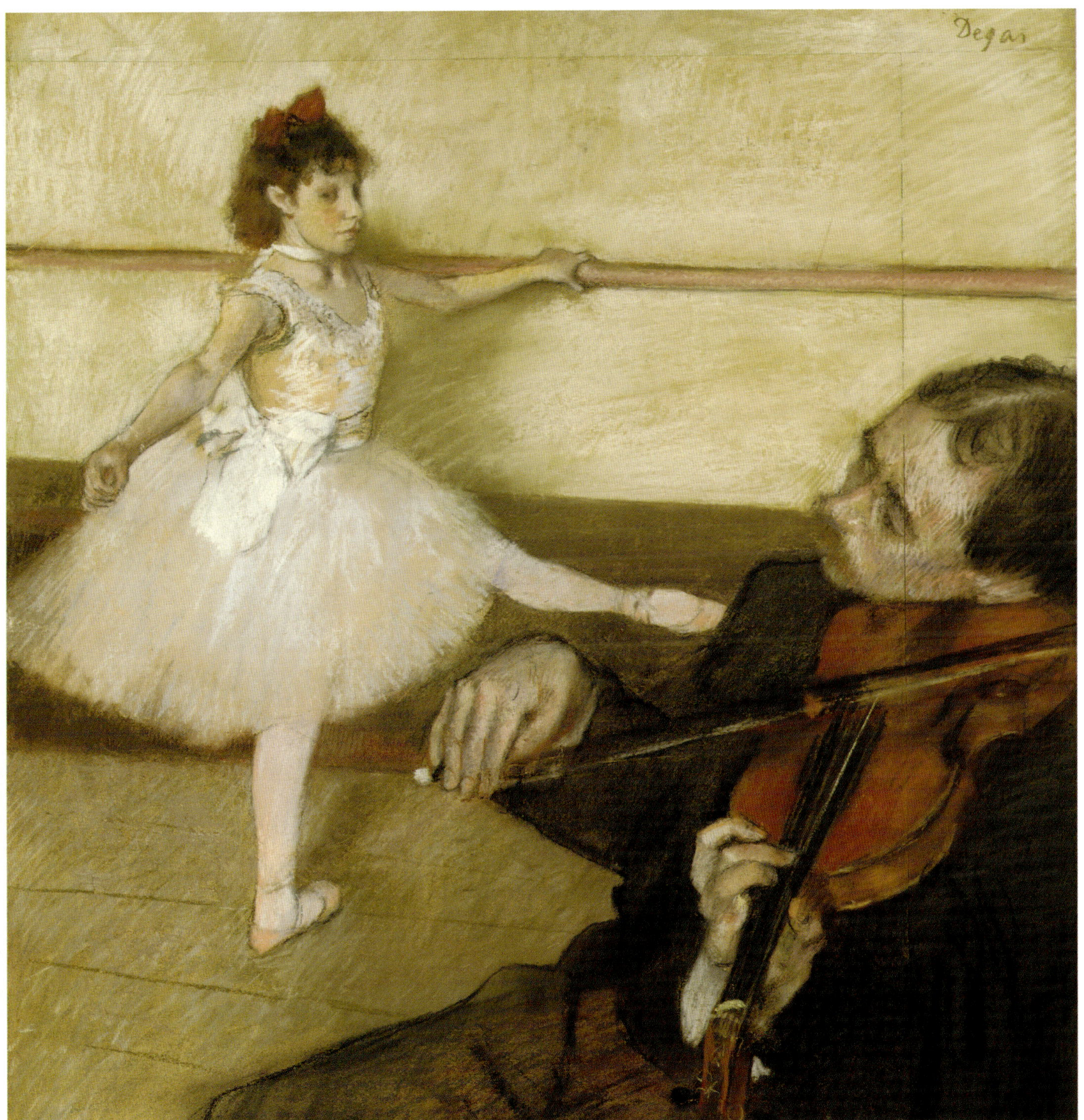

The Dance Lesson, *c.* 1879
Pastel, 65 x 56 cm (25$\frac{1}{2}$ x 22 in)
• Metropolitan Museum of Art, New York

In this view we are standing where the dance master or examiner would stand, next to the musician, possibly tapping out the rhythm with his cane. The dancer appears to be looking towards the viewer (the dance master).

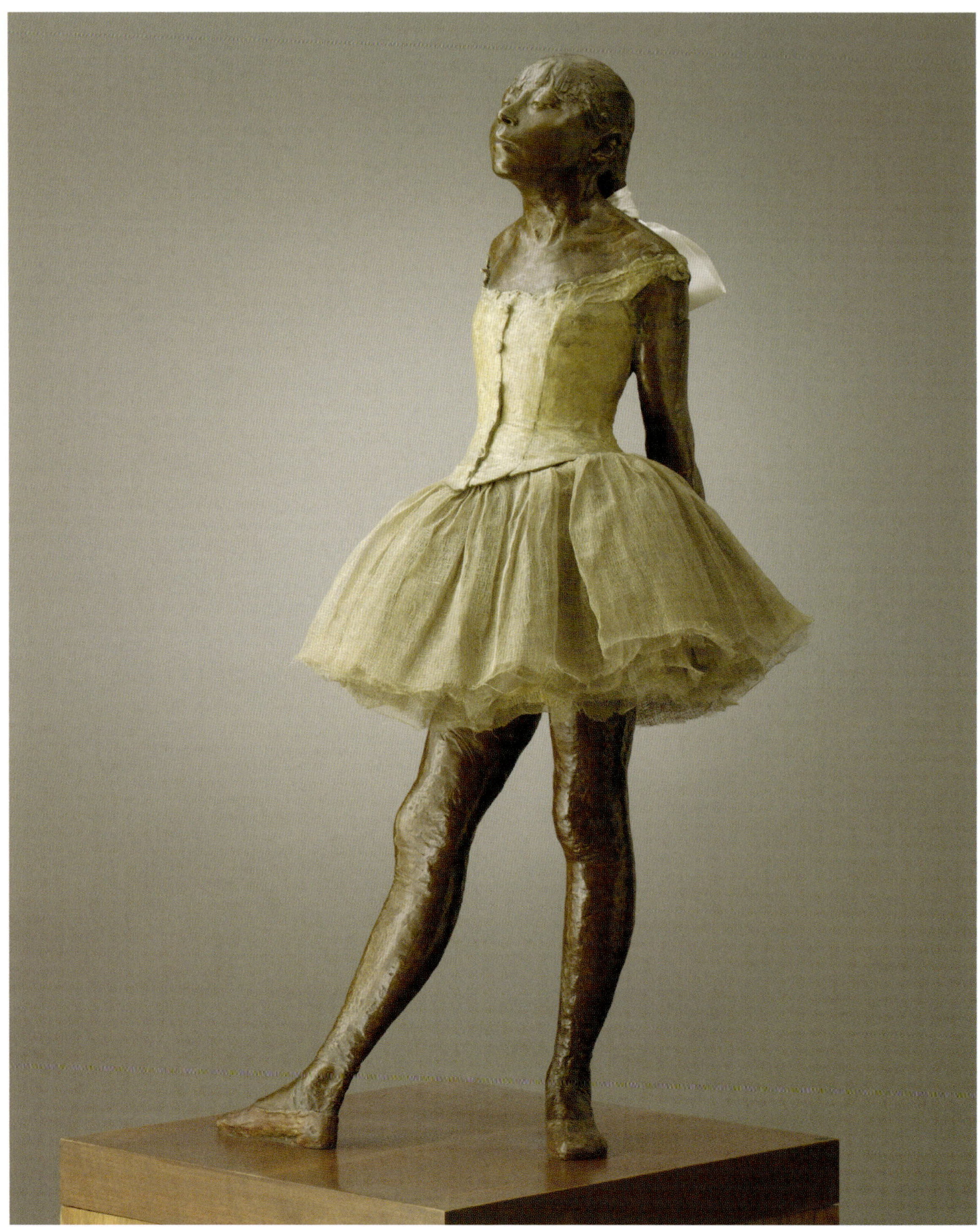

Little Dancer Aged Fourteen, modelled 1879–81, cast 1919–21
Bronze with gauze tutu and silk ribbon on a wooden base, height 99 cm (39 in)
• Clark Institute of Art, Williamstown, Massachusetts

Originally made in wax by Degas when it was exhibited in 1881, the artist used real hair on his sculpture. Many critics were alarmed at the breaking of artistic conventions and its sense of realism.

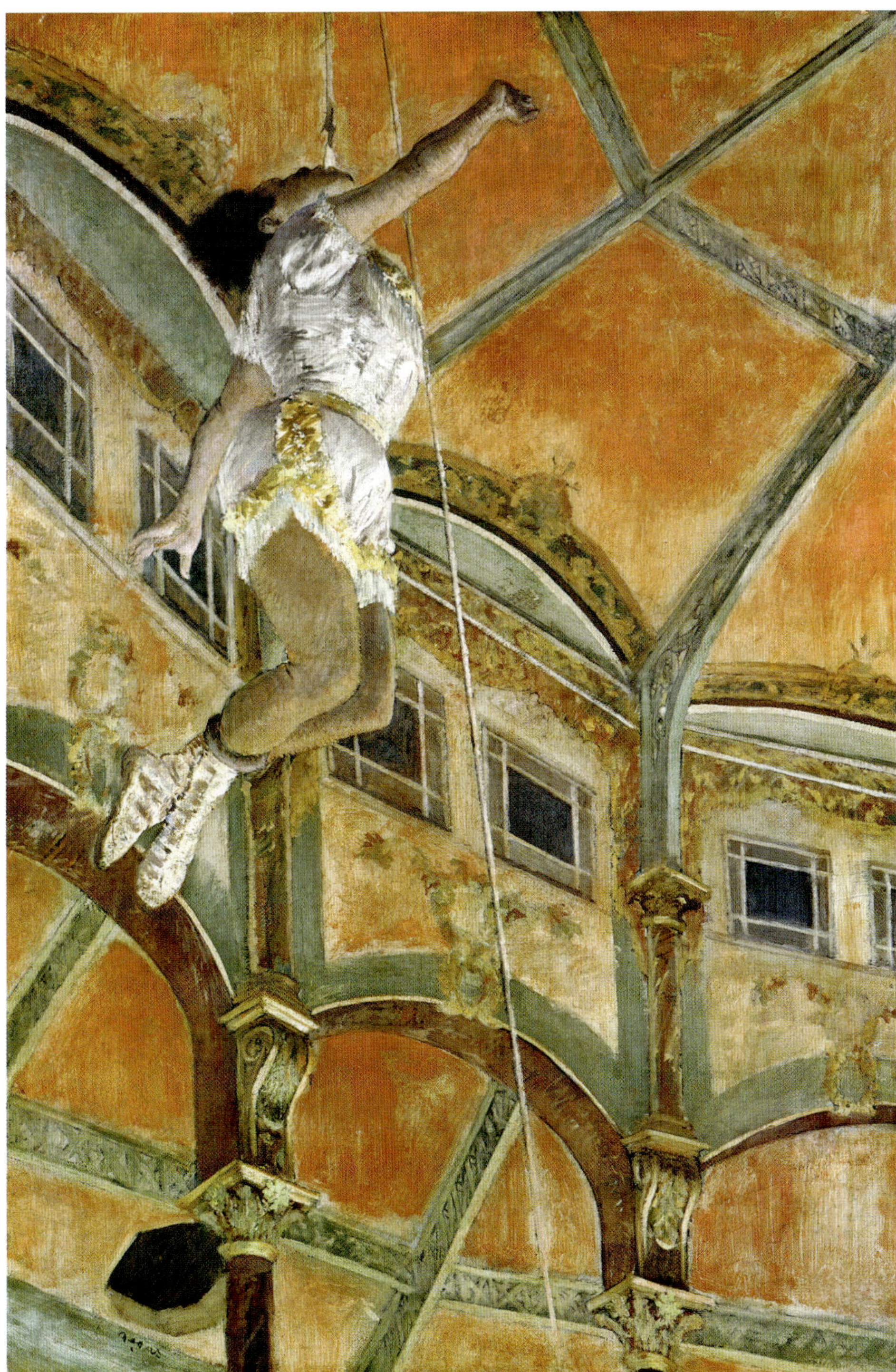

Miss La La at the Cirque Fernando, 1879
Oil on canvas, 116.8 x 77.5 cm (46 x 30½ in)
• National Gallery, London

Miss La La was an acrobat, shown here suspended by a rope clenched between her teeth.
The painting was exhibited at the fourth Impressionist exhibition in 1879.

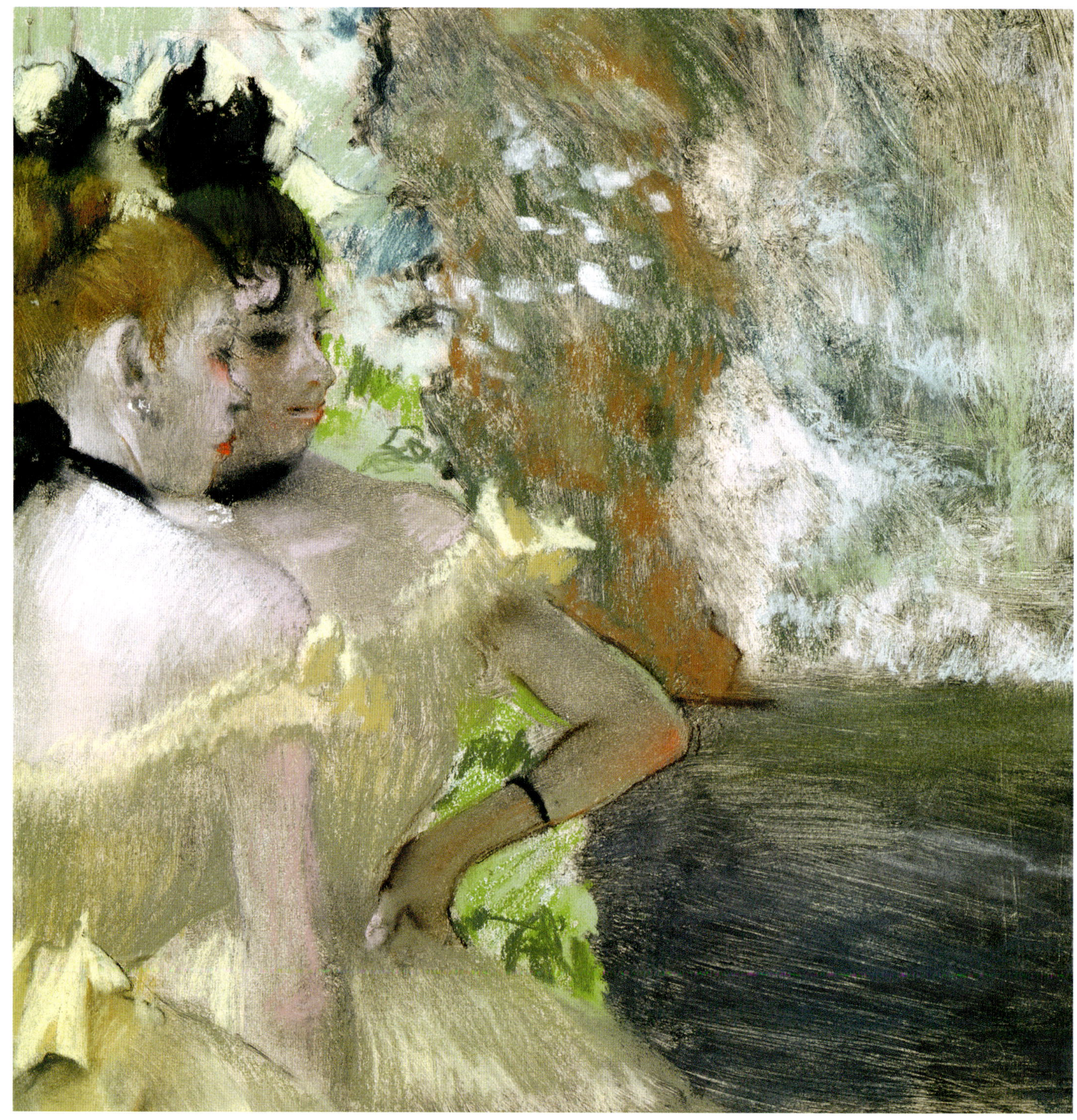

Dancers in the Wings, *c.* 1878–79
Pastel on paper, 29 x 26 cm (11$\frac{1}{2}$ x 10$\frac{1}{4}$ in)
• Private Collection

The nondescript background is a foil to the focus of the viewer's attention, the dancers themselves. Degas produced a number of these images, which show dancers waiting for the performance, or their part in it, to begin.

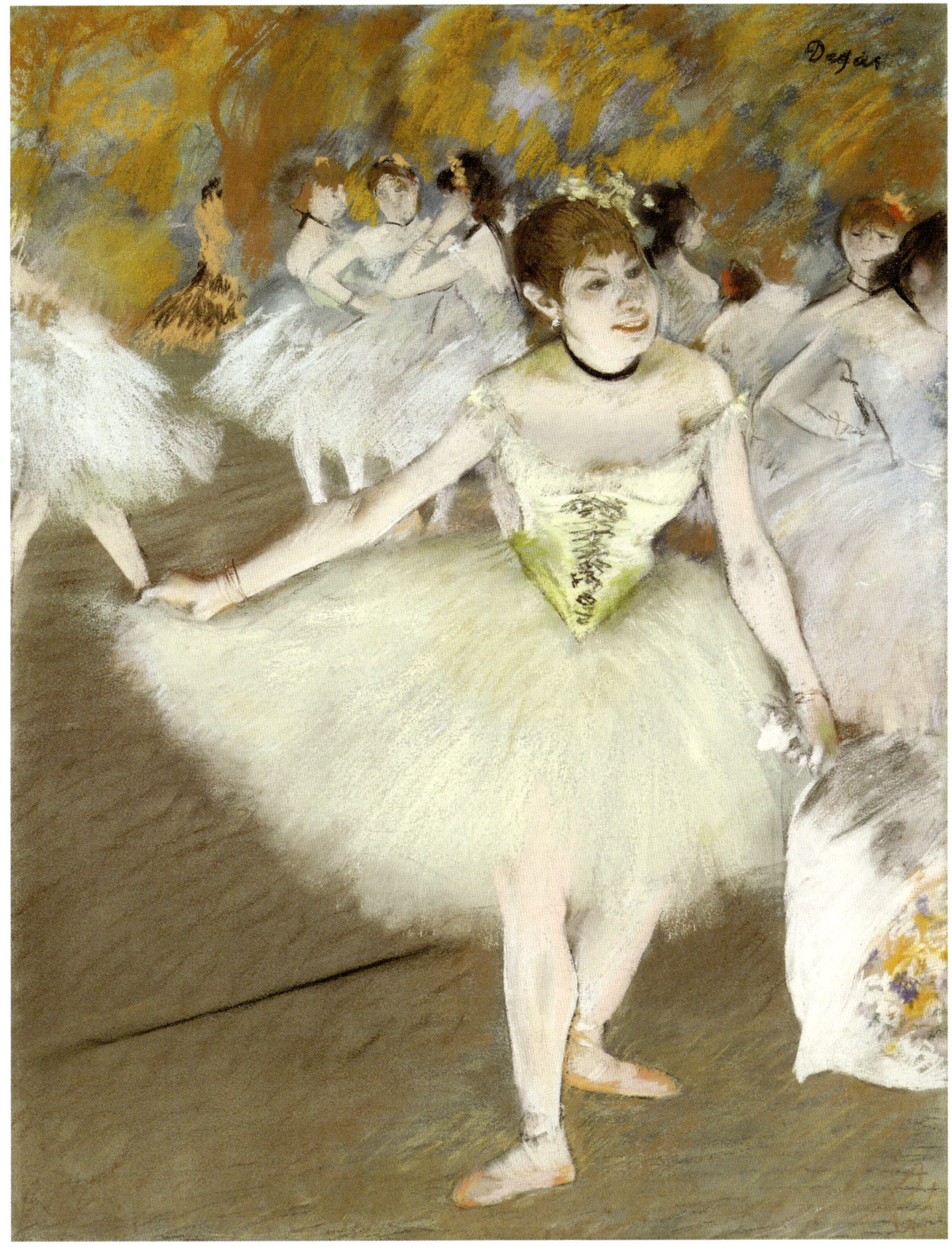

On Stage, 1879–81
Pastel on paper, 58.5 x 44.8 cm (23 x 17²/₃ in)
• Private Collection

The diagonal line across the stage emphasises the location of the prima ballerina, who is enjoying the applause from an unseen audience. Unlike many of Degas' ballet performance pictures, there is no sense of fatigue in her stance.

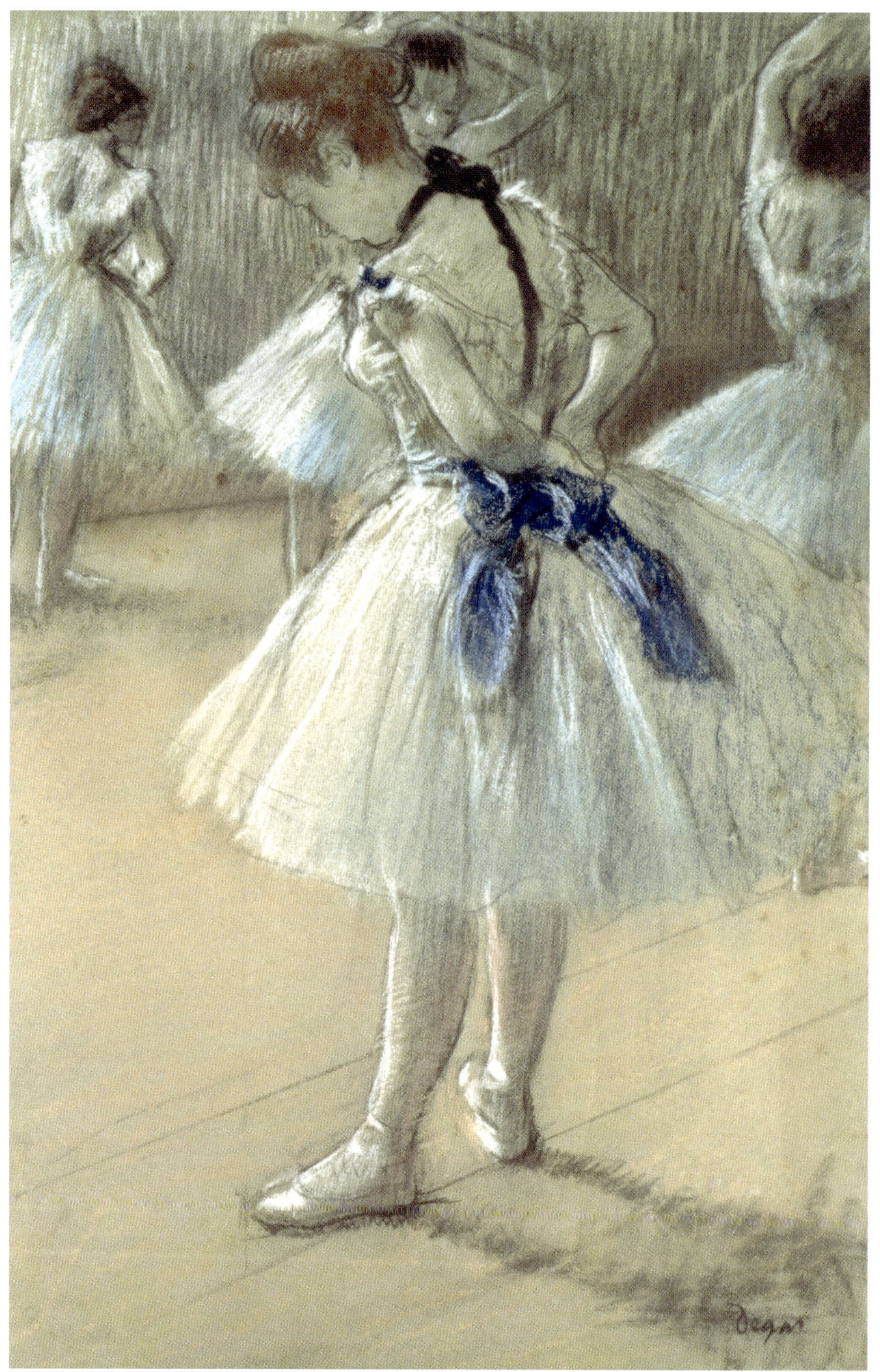

Dancer, _c._ 1880
Pastel, 49 x 32 cm (19^1/$_3$ x 13 in)
• Private Collection

This delicate pastel drawing is most likely a study for a larger picture, possibly _The Dance Lesson_ (_see_ page 44), exhibited at the fifth Impressionist exhibition in 1880. The dancer is apparently unaware of the artist's presence.

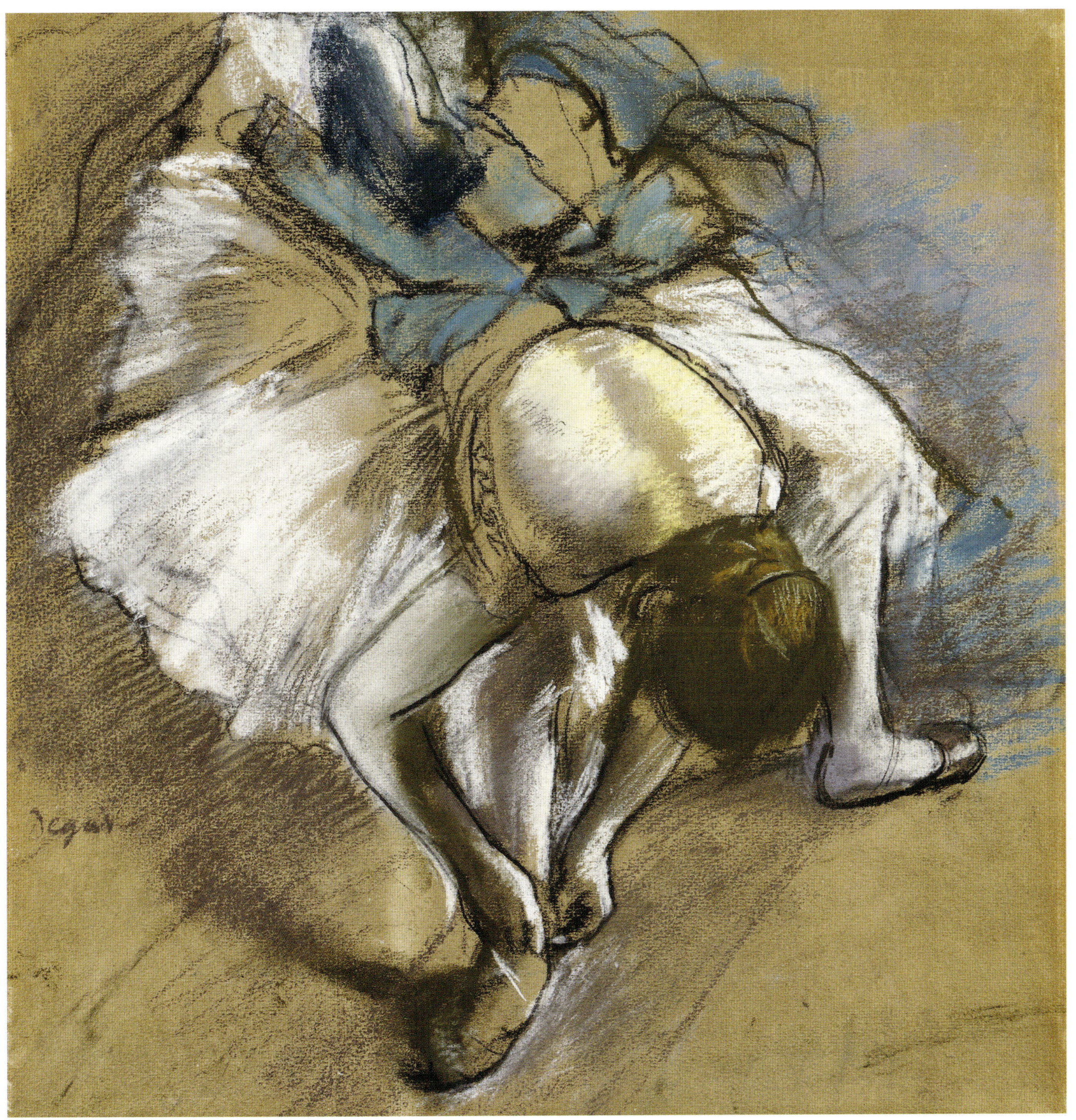

Dancer Putting on her Shoes, *c.* **1880–85**
Pastel and chalk on buff paper, 47.2 x 43 cm (18$\frac{1}{2}$ x 17 in)
• Private Collection

An off-guard moment caught by Degas, who would have completed a number of sketches prior to executing this work in his studio. Degas has chosen a darker background than usual, to give more emphasis to the white chalk.

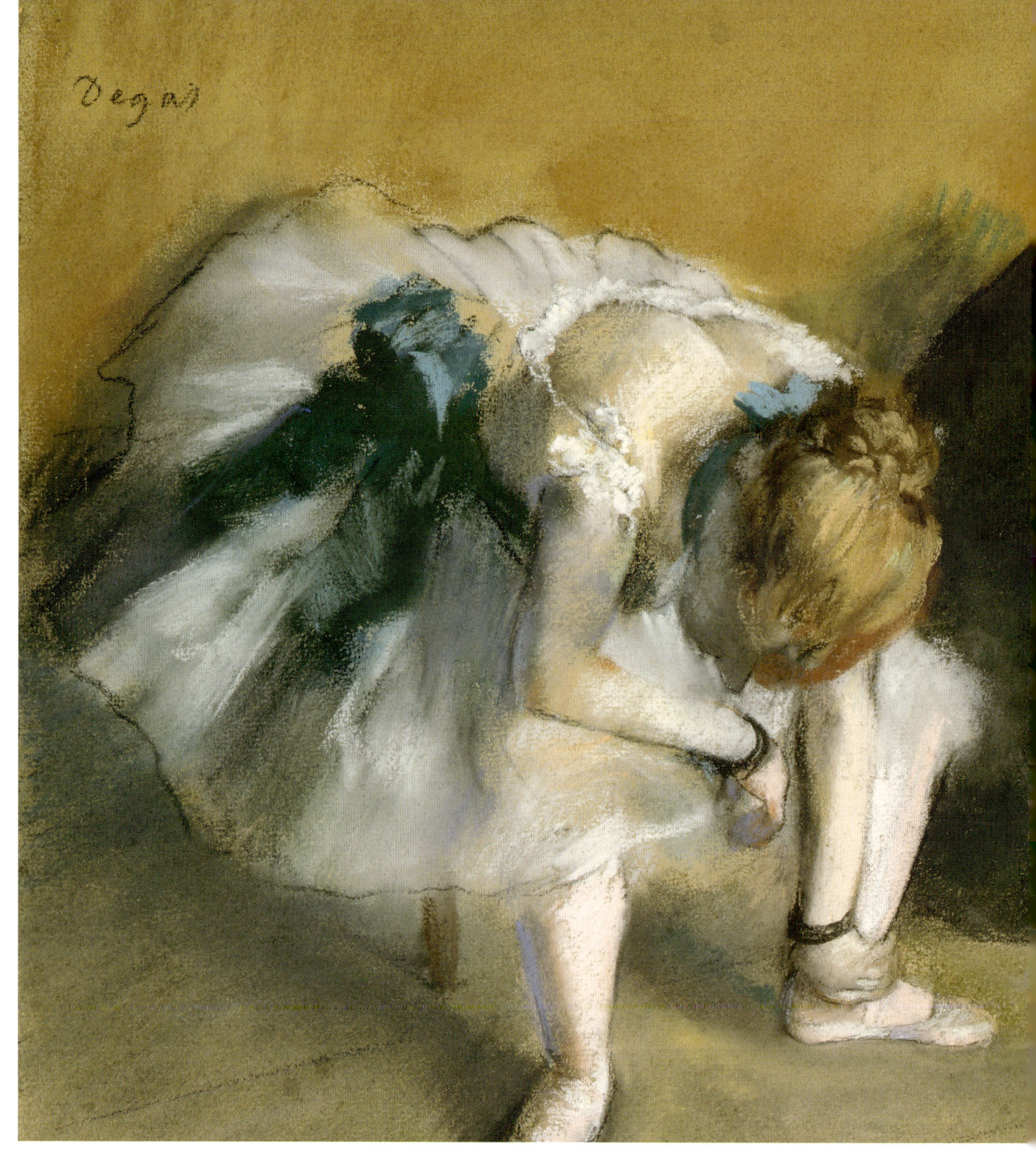

Waiting, *c.* **1882**
Pastel on paper, 48.2 x 61 cm (19 x 24 in)
• Getty Museum, Los Angeles

An aspect of Degas' dance pictures that differs from the mainstream is the way he depicted them fatigued after their class, examination or performance. This dancer is rubbing her sore ankle, the exhaustion palpable in her body language.

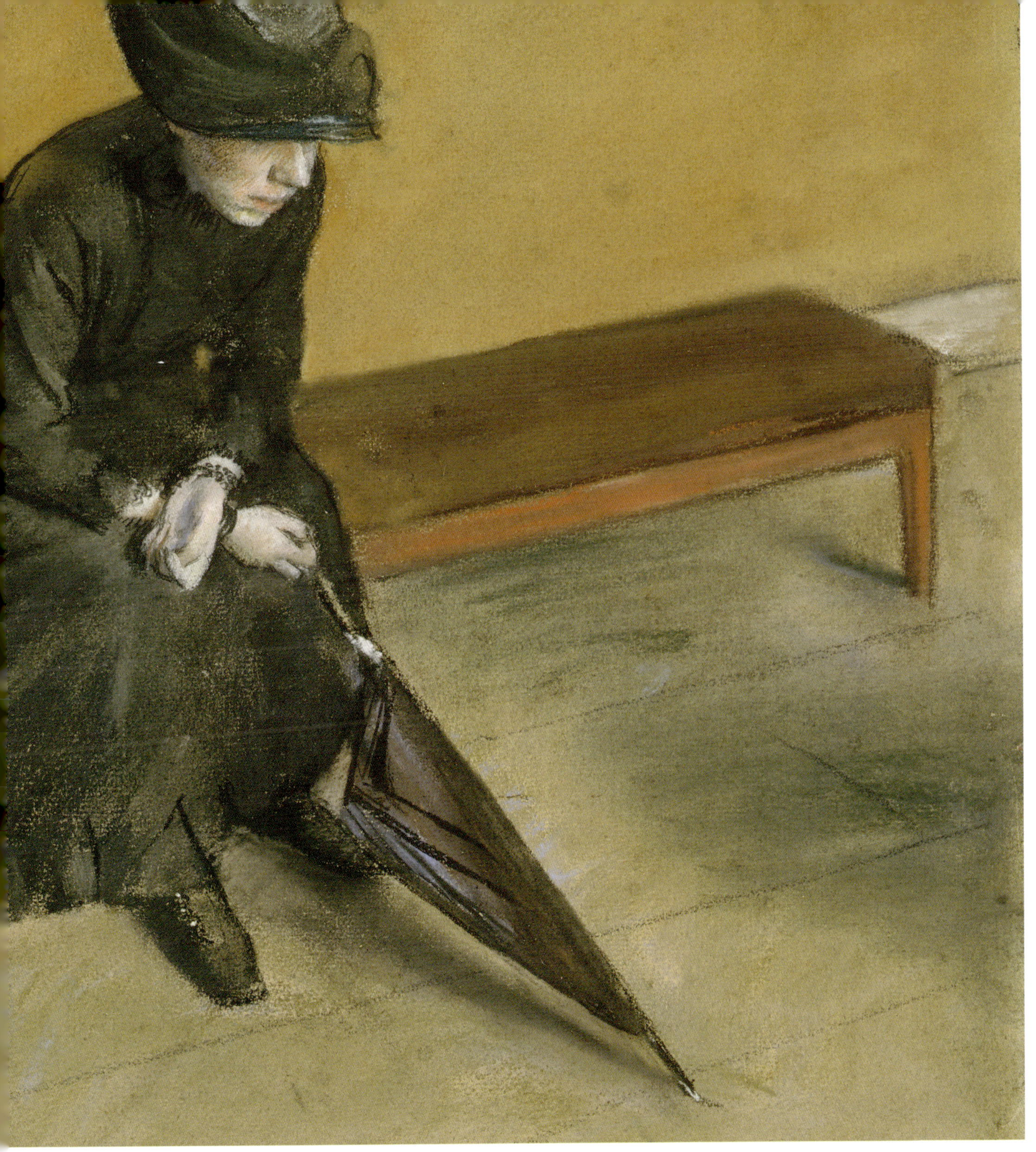

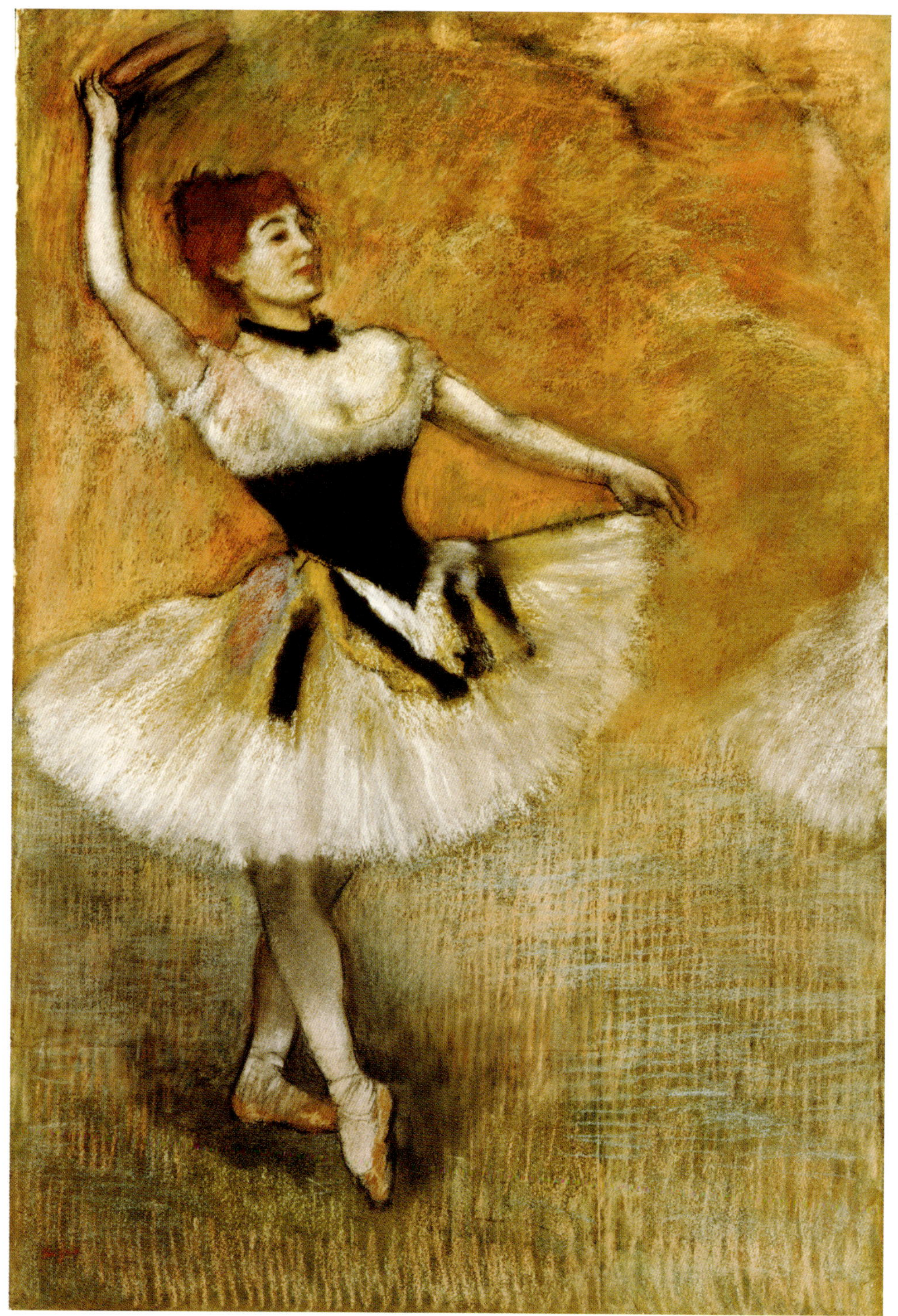

Dancer with Tambourine, 1882
Pastel on paper, 97 x 65 cm (38¼ x 25½ in)
• Private Collection

Three years after this drawing was made, Degas created the same posed figure as a sculpture, without her dress. Like his other sculptures, it was not cast until after his death.

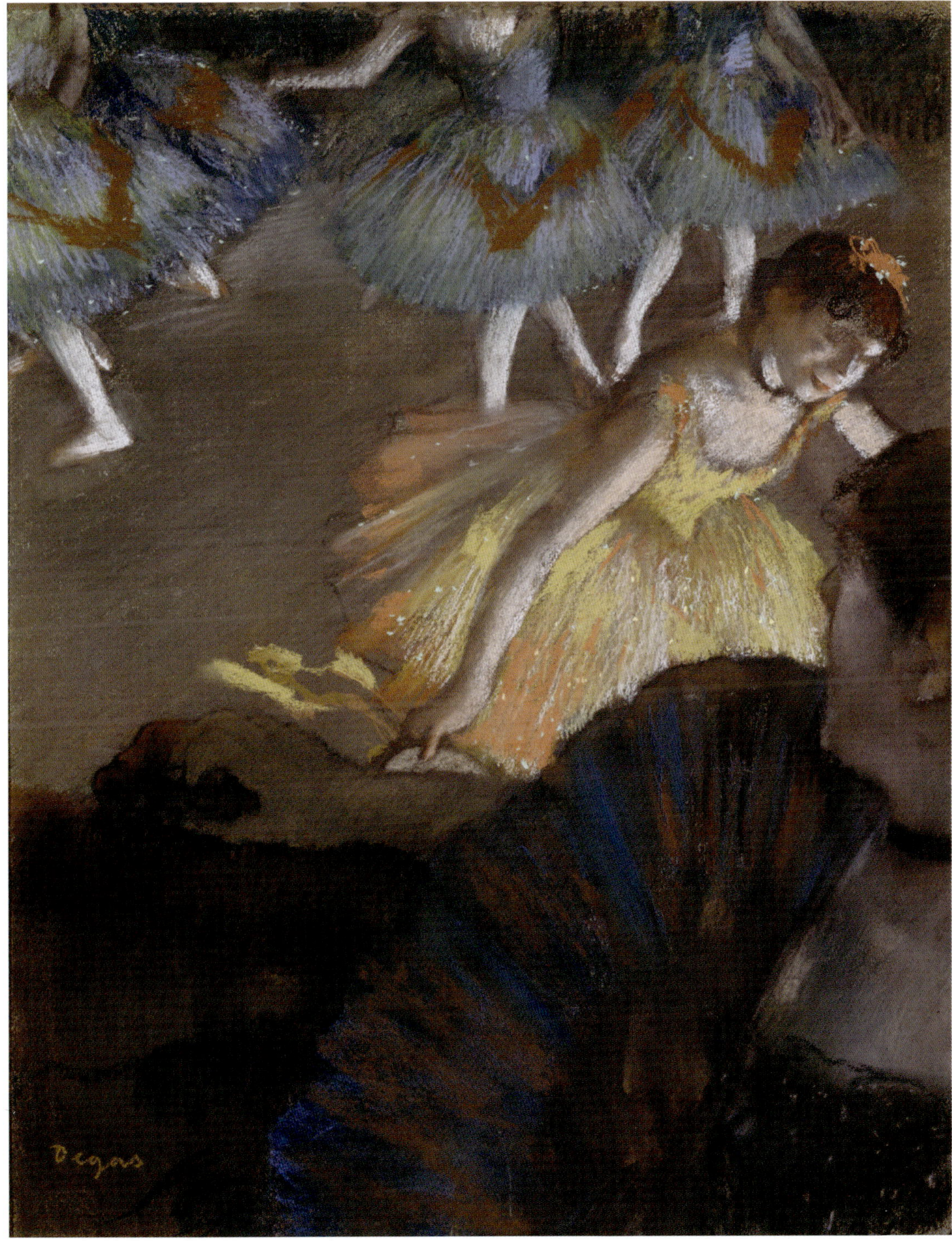

Ballet from an Opera Box, *c.* 1884
Pastel on paper, 65.4 x 50.5 cm (25³/₄ x 20 in)
• Philadelphia Museum of Art, Pennsylvania

A view such as this is one of privilege, as it's from a box, or *loge*. The viewer accompanies the lady in the *loge*, enjoying the spectacle. The top of the background is cut off, focusing the eye on the main dancer.

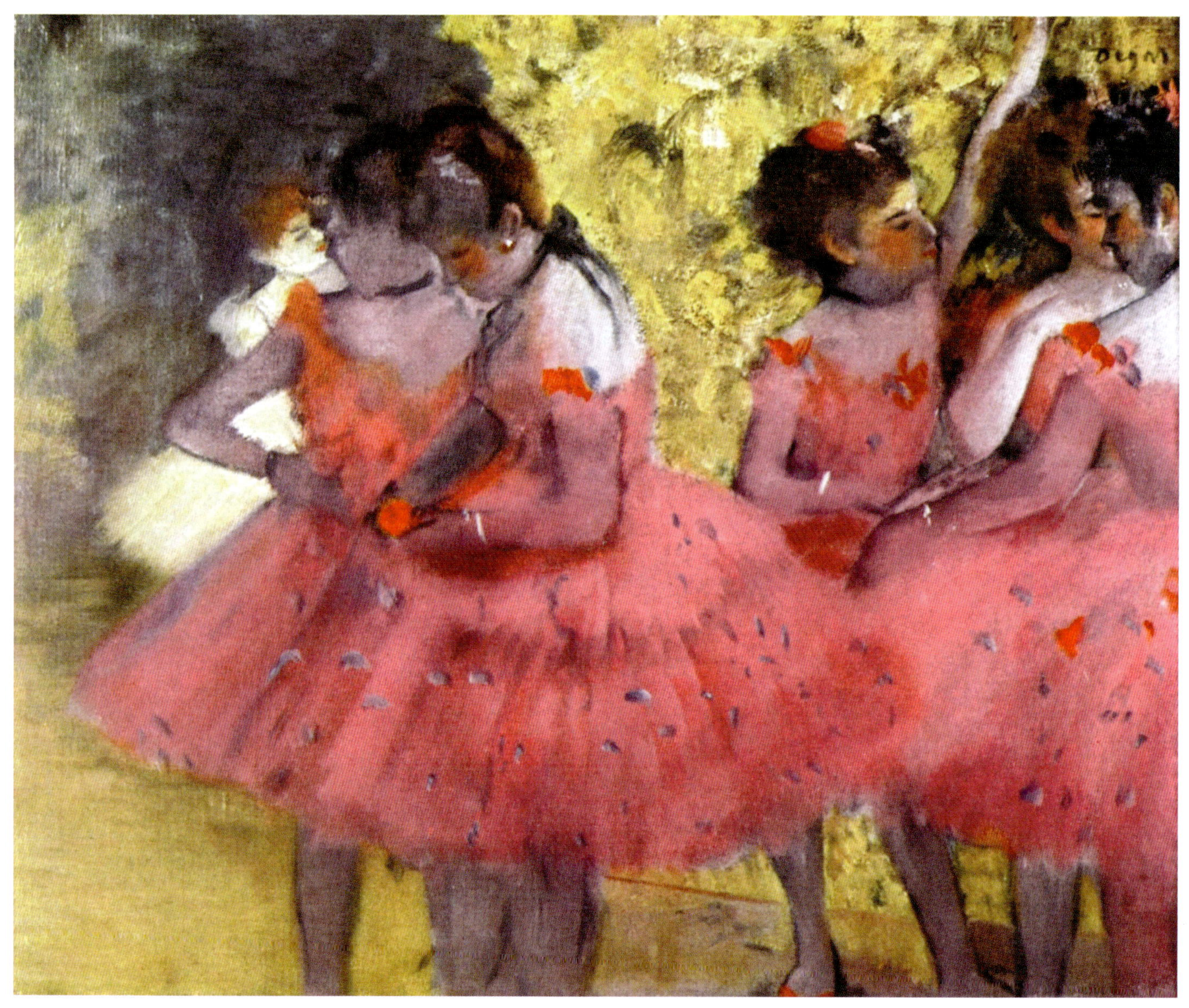

Dancers in Red Skirts, *c.* 1884
Oil on canvas, 38 x 44.5 cm (15 x 17½ in)
• Ny Carlsberg Glyptotek, Copenhagen

A gloriously coloured painting that depicts the *corps de ballet* waiting to go on stage, making last-minute adjustments to their attire. In the background is possibly the prima ballerina in a pale-coloured tutu.

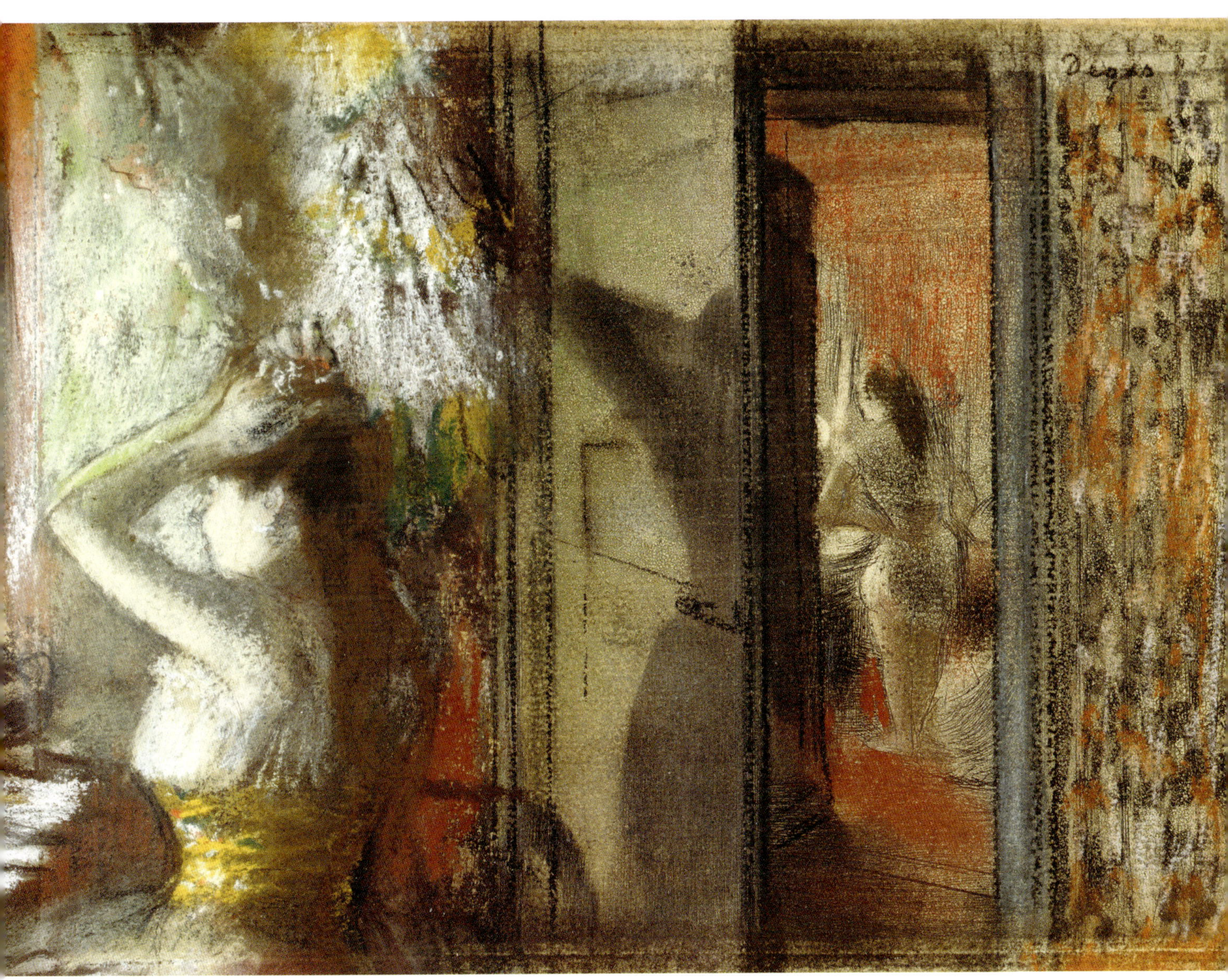

Actresses' Dressing Room, _c._ 1885
Pastel over etching on paper, 16.5 x 23 cm (6$^{1}/_{2}$ x 9 in)
• Private Collection

This 'privileged' view was reserved for those well connected to the theatre management. There is a sense of voyeurism created by Degas in his use of the partially opened door, suggesting that we are not supposed to be there.

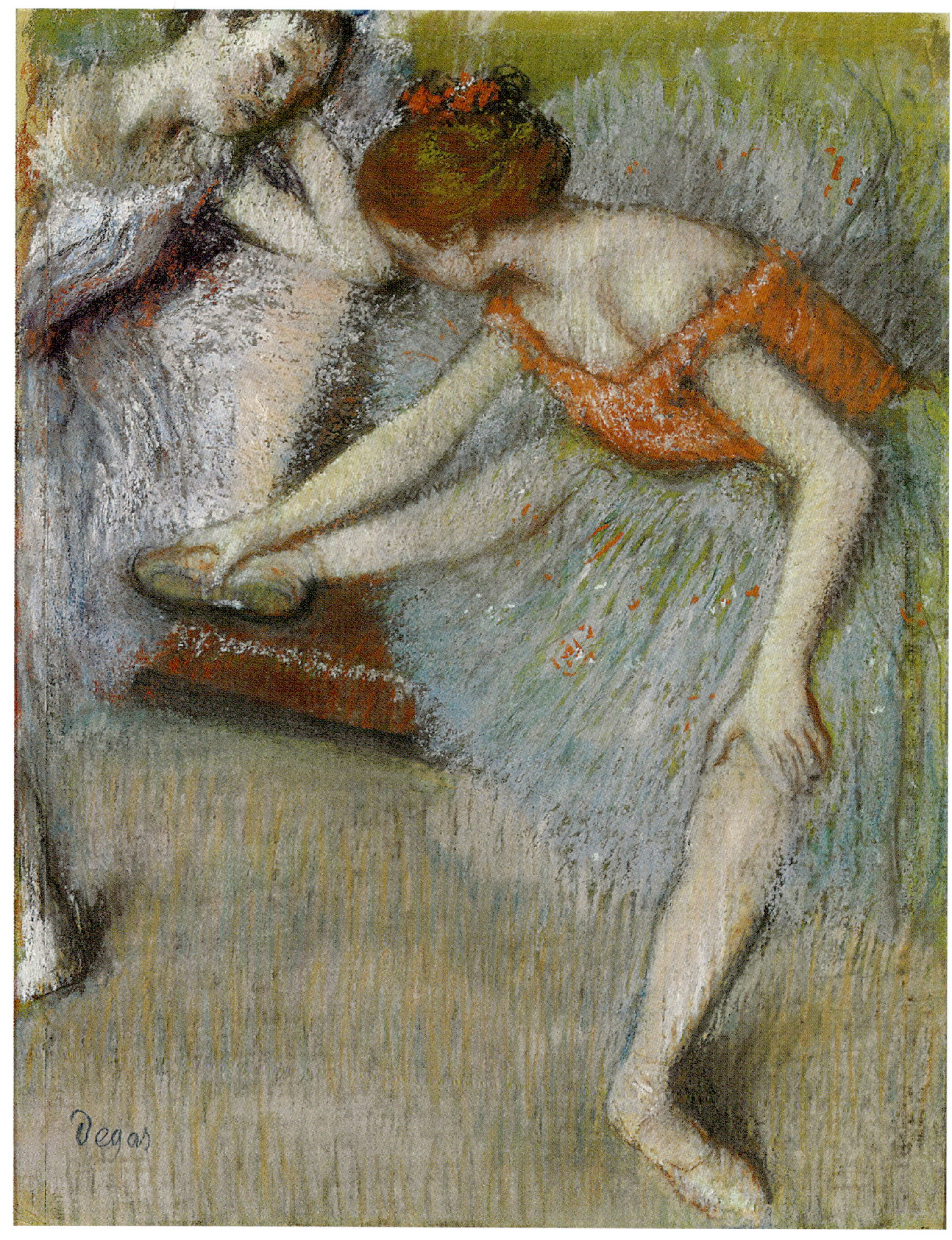

Dancers, _c._ 1896
Pastel on paper, 51.1 x 40 cm (20 x 15¾ in)
• Private Collection

These two dancers are looking exhausted after their performance, the one in red checking her feet, or possibly an aching ankle. At this stage in Degas' career his strokes are becoming much broader and more pronounced.

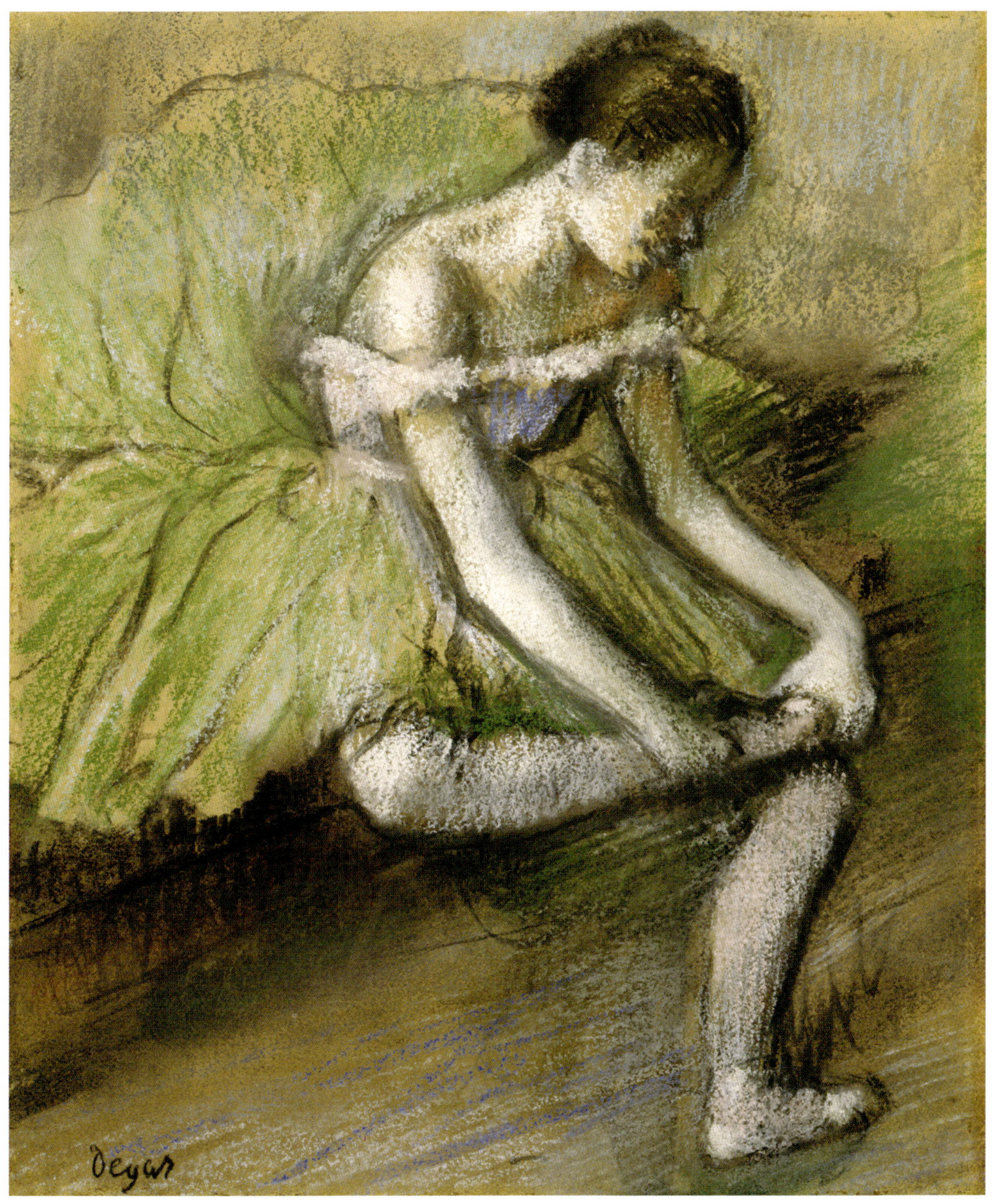

La Jupe Verte, *c.* 1896
Pastel on paper, 45 x 37 cm (17³/₄ x 14¹/₂ in)
• Private Collection

With Degas' eyesight failing his draughtsmanship is seen to suffer, as evidenced in this drawing of the dancer's legs. Instead the viewer's attention is drawn to the dancer's green skirt, which dominates the picture.

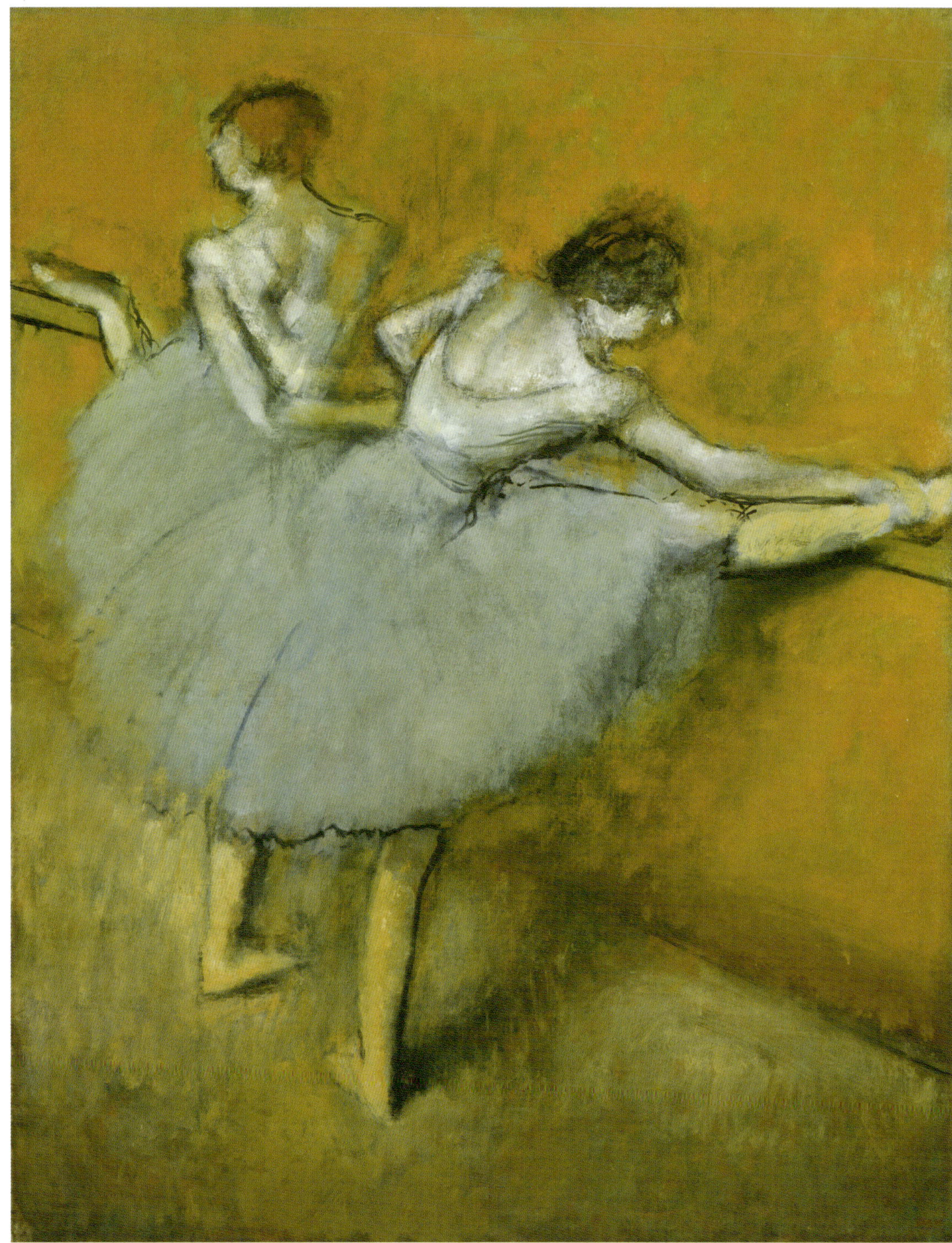

Dancers at the Bar, *c.* 1900
Oil on canvas, 130.1 x 97.7 cm (51$\frac{1}{4}$ x 38$\frac{1}{2}$ in)
• Phillips Collection, Washington D.C.

A large format was used for this ballet painting in oil, one of the last Degas painted in this medium due to his failing eyesight. There is little detail and the figures lack any personality.

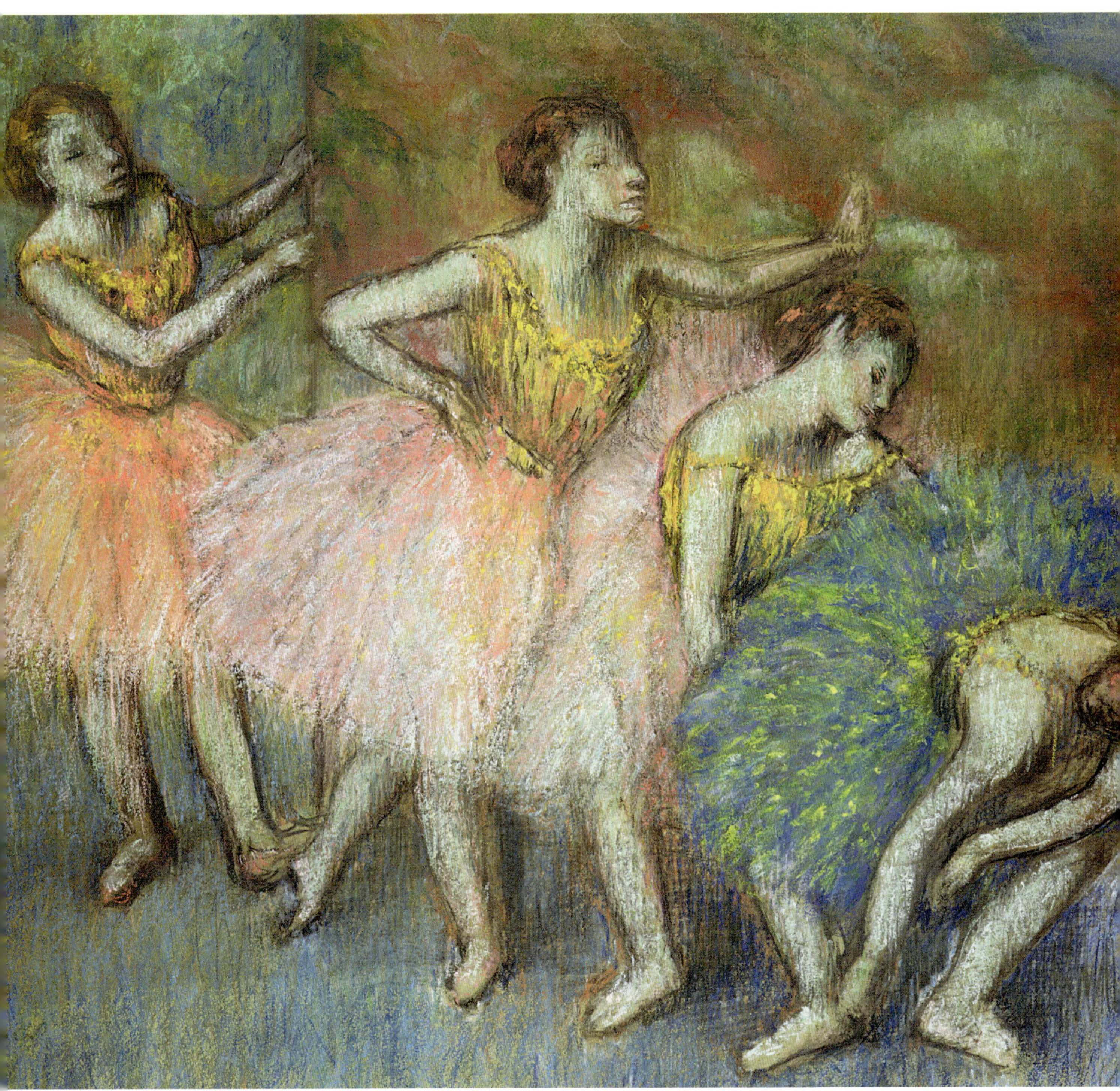

Four Dancers, 1903
Pastel, 77.5 x 88.3 cm (30½ x 34¾ in)
• Private Collection

These four dancers from the *corps* look exhausted and are depicted in various states of collapse, the rear two holding on to the wings to prevent them falling over.

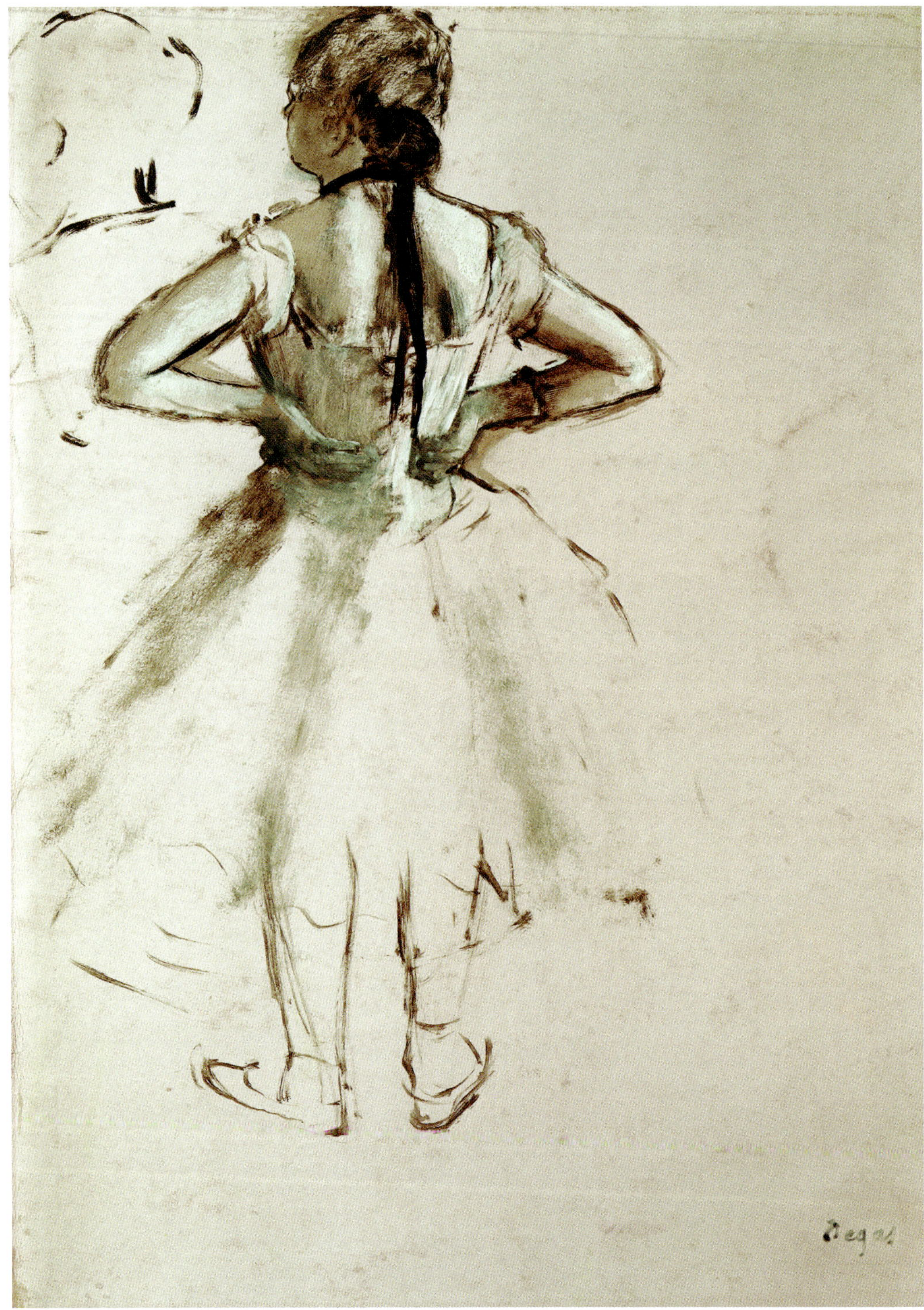

Dancer Viewed from the Back, undated
Sketch, 50 x 39 cm (19³/₄ x 15¹/₃ in)
• Louvre Museum, Paris

Degas once remarked to the art dealer Ambroise Vollard: 'people call me the painter of dancing girls … has it ever occurred to them that my chief interest in dancers lies in rendering movement and painting pretty clothes?'

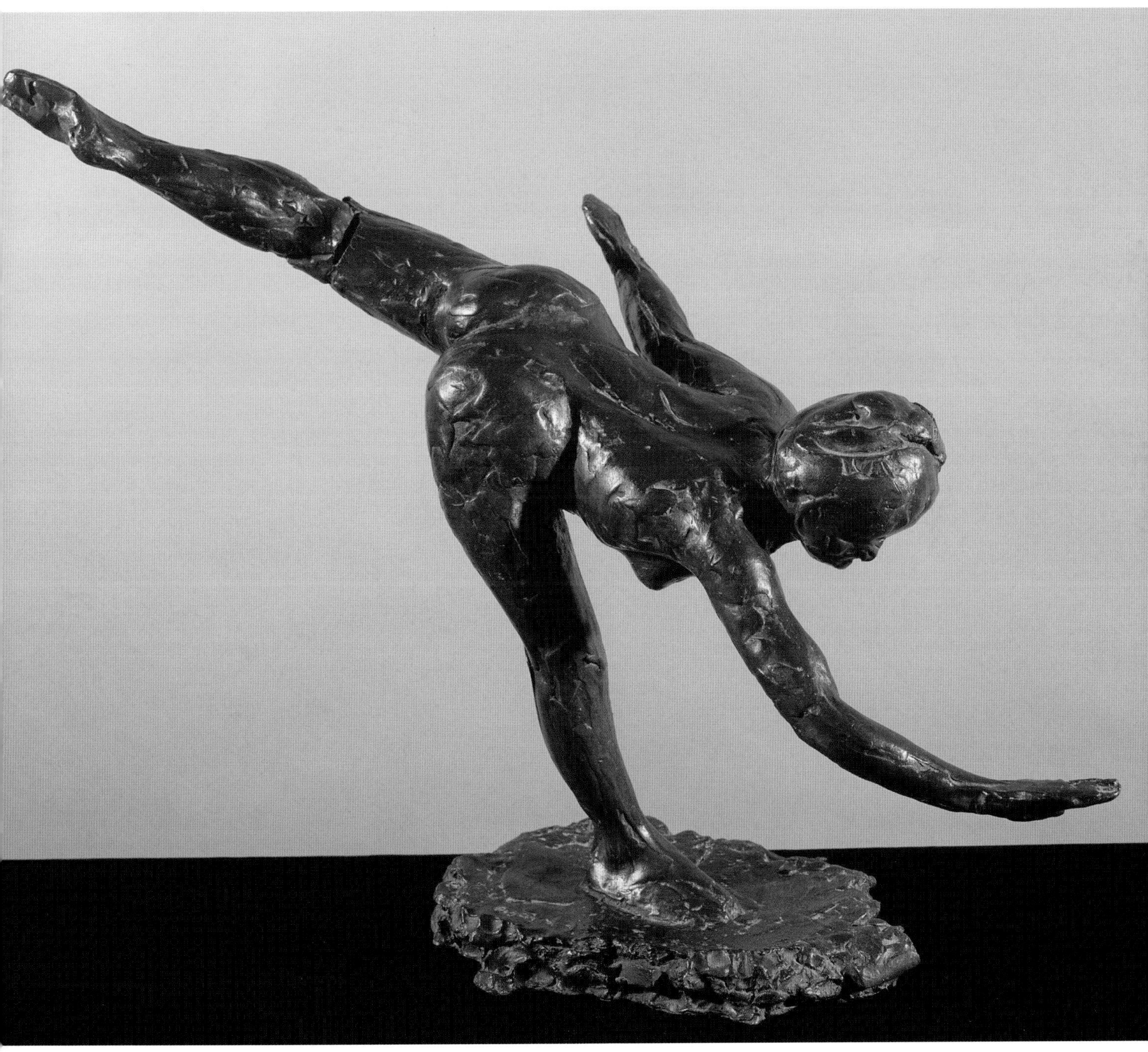

Large Arabesque, third state, c. 1921–31
Bronze, height 43.5 cm (17 in)
• Private Collection

Degas' sculptures are not academic in either their rendering or the poses adopted.
He was after all an untrained sculptor, who was interested in recording the movement
of the dancers he had seen perform.

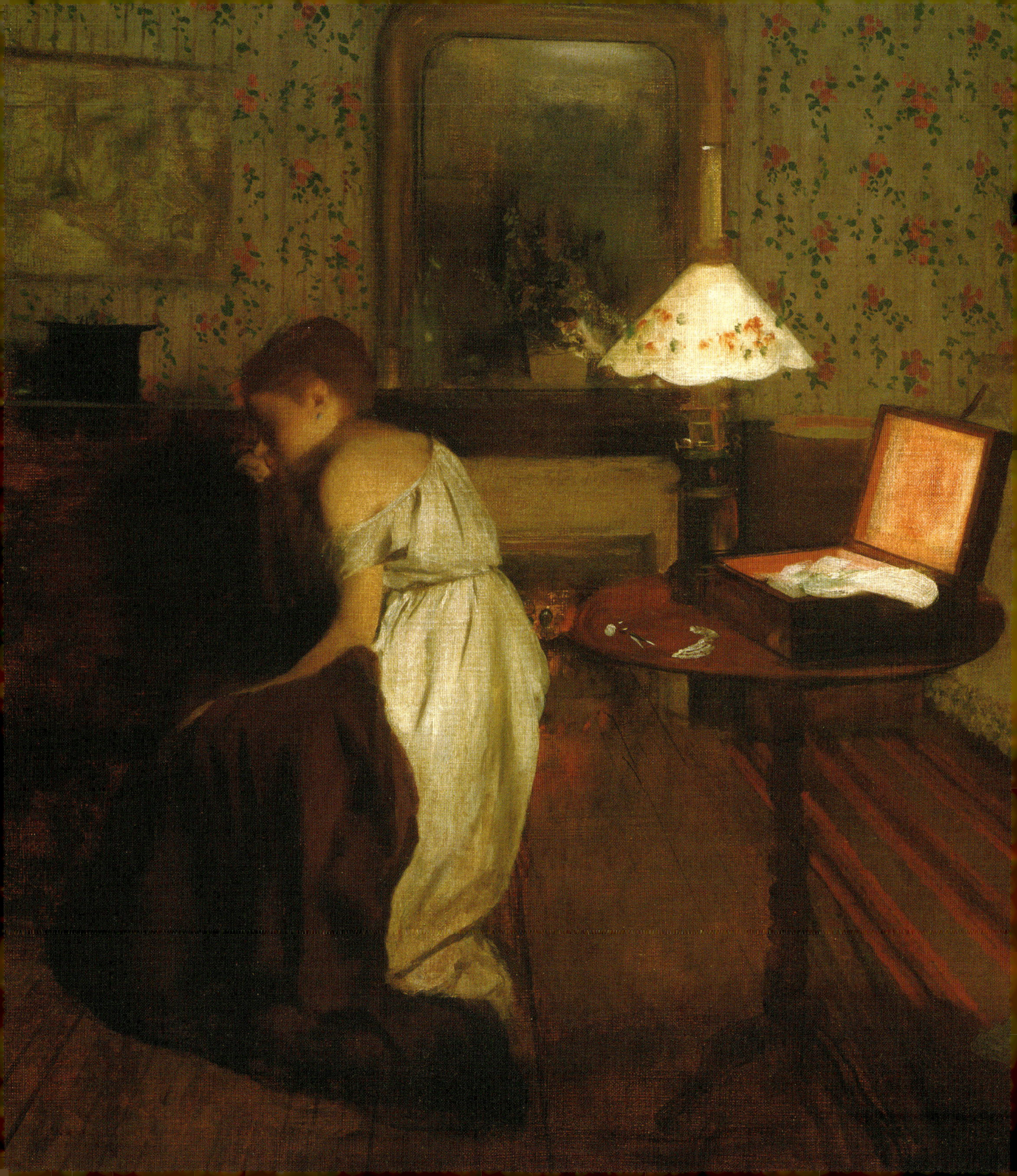

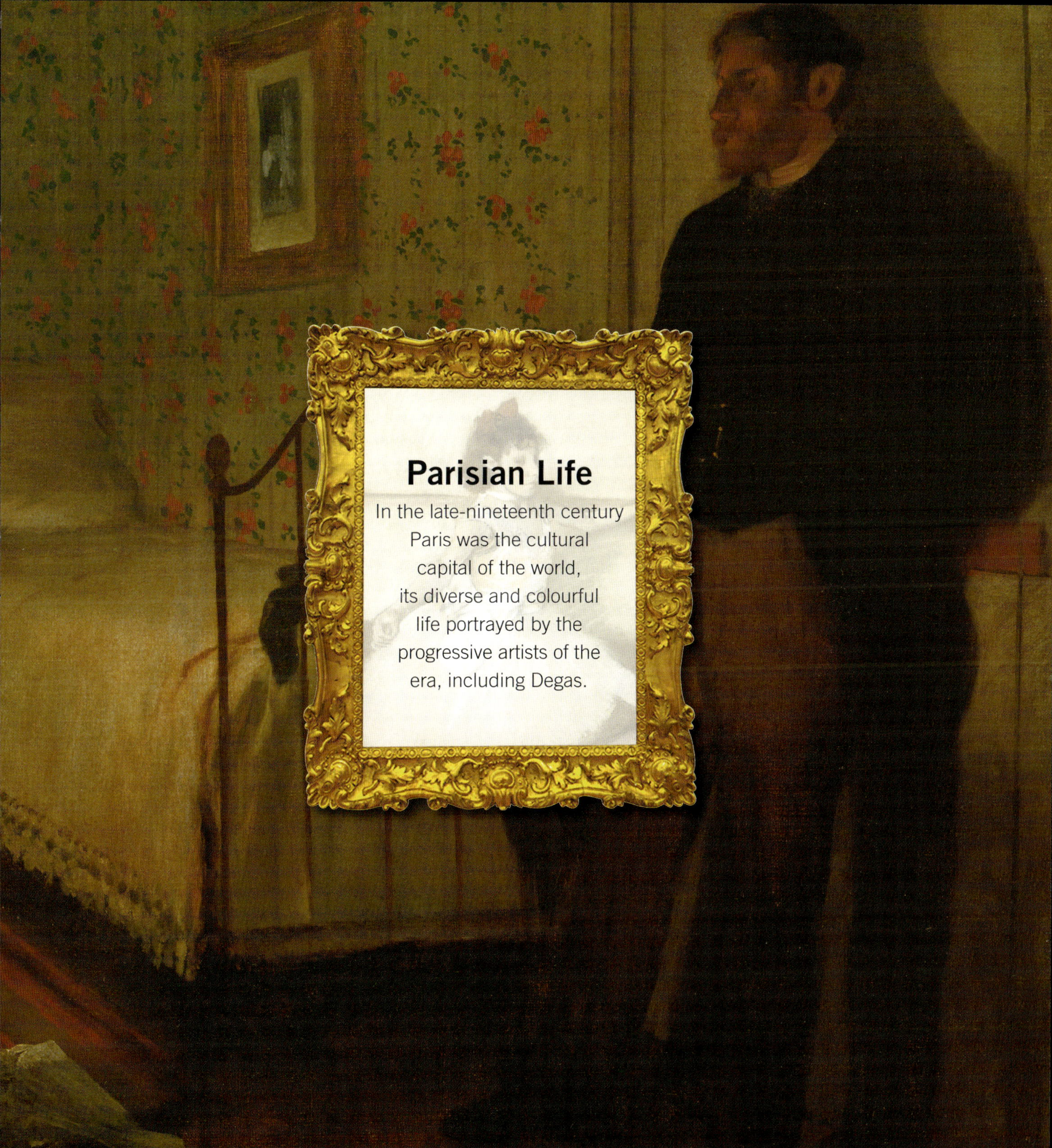

Parisian Life

In the late-nineteenth century
Paris was the cultural
capital of the world,
its diverse and colourful
life portrayed by the
progressive artists of the
era, including Degas.

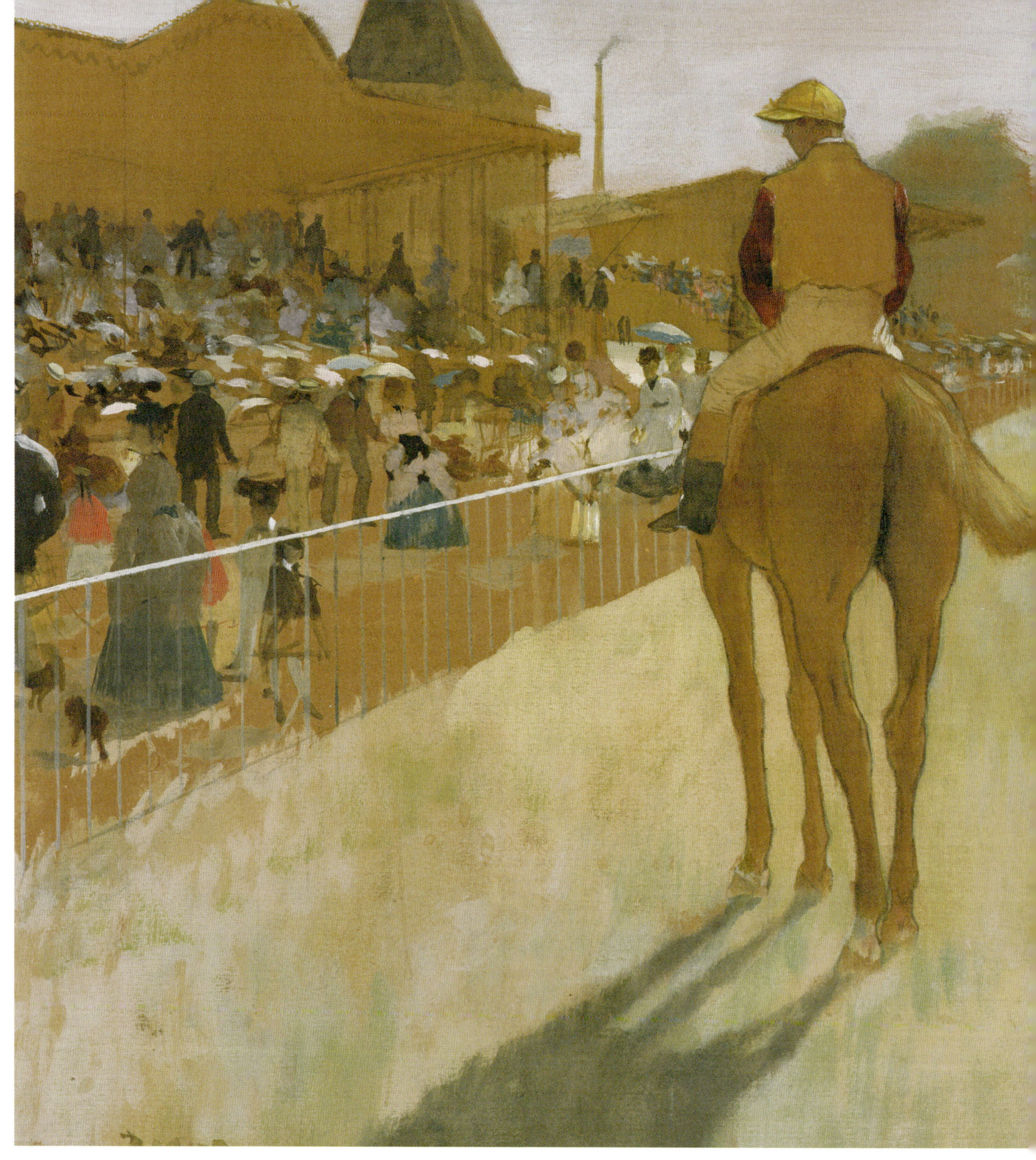

Racehorses in Front of the Stands, *c.* **1866–68**
Oil on paper, 46 x 61 cm (18 x 24 in)
• Musée d'Orsay, Paris

The location of the racecourse is unclear, since Longchamp did not have a view towards factories at this time. It may well have been a ruse by Degas to give the picture its modernity.

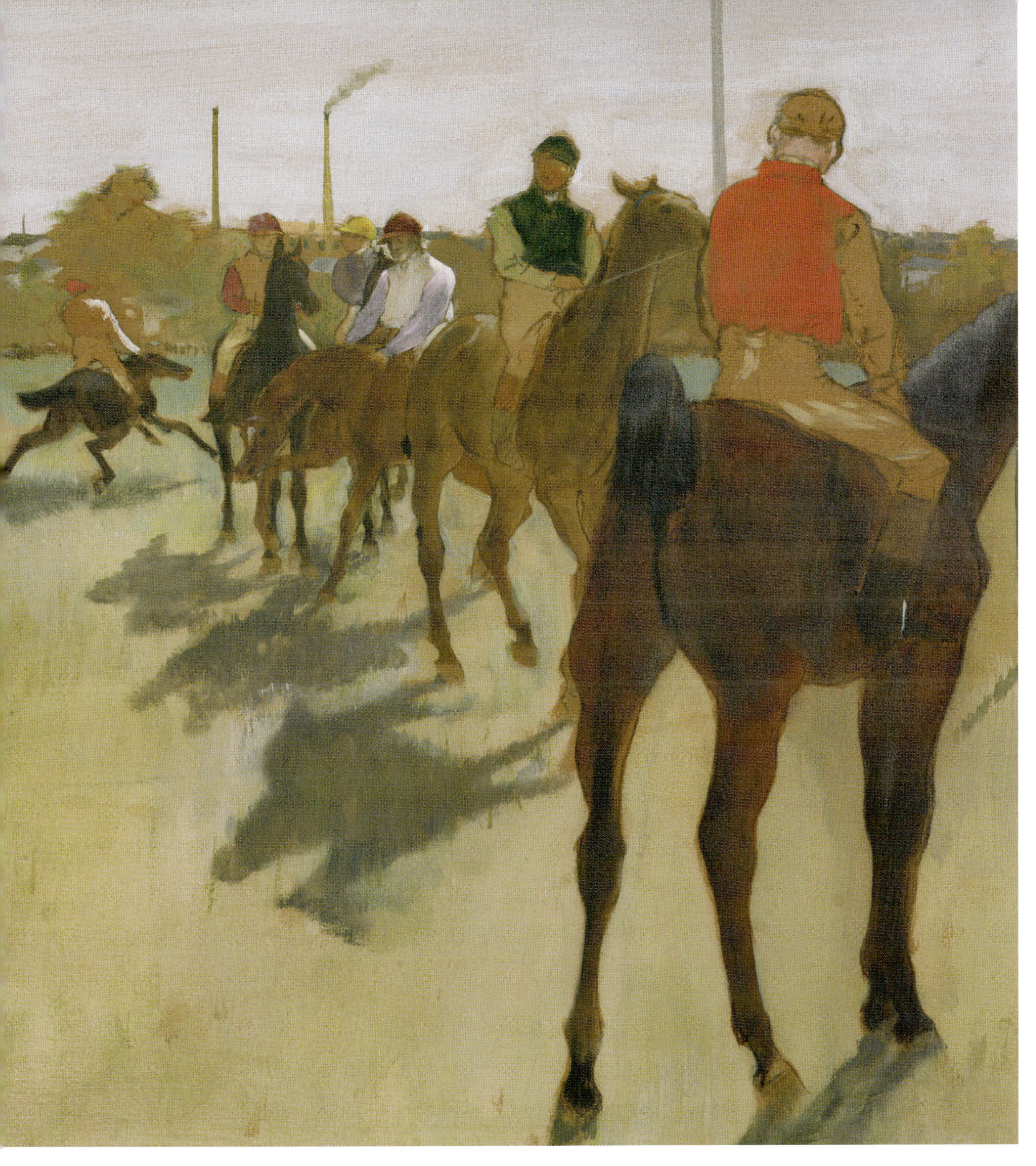

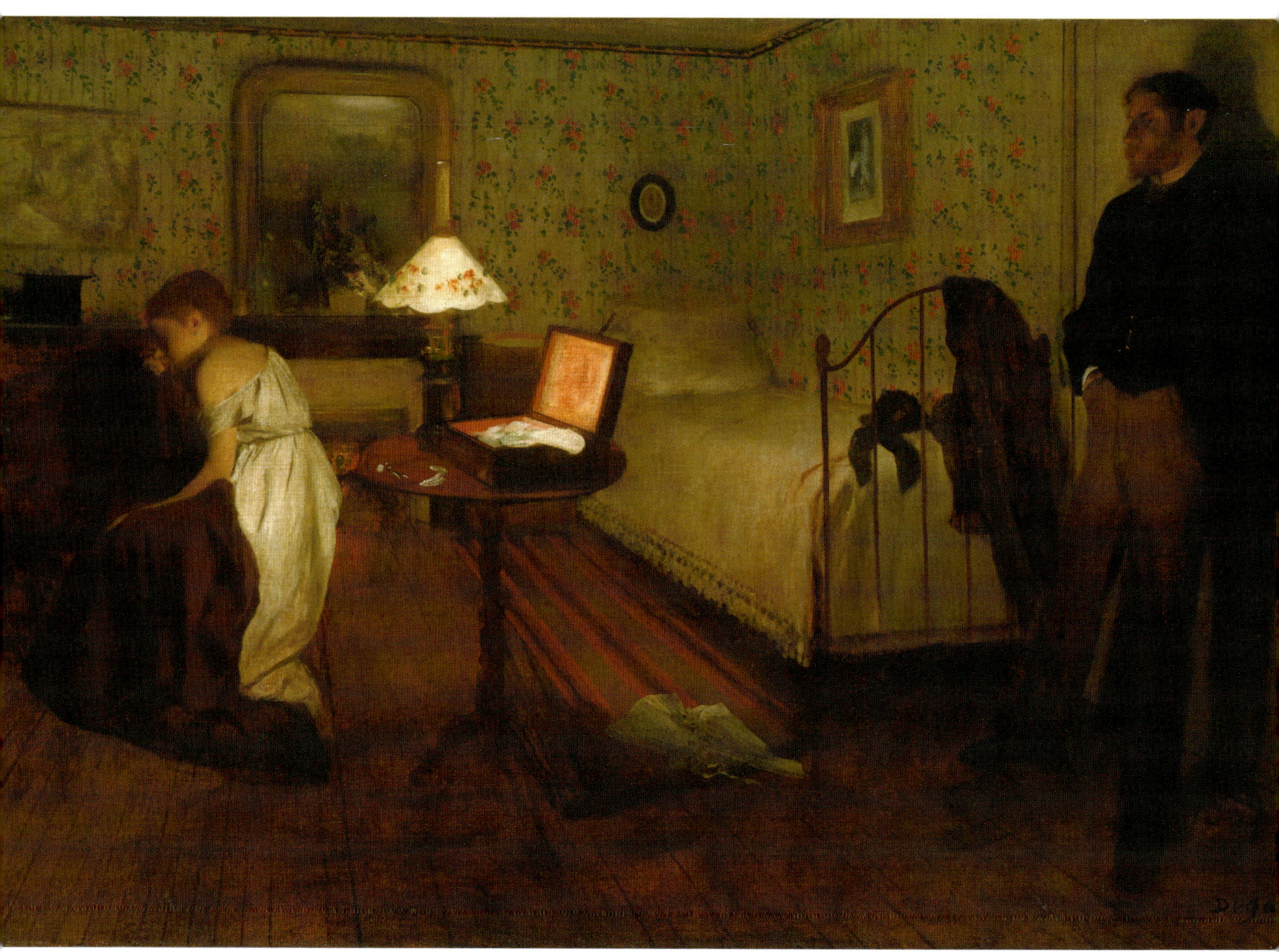

Interior, 1868–69

Oil on canvas, 81.3 x 114.3 cm (32 x 45 in)

• Philadelphia Museum of Art, Pennsylvania

Degas referred to this painting as 'my genre picture', refusing to discuss its narrative. Its possible literary source is Emile Zola's novel *Thérèse Raquin*, published in 1867, in which both protagonists are responsible for killing Thérèse's husband.

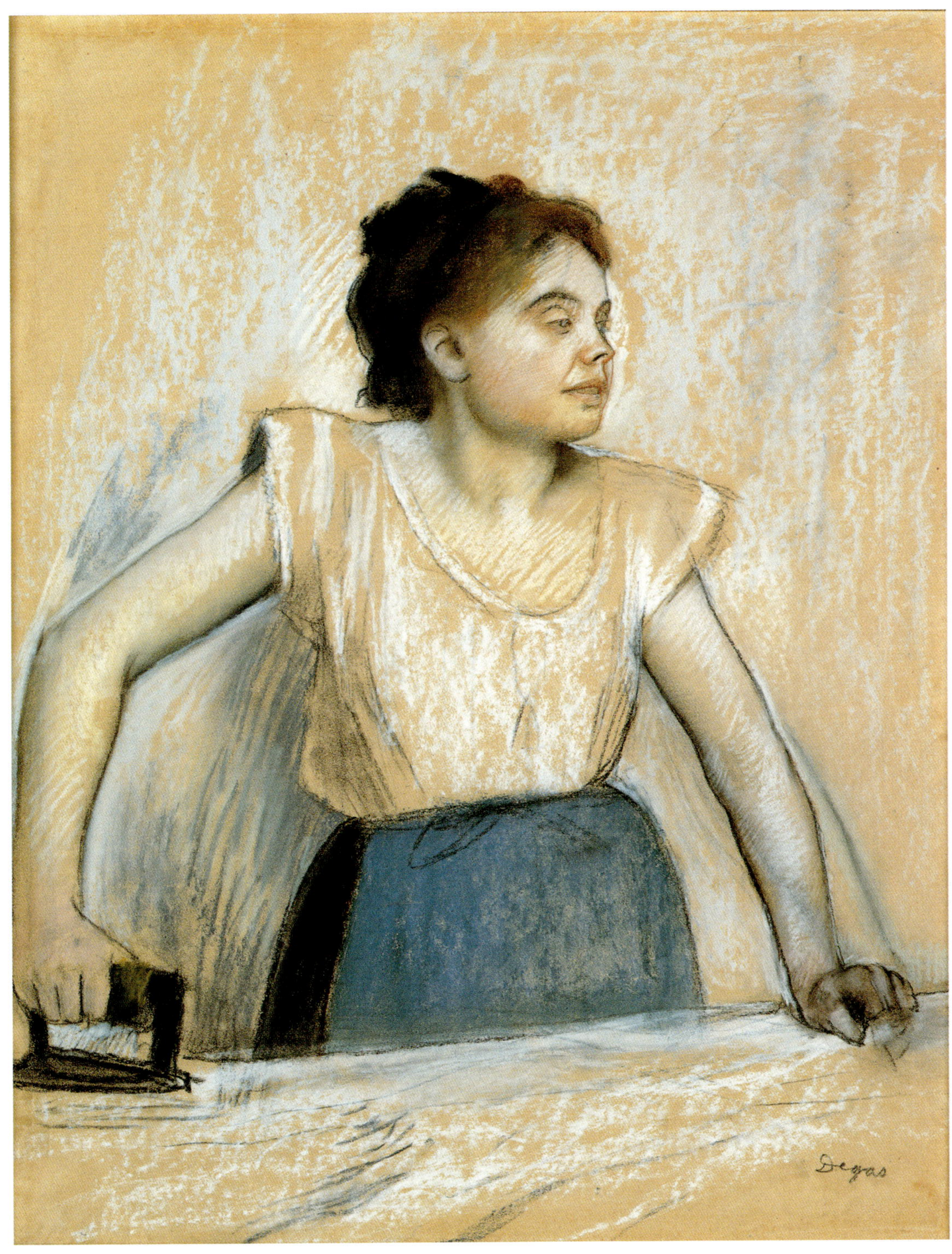

Woman Ironing, 1869
Pastel on paper, 74 x 61 cm (29 x 24 in)
• Musée d'Orsay, Paris

The model for this pastel was Emma Dobigny, who posed for Degas a number of times.
The work was not exhibited in Degas' lifetime and may well have been a preparatory sketch.

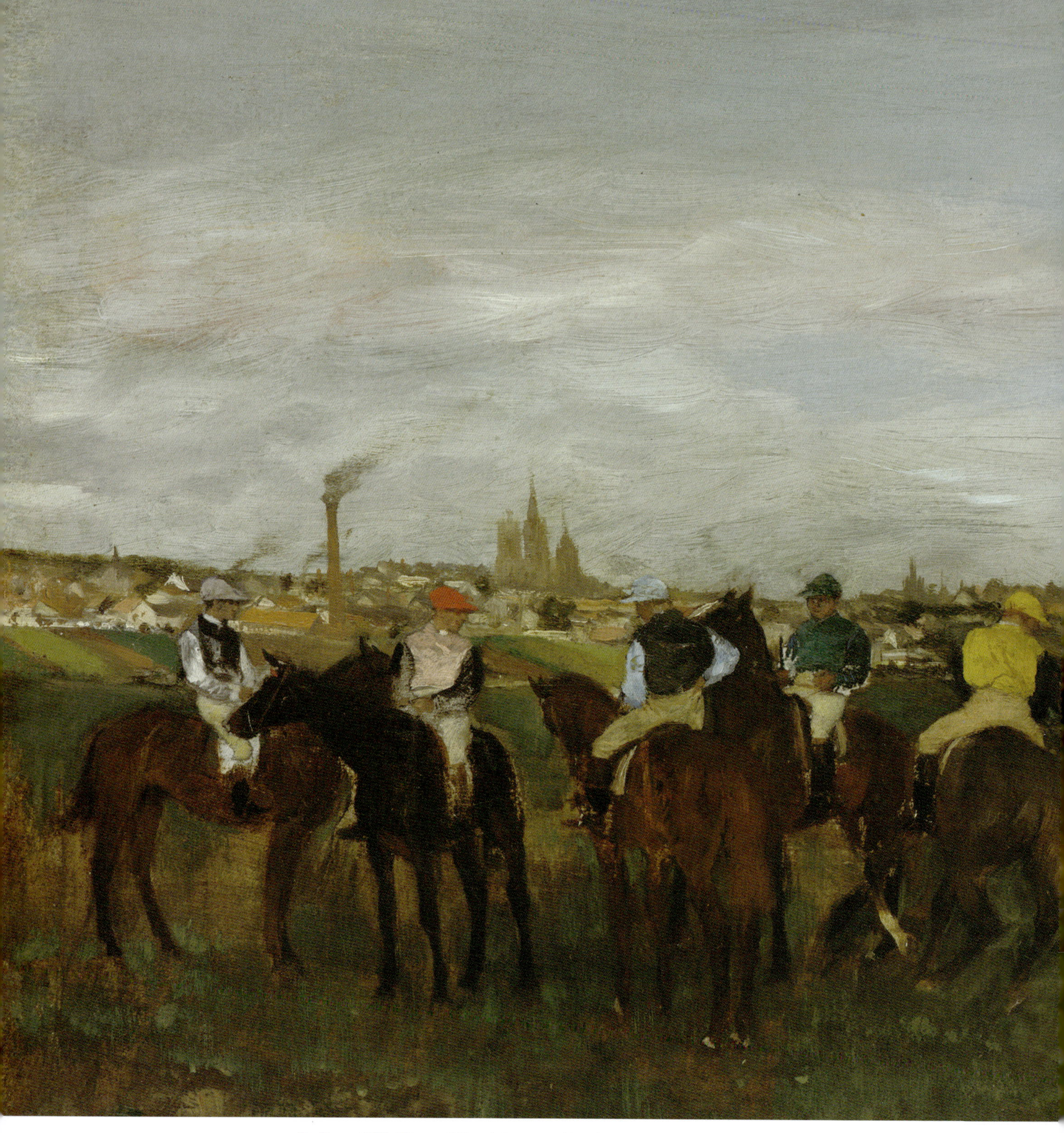

The Races, 1871–72
Oil on wood, 26.6 x 35.1 cm (10$\frac{1}{2}$ x 13$\frac{4}{5}$ in)
• National Gallery of Art, Washington DC

This painting was sold to the opera singer Jean-Baptiste Faure (1830–1914) in 1873. Faure was a baritone much in demand in Paris and London, and an avid collector of Impressionist work.

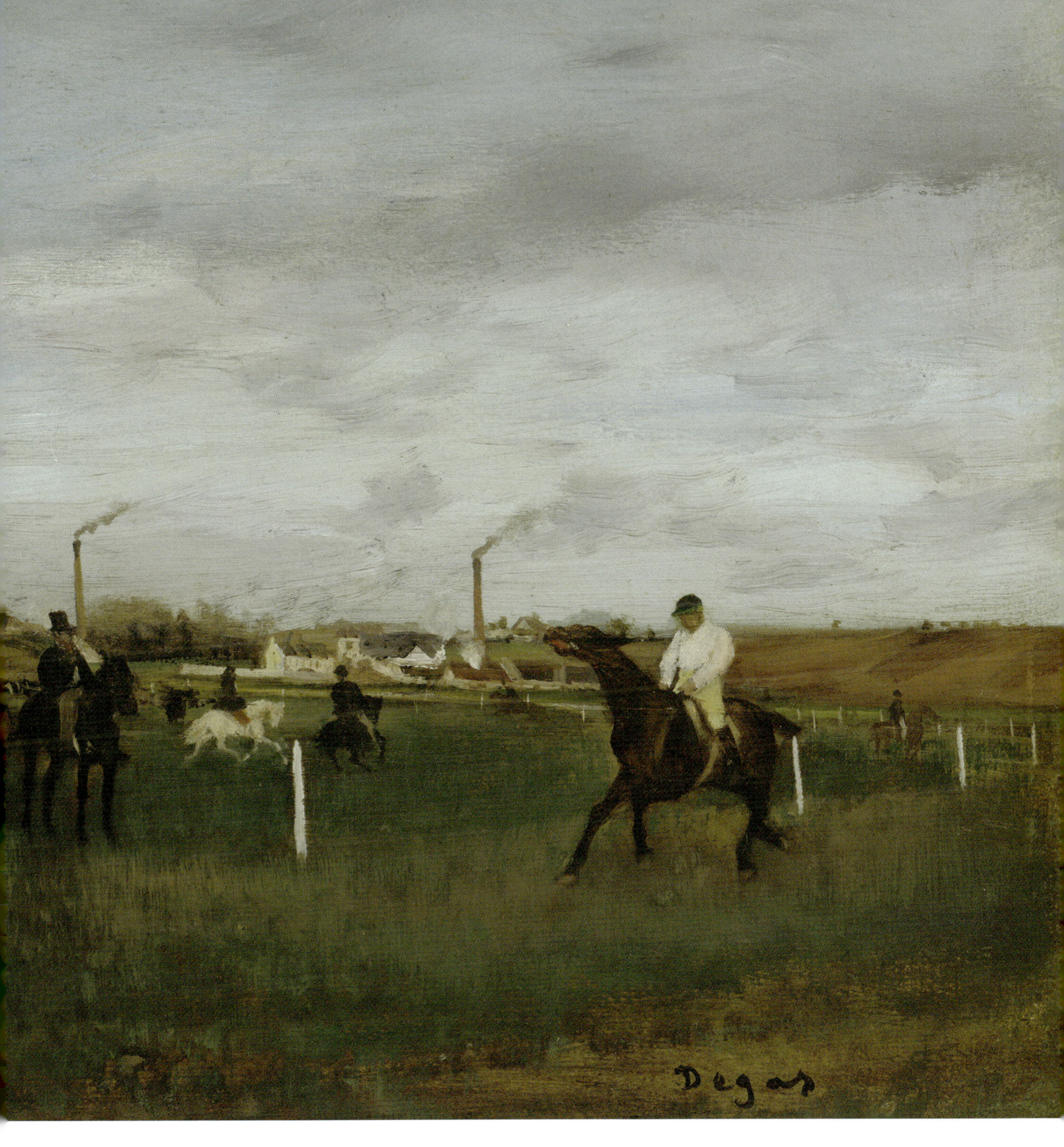

Degas

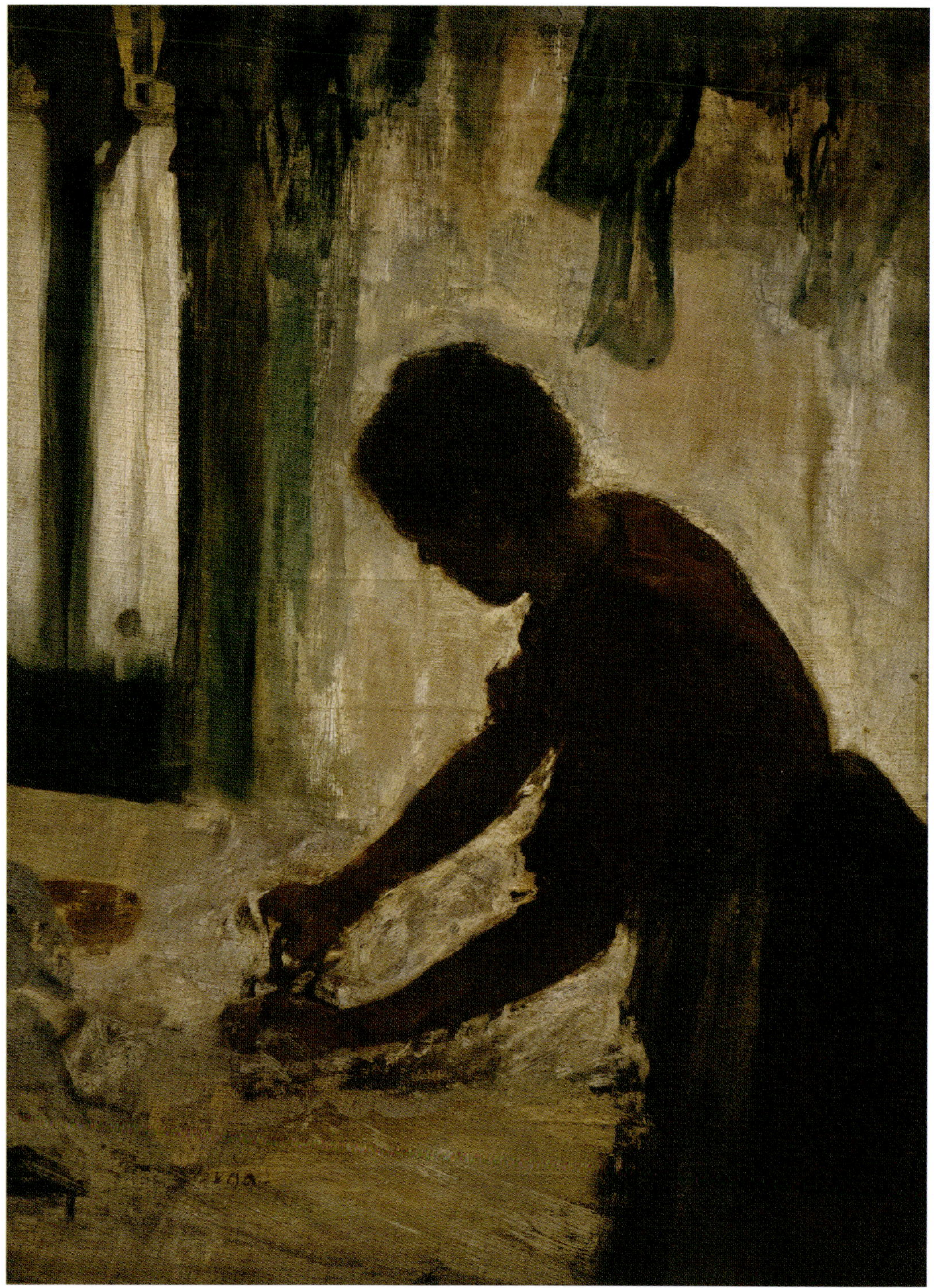

A Woman Ironing, 1873
Oil on canvas, 54 x 39 cm (21$\frac{1}{4}$ x 15$\frac{1}{3}$ in)
• Metropolitan Museum of Art, New York

The figure is in silhouette, suggesting that Degas was more interested in the play of light on the washing hanging up to dry and the ethereal effects of the steam emanating from the iron.

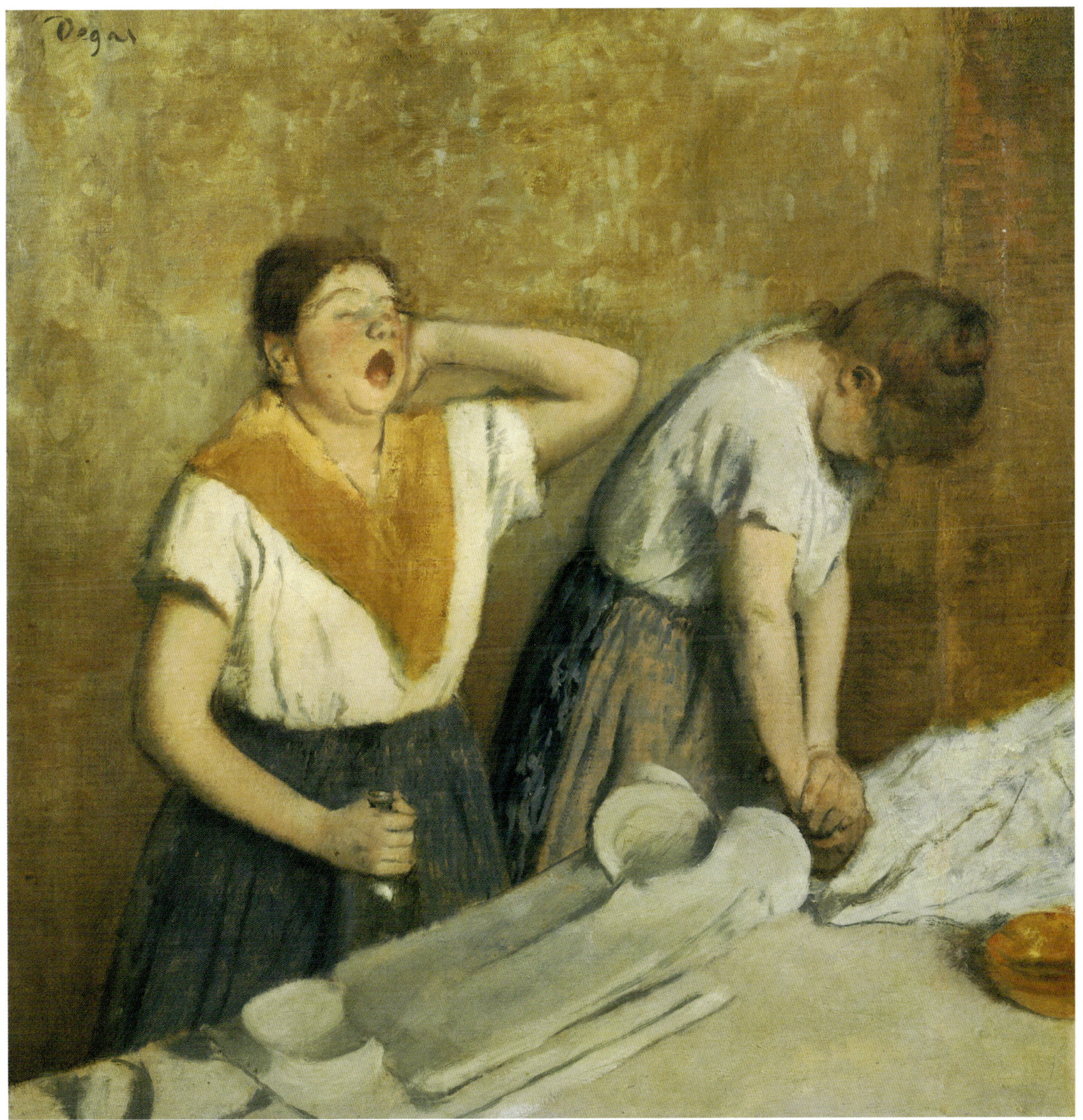

The Laundresses (The Ironing), *c.* **1874–76**
Oil on canvas, 76 x 81.5 cm (30 x 32 in)
• Musée d'Orsay, Paris

This is one of Degas' best-known images of lower-class workers, and one of several images of its type. This one has a much rougher texture, and the two women are much larger than in previous depictions of both laundresses and other lower-class workers.

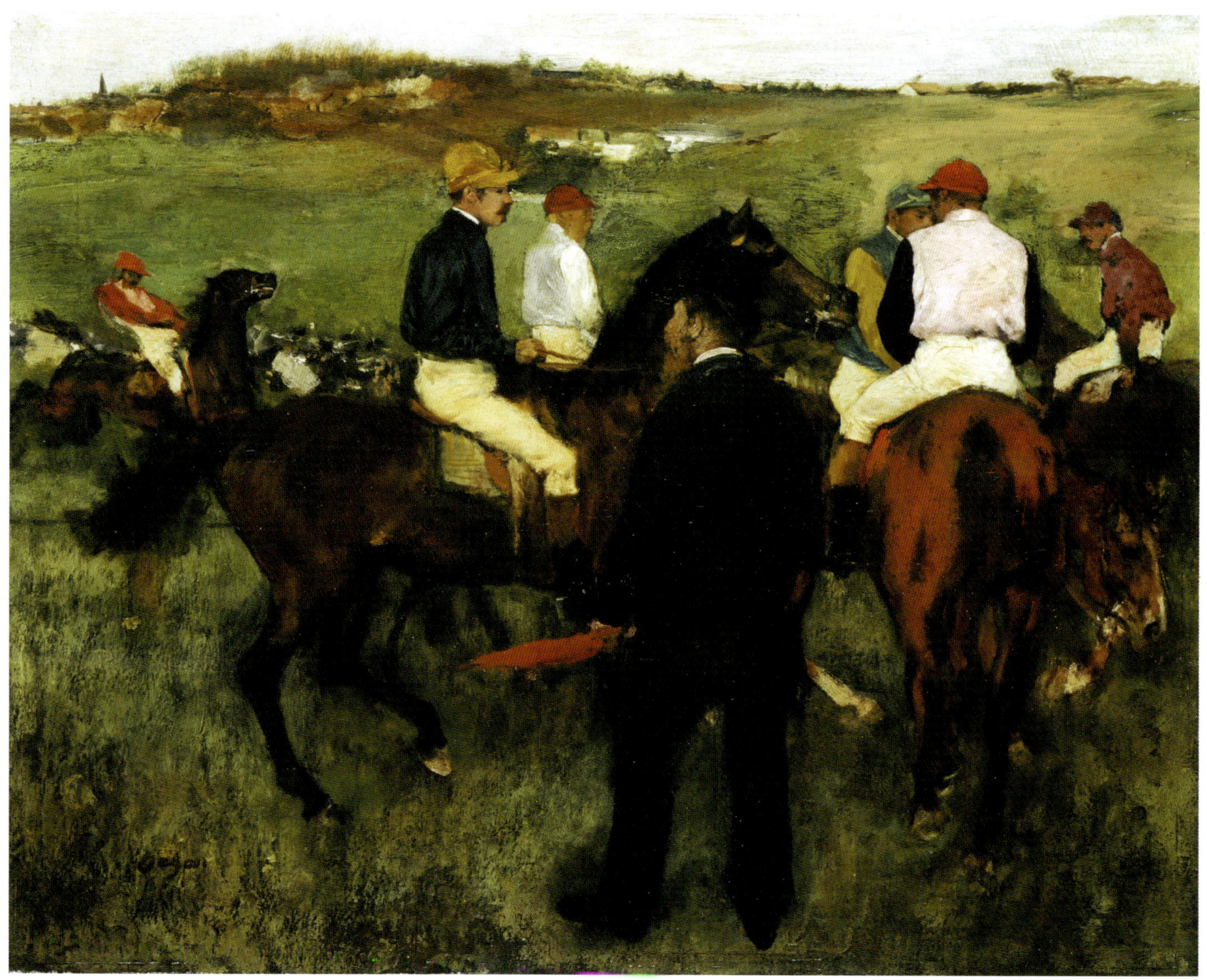

Racehorses (Leaving the Weighing), *c.* **1874–78**
Oil on panel • Private Collection

Traditionally jockeys and their equipment, including the saddle, have to weigh in prior to the start of a race to ensure they are carrying the correct weight.

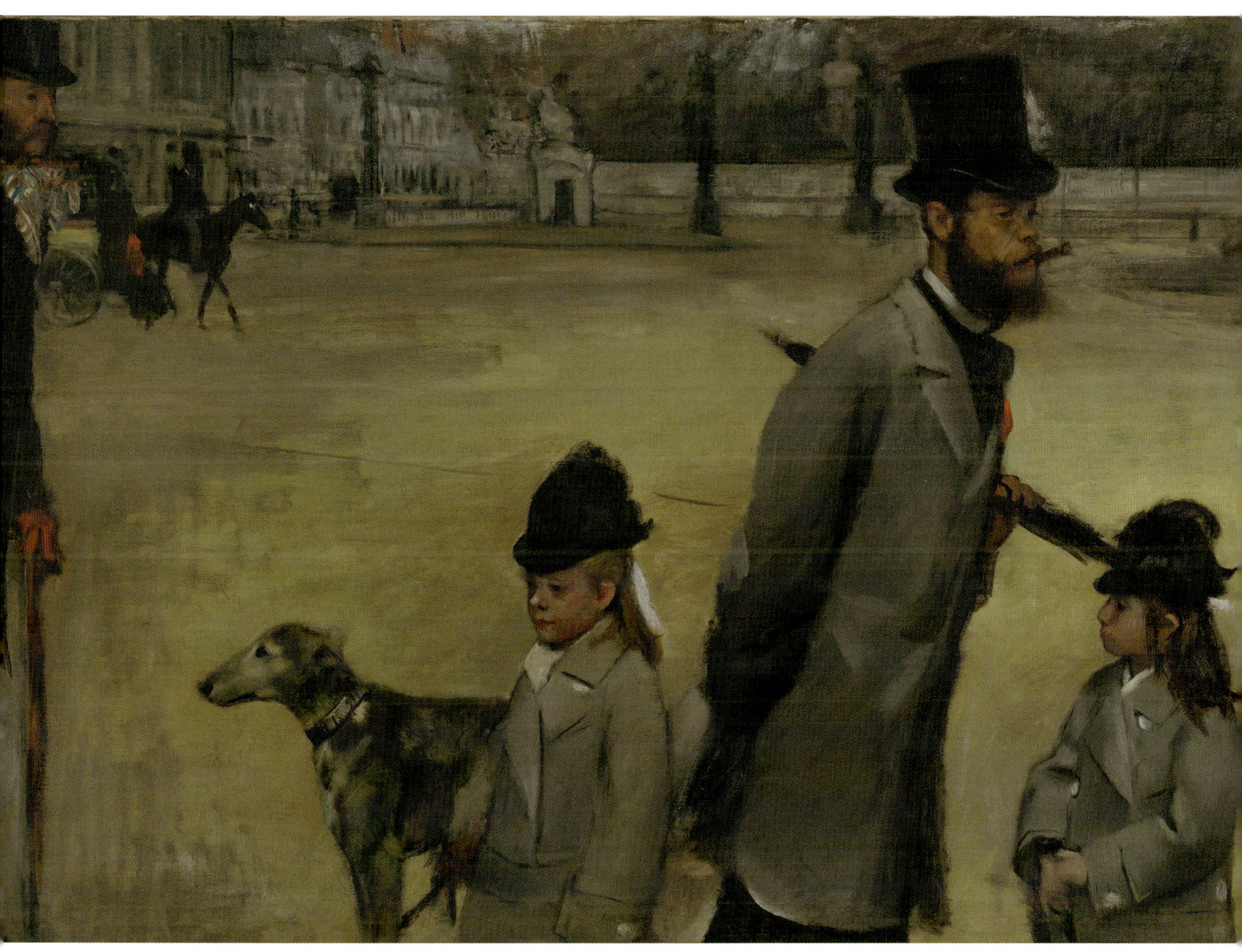

Place de la Concorde, 1875
Oil on canvas, 78 x 118 cm (30¾ x 46½ in)
• Hermitage State Museum, St Petersburg

Baron Lepic is shown smoking a small cigar while crossing the Place de la Concorde with his two daughters and dog. Degas' composition suggests this is a transitory moment for the viewer.

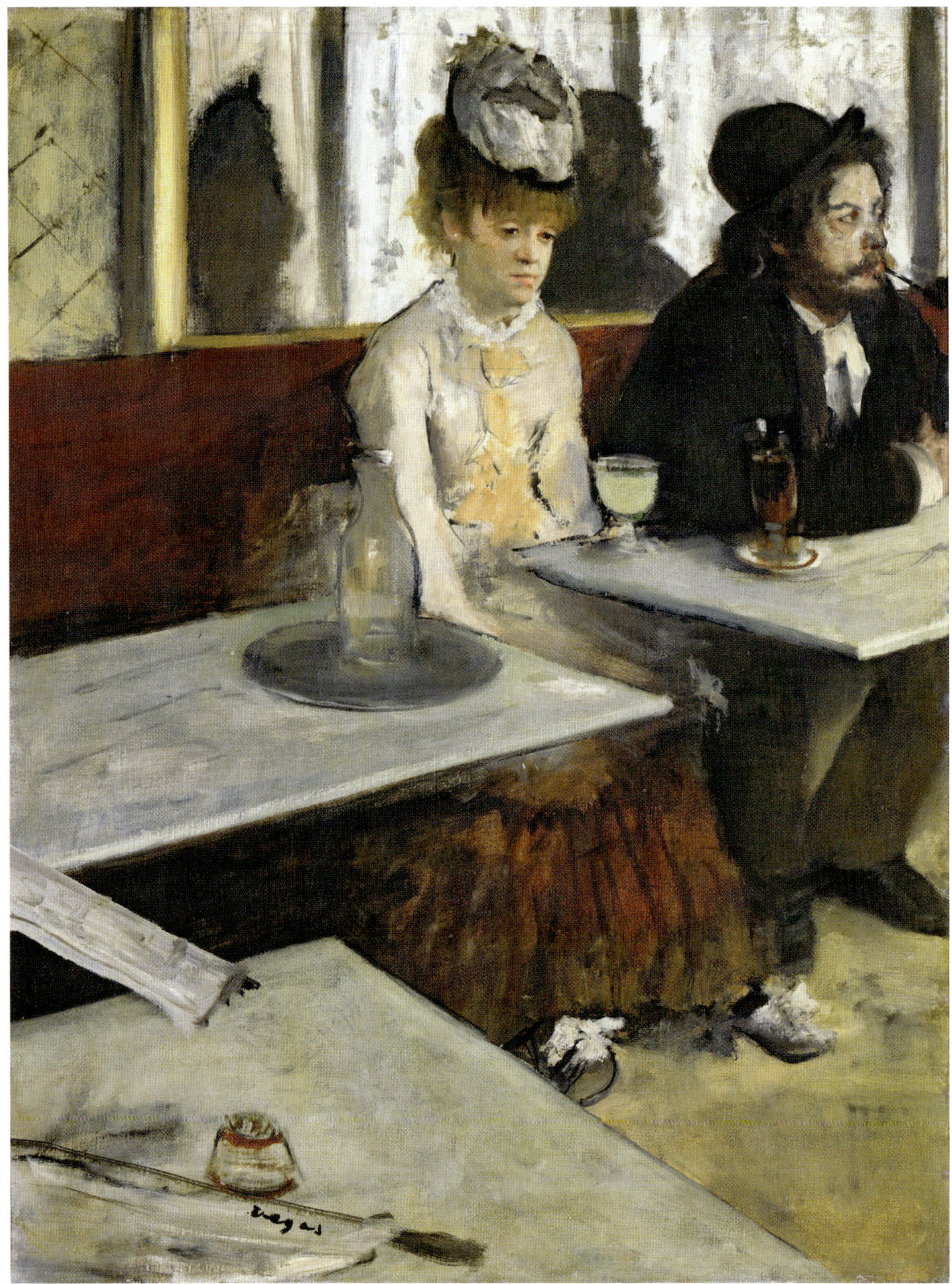

In a Café, or The Absinthe, *c.* 1875–76
Oil on canvas, 92 x 68 cm (36¼ x 26¼ in)
• Musée d'Orsay, Paris

The scene of this tragic picture is inside the Nouvelle Athènes Café in Paris, which became the haunt of Degas and the Batignolles Group after the Franco-Prussian War.

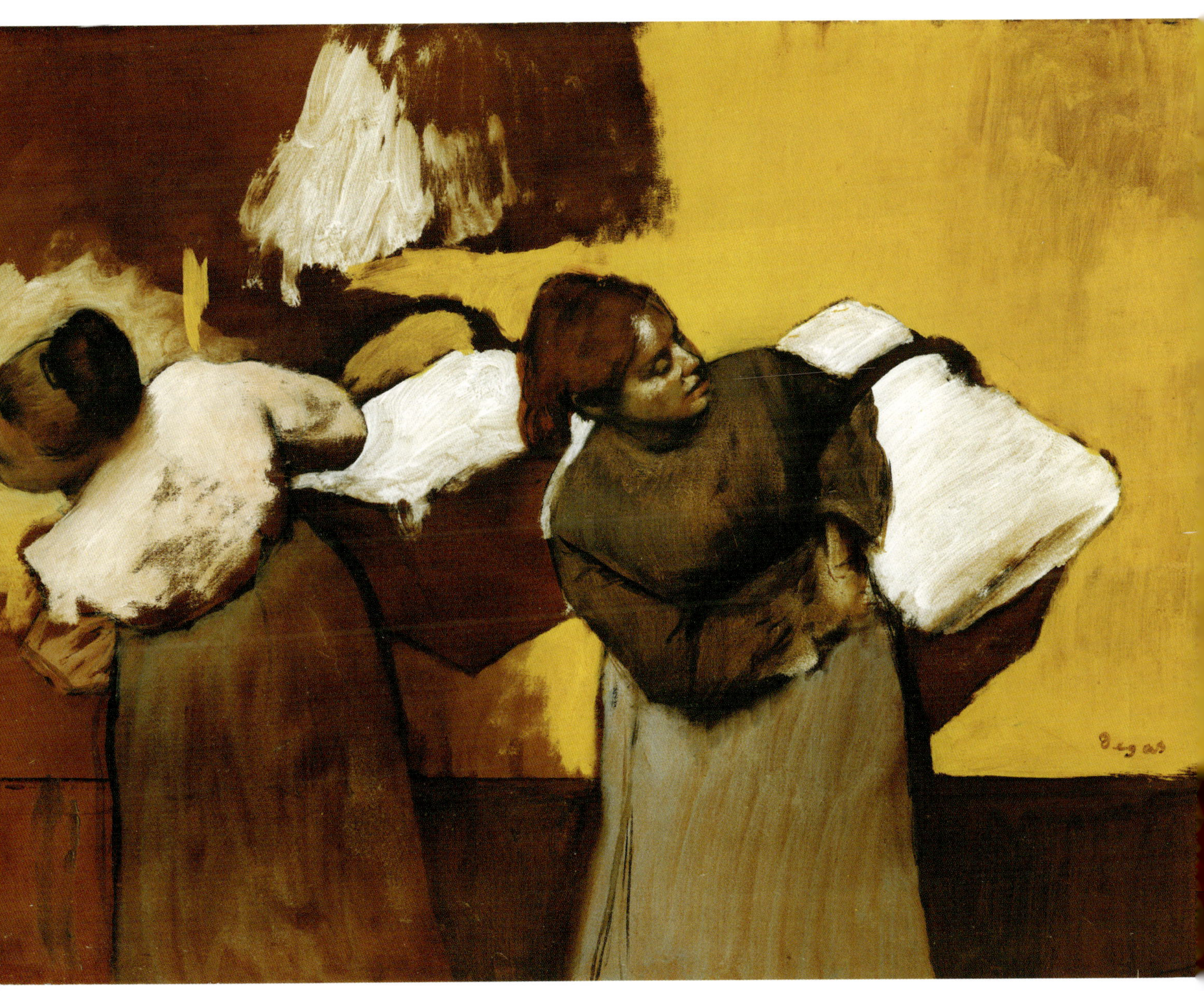

Laundresses, *c.* **1876**
Oil on canvas, 46 x 61 cm (18 x 24 in)
• Private Collection

This early image of laundresses by Degas borrows heavily from the artist Honoré Daumier (1808–79), who tended to emphasize the plight of working people in a similar style.

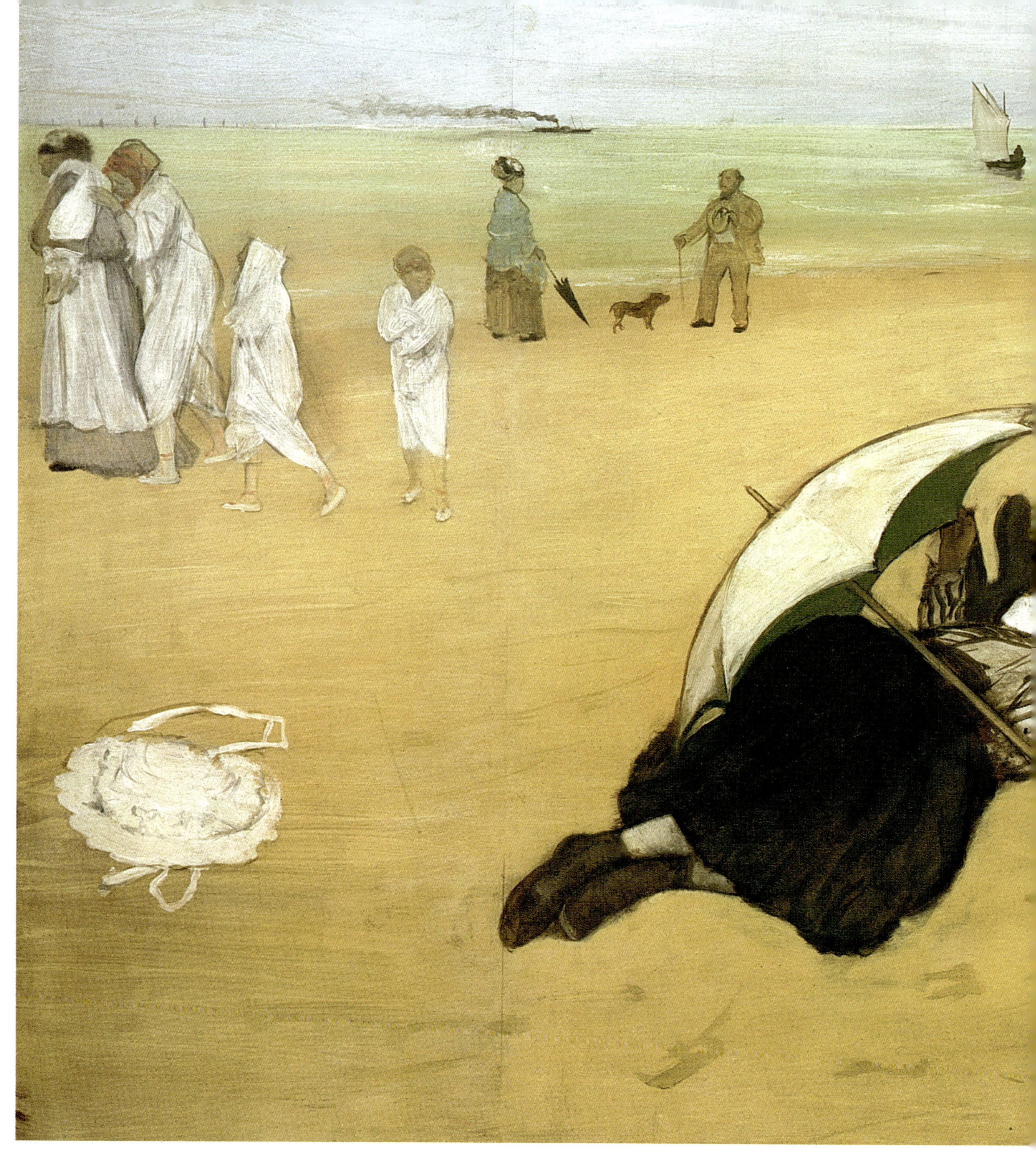

Beach Scene: Little Girl Having her Hair Combed by her Nanny, *c.* **1876–77** Oil on paper, 47 x 82.6 cm (18$^1/_2$ x 32$^1/_2$ in)
• National Gallery, London

In something of a departure for Degas, he has executed a landscape painting. However, the emphasis is very much on the two figures at the centre of the scene, rather than the landscape.

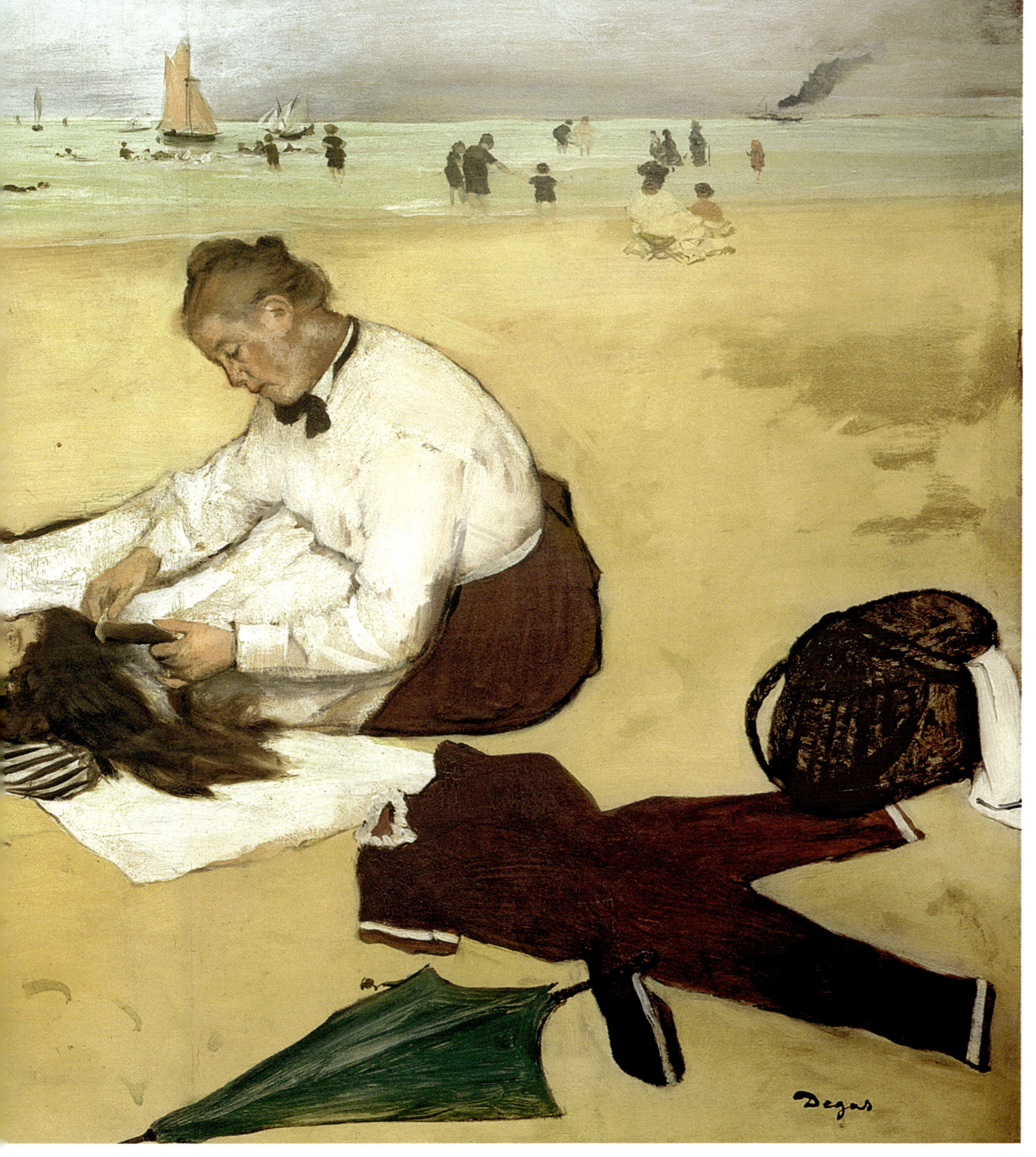

Degas

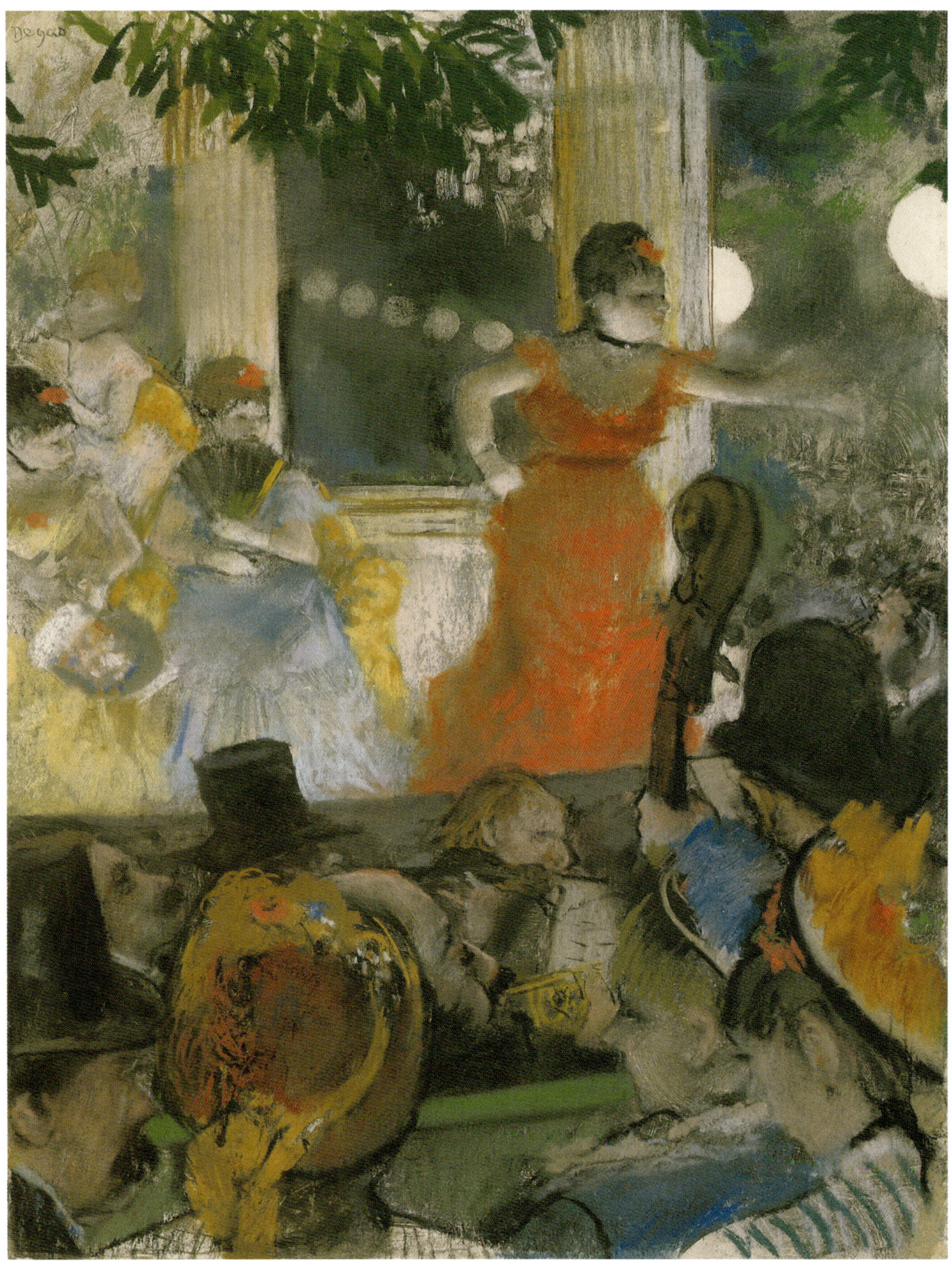

Café Concert at Les Ambassadeurs, 1876–77
Pastel on paper, 37 x 26 cm (14¹/₂ x 10¹/₄ in)
• Musée des Beaux Arts, Lyon

Another feature of the outdoor café concert was the use of over-large gas lanterns, which Degas shows to great effect in the picture, most notably along one side of the performer's face.

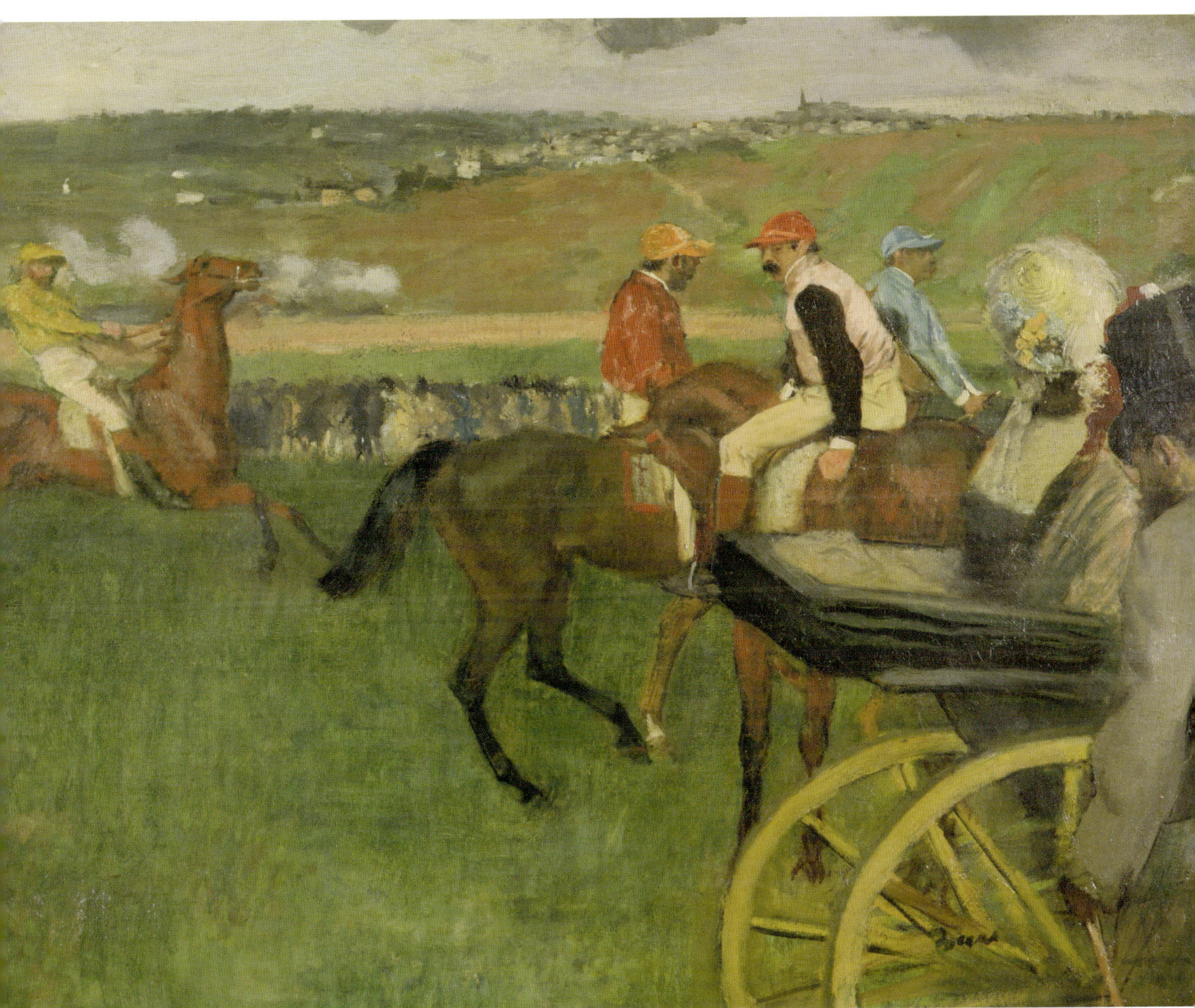

The Racecourse – Amateur Jockeys near a Carriage, *c.* 1876–87
Oil on canvas, 66 x 81 cm (26 x 32 in)
• Musée d'Orsay, Paris

The scene is another spectacle for Degas to explore as the *flâneur* artist, seeking all that is modern. The modernity is explicit in the presence of the steam train and the fashionable attire of the couple in the foreground.

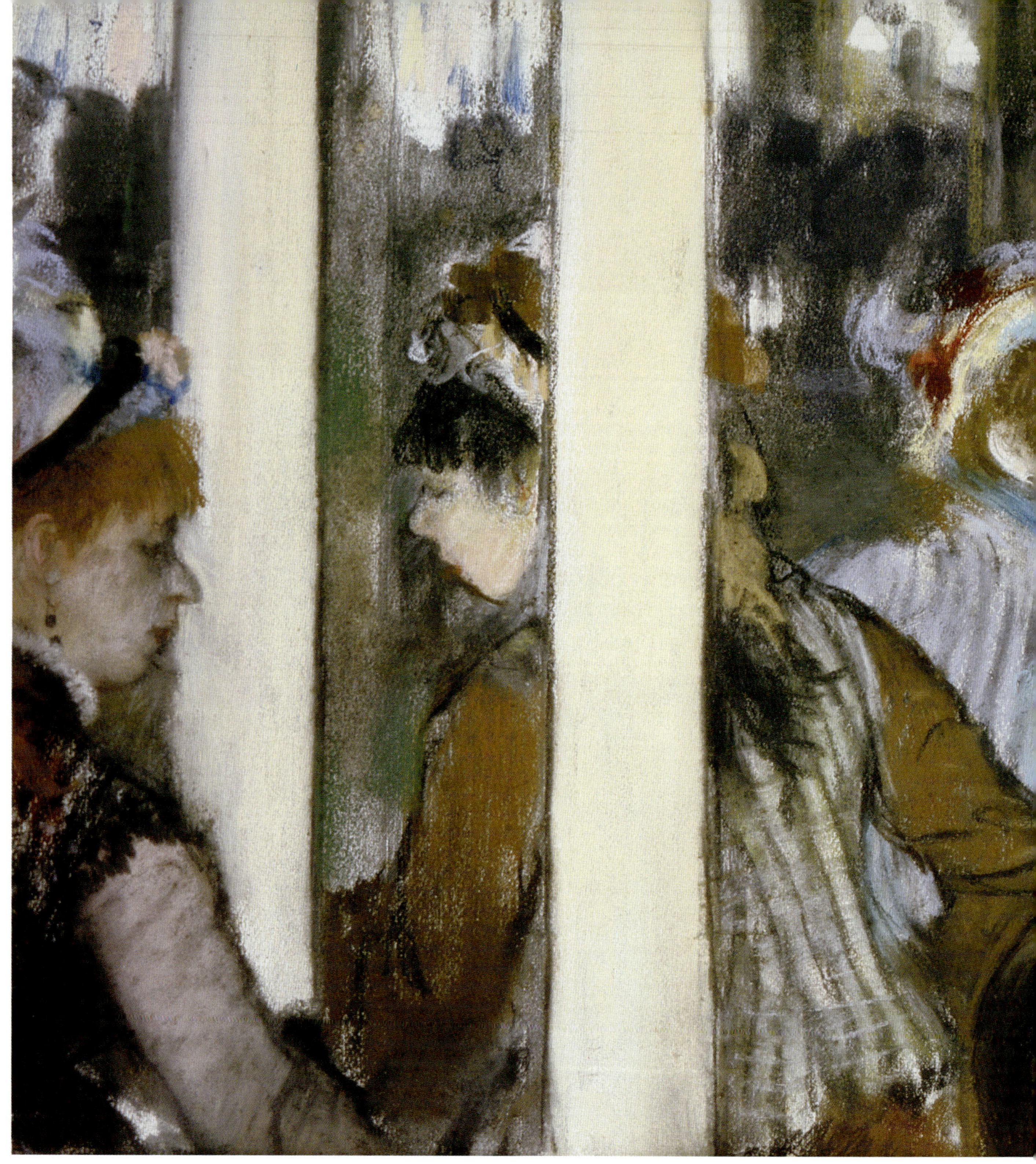

Women on a Café Terrace, Evening, 1877
Pastel on monotype, 54.5 x 71.5 cm (21½ x 28 in)
• Musée d'Orsay, Paris

The scene depicts a group of prostitutes waiting for potential clients. Notice the man walking off to the right of the picture. Was he a possible client who rejected their advances, to the annoyance of the central figure in blue?

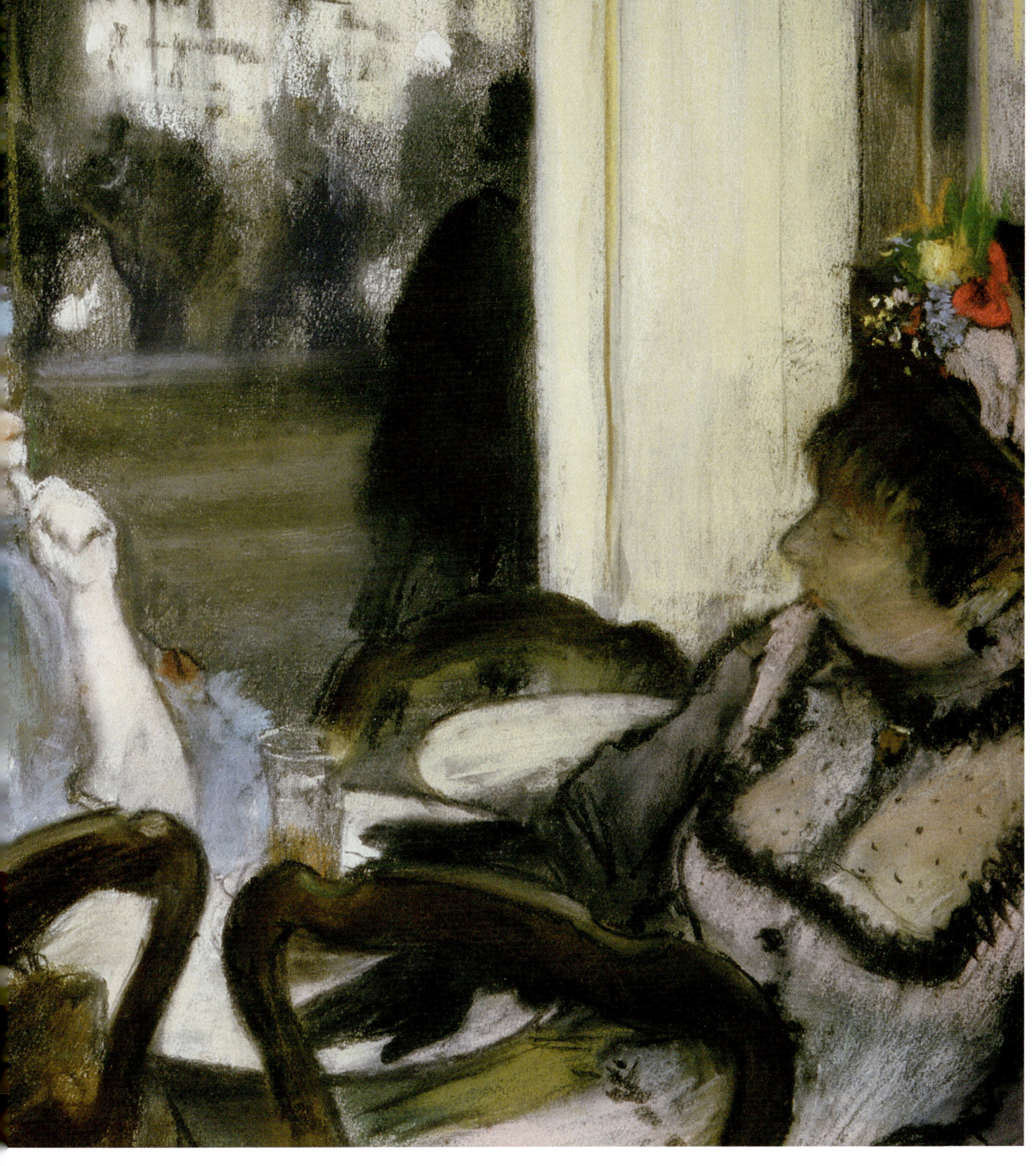

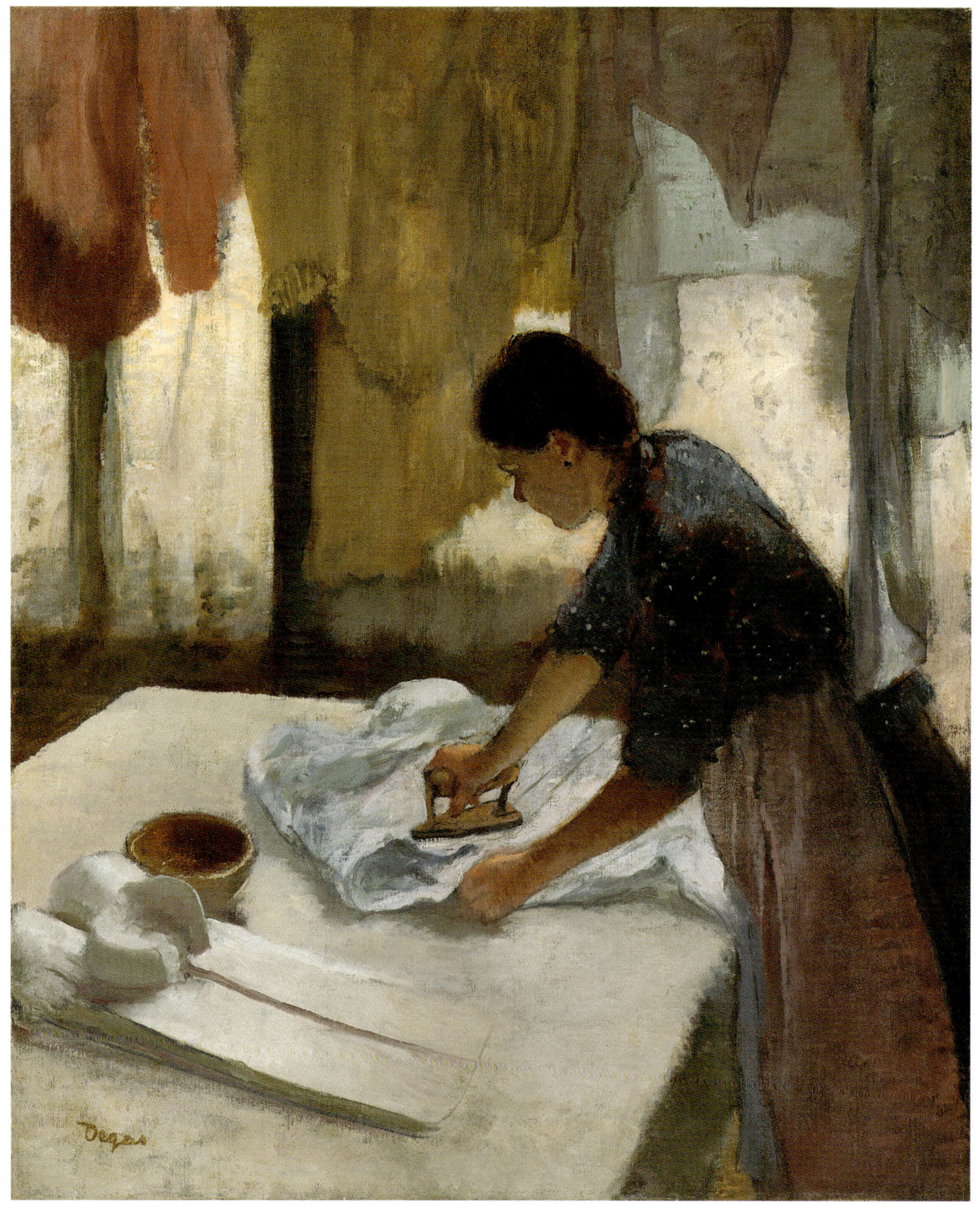

Woman Ironing, *c.* 1876–87
Oil on canvas, 81.3 x 66 cm (32 x 26 in)
• National Gallery of Art, Washington DC

Degas has introduced a number of textures into the picture, from the hard ironing surface to the crisply starched shirt, to the soft translucence of the damp clothes hanging up to dry.

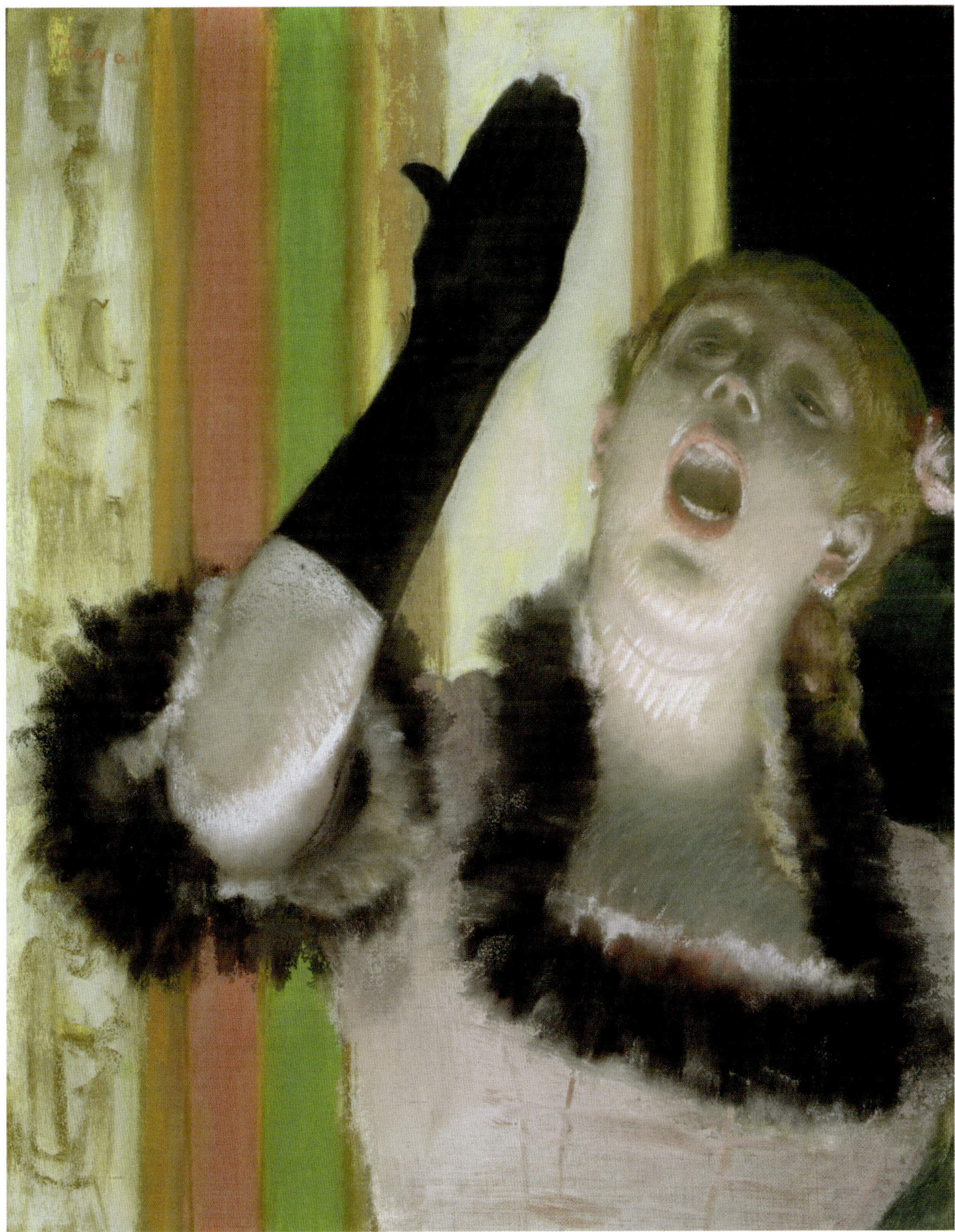

Chanteuse de Café, *c.* 1878
Pastel on canvas, 51.4 x 40 cm (20¼ x 15¾ in)
• Fogg Art Museum, Cambridge, Massachusetts

Degas loved the characteristic gestures of those performing at the café concerts, as they sought to engage with their audience. The painting was exhibited at the fourth Impressionist exhibition in 1879.

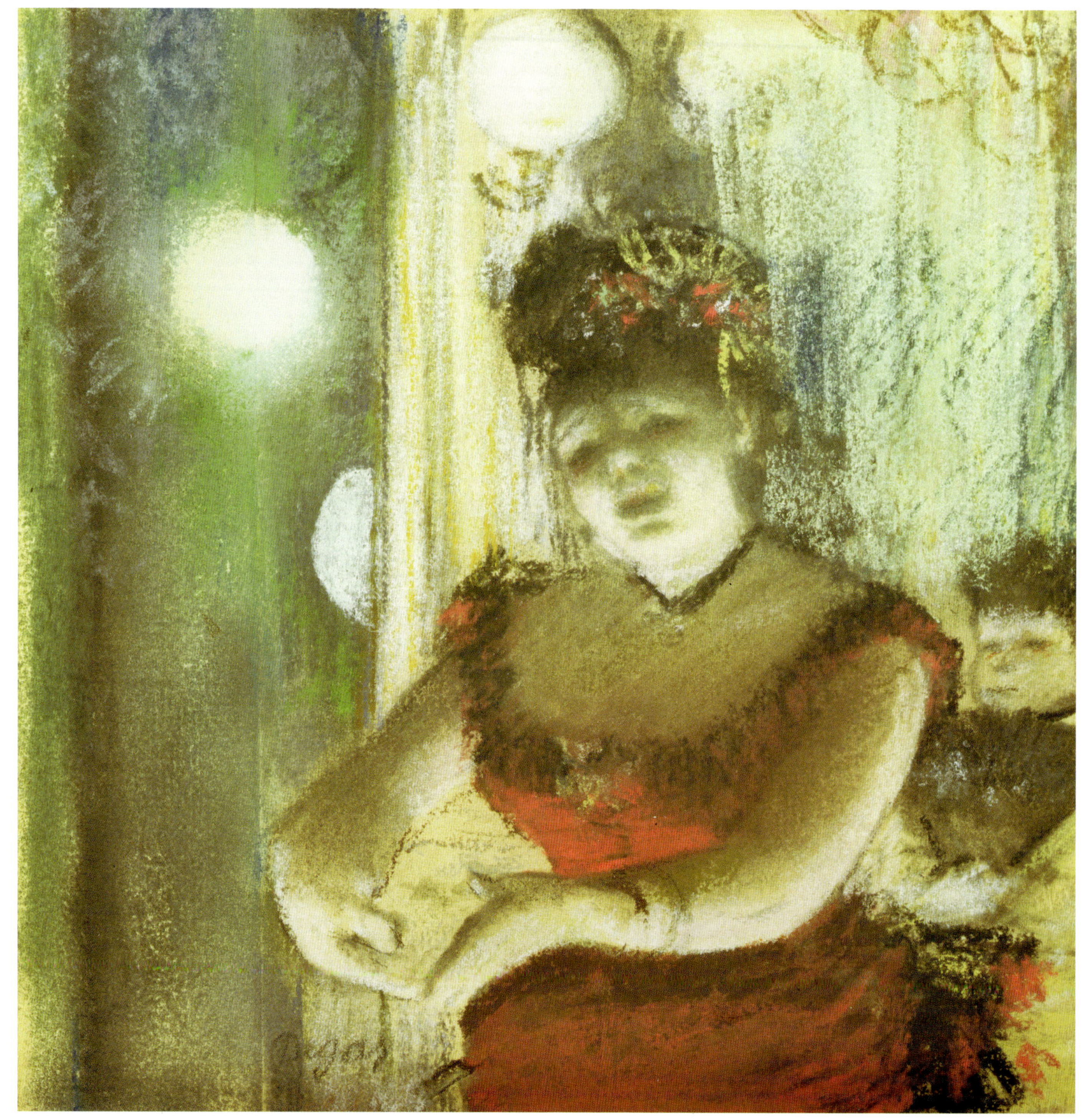

Café-Concert Singer, *c.* 1878
Pastel on paper, 16.8 x 15.9 cm (6²/₃ x 6¹/₄ in)
• Private Collection

Although small in scale, this pastel is wonderfully finished in detail. The performer is Mlle Dumay, who was well known as a café-concert singer, Degas having sketched her a number of times.

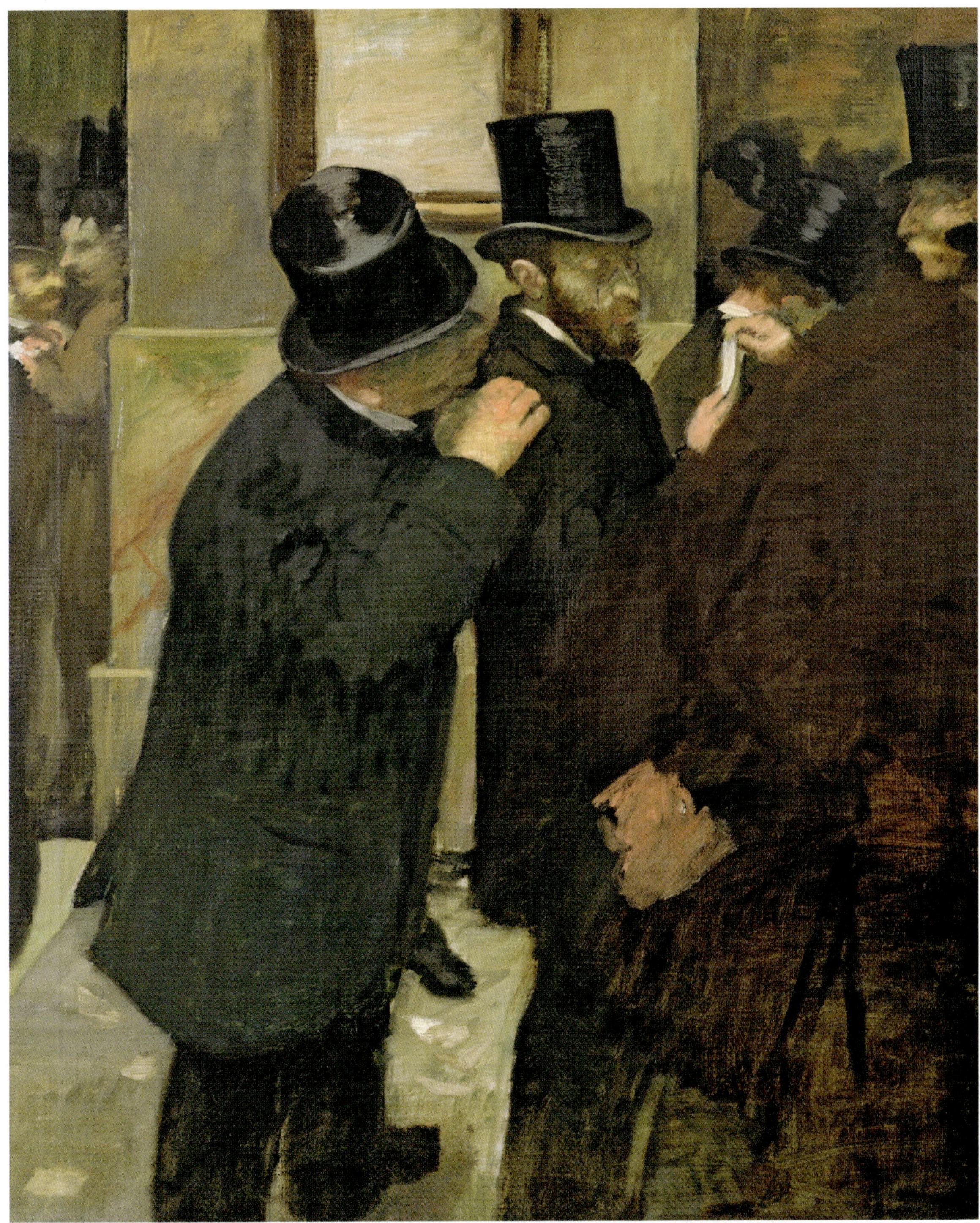

Portraits at the Stock Exchange, 1878–79
Oil on canvas, 100 x 82 cm (39$^{1}/_{3}$ x 32$^{1}/_{3}$ in)
• Musée d'Orsay, Paris

The central figure in the composition is Ernest May, a financier and art collector known to Degas. He appears to be privy to some inside information, which the two characters on the left are trying to overhear.

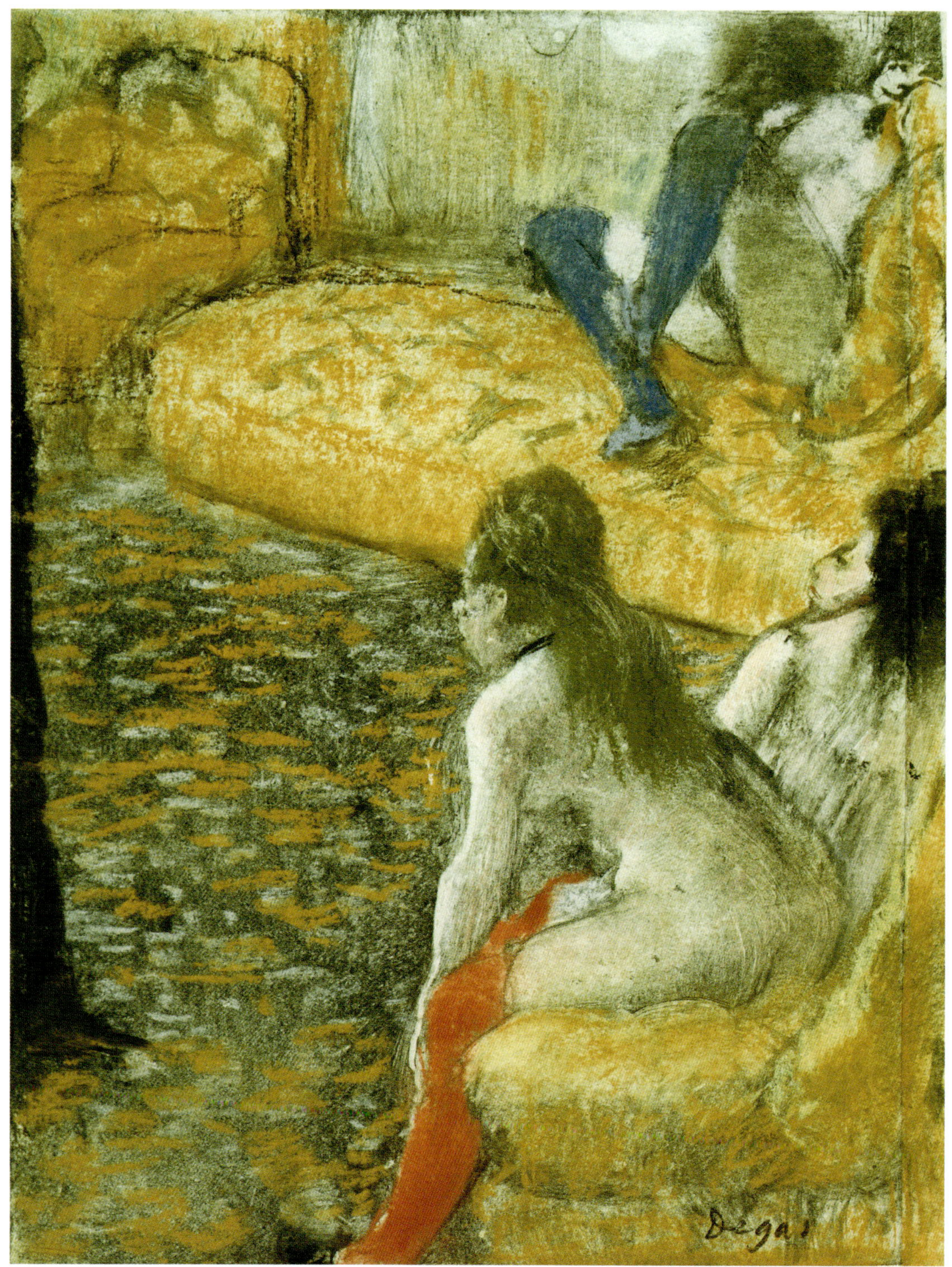

Waiting for a Client, *c.* 1879
Pastel and charcoal on paper, 17 x 12 cm (6²/₃ x 4³/₄ in)
• Private Collection

Degas is in the brothel as an observer of the transaction rather than the sexual act. He depicts a male 'intruder' on the extreme left, almost a shadowy figure, suggesting that the transaction itself is sordid.

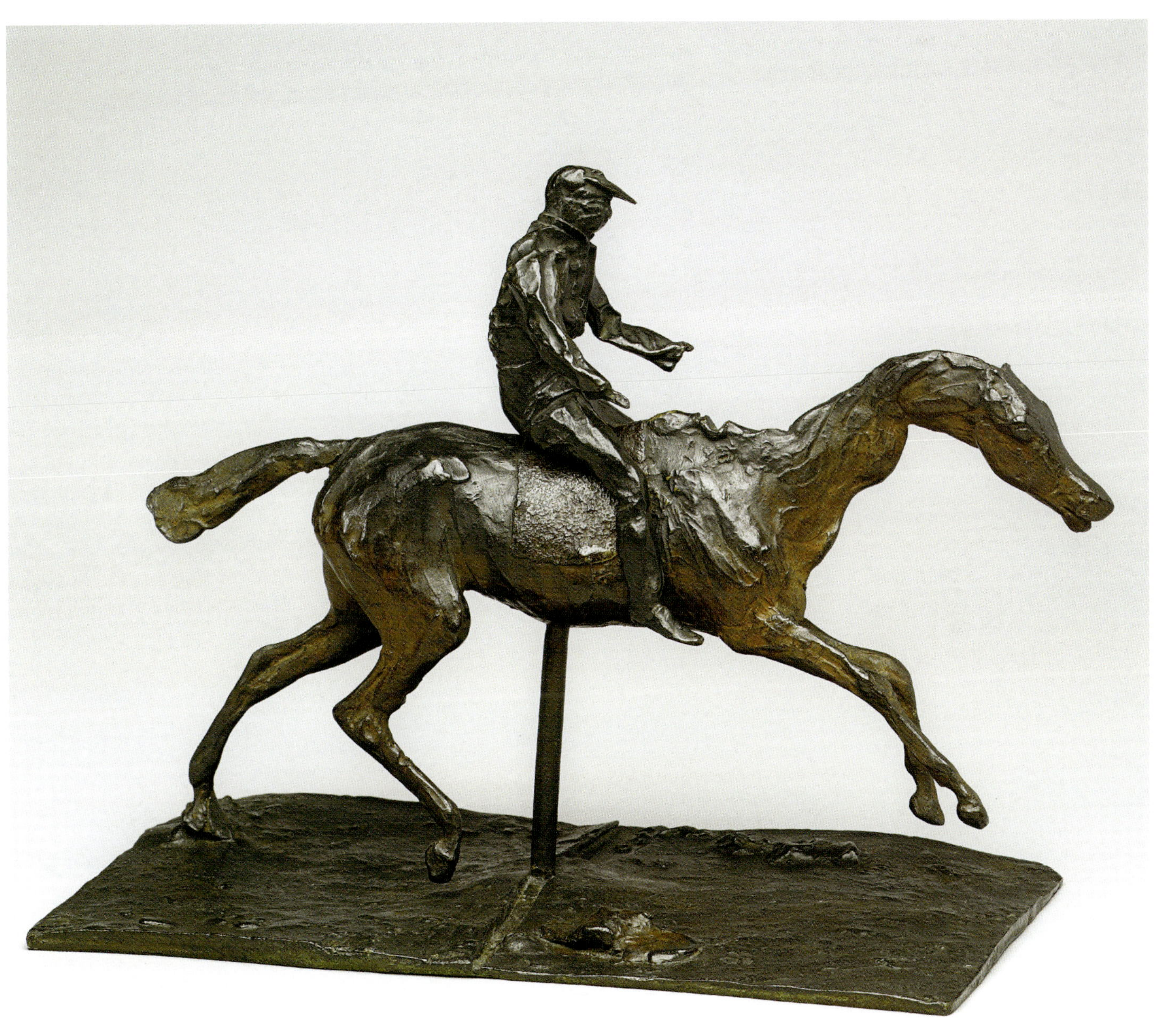

Horse with Jockey, created 1878-81 or early 1890s, cast 1919–21
Bronze, 24.6 x 17.8 x 34 cm (9²/₃ x 7 x 13¹/₃ in)
• Art Gallery of Ontario, Toronto

Degas was fascinated by movement, whether equine or human. He carefully studied the photographic images of Eadweard Muybridge, who had pioneered the study of moving images in photography.

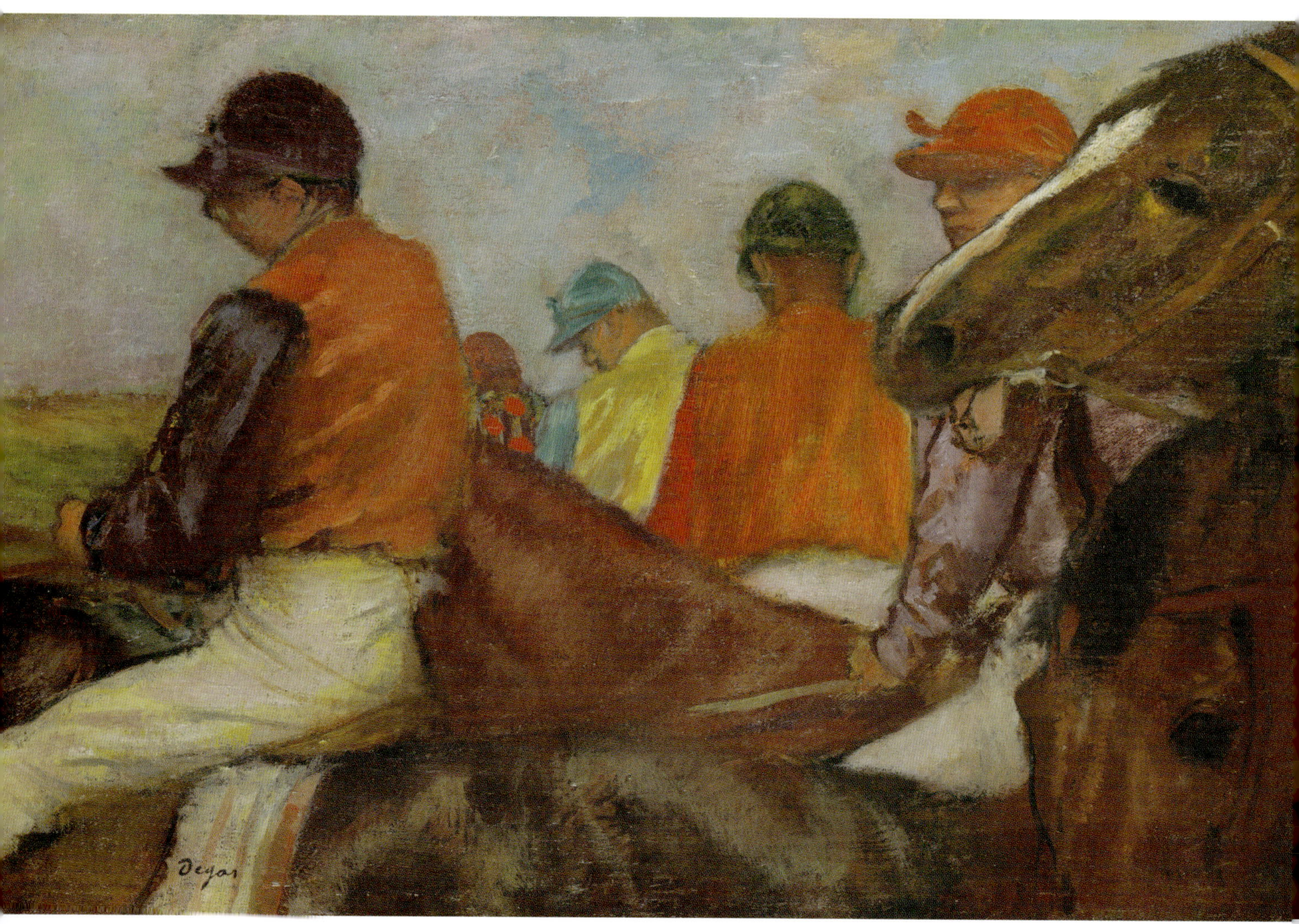

The Jockeys, *c.* 1882
Oil on canvas, 26.4 x 39.8 cm (10$^{1}/_{3}$ x 15$^{2}/_{3}$ in)
• Yale University Museum, New Haven, Connecticut

Degas places the viewer in the midst of this bustling scene, as the jockeys prepare for the race.
Usually Degas gives the viewer space to contemplate the scene, but here we are confined and
excited by their presence.

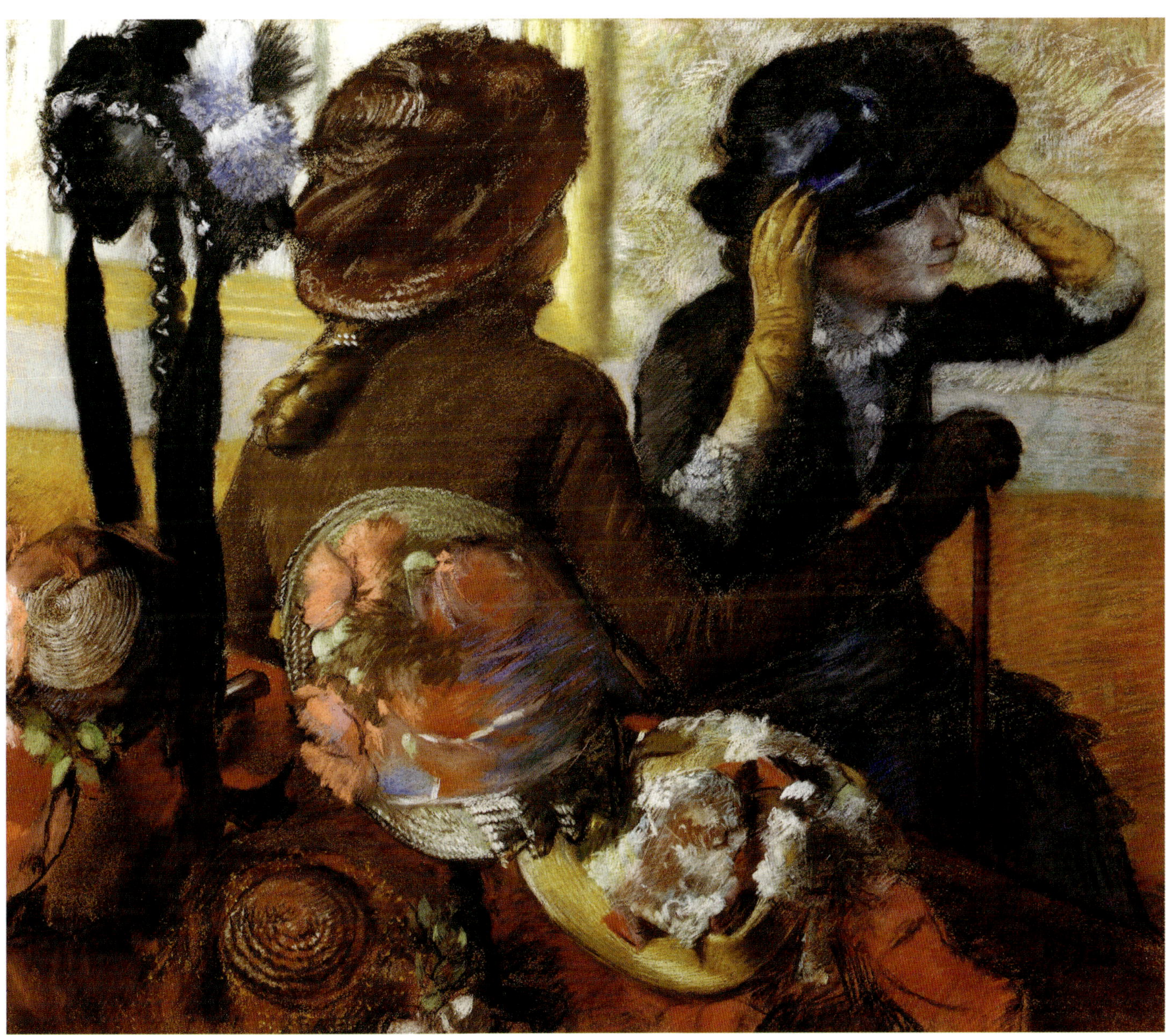

At the Milliner's, 1882
Pastel on paper, 75.5 x 85.5 cm (29³/₄ x 33²/₃ in)
• Museo Thyssen-Bornemisza, Madrid

A young woman tries on a hat in the presence of an older lady, possibly her mother.
We are not able to see the mirror, but the light reflecting on the young woman's face
makes us aware of its presence.

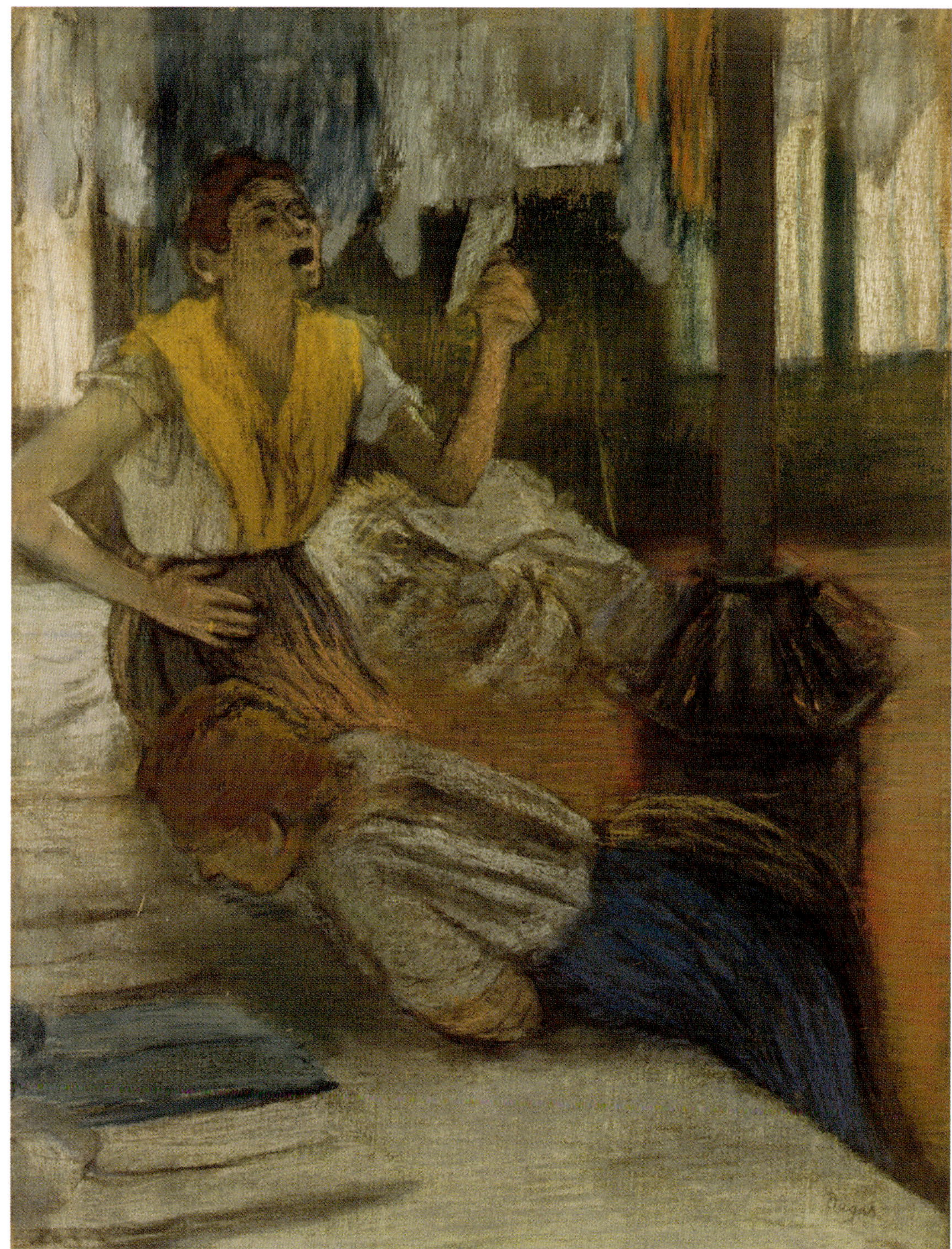

Reading a Letter, *c.* **1884**
Pastel on paper, 63 x 45 cm (24⁴/₅ x 17³/₄ in)
• Glasgow Art Gallery and Museum, Glasgow

The two laundresses are taking a rest from their labours as one reads a letter out loud.
The power of this image is in the heavy use of complementary colours (yellow and blue)
and the broad strokes.

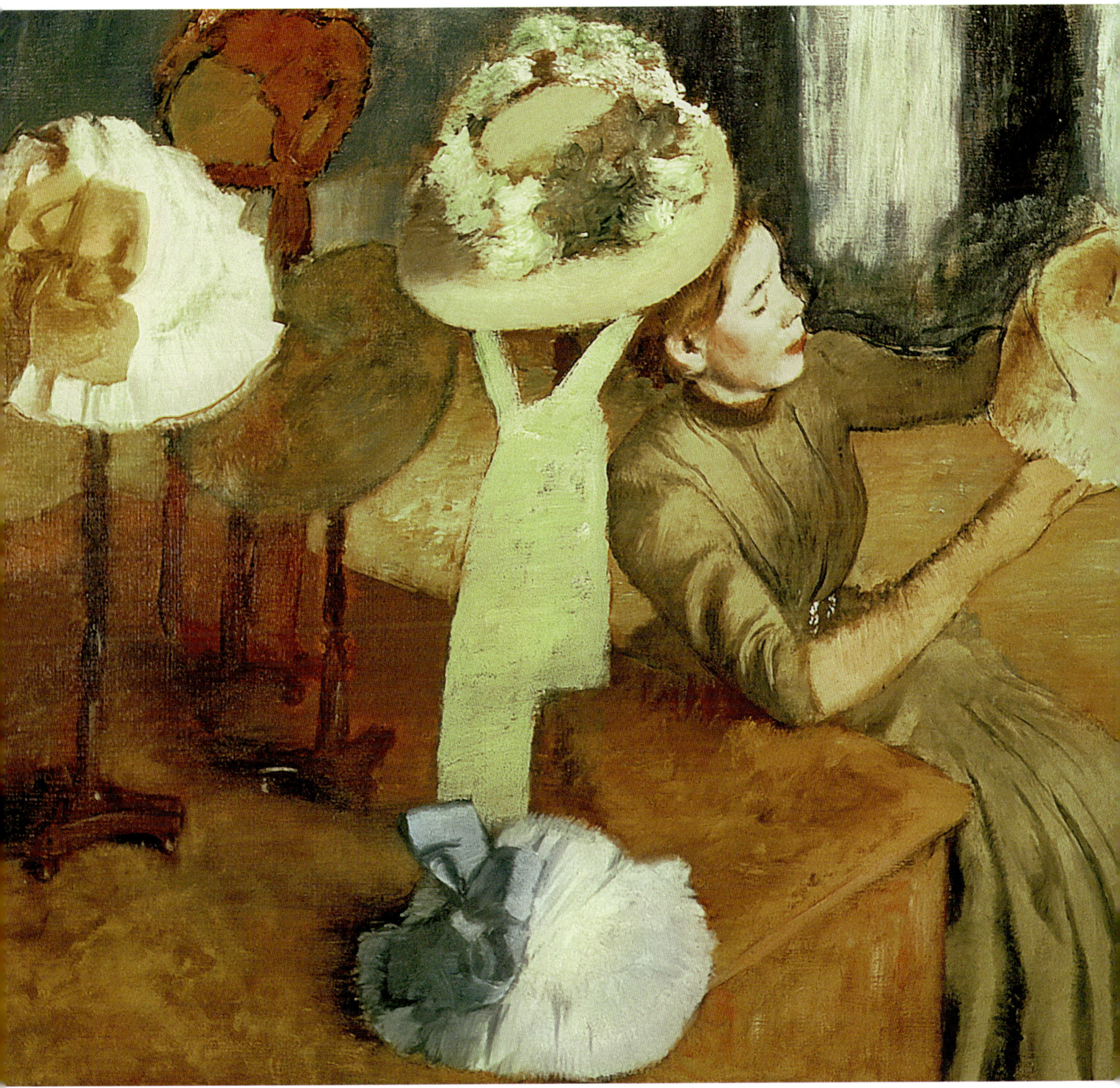

The Millinery Shop, 1882–86
Oil on canvas, 100 x 110.7 cm (39$\frac{1}{3}$ x 45$\frac{1}{2}$ in)
• Art Institute of Chicago, Illinois

The young milliner is completely unaware of the artist's or the viewer's presence as she prepares her display of hats, which appear to be hovering above the picture plane.

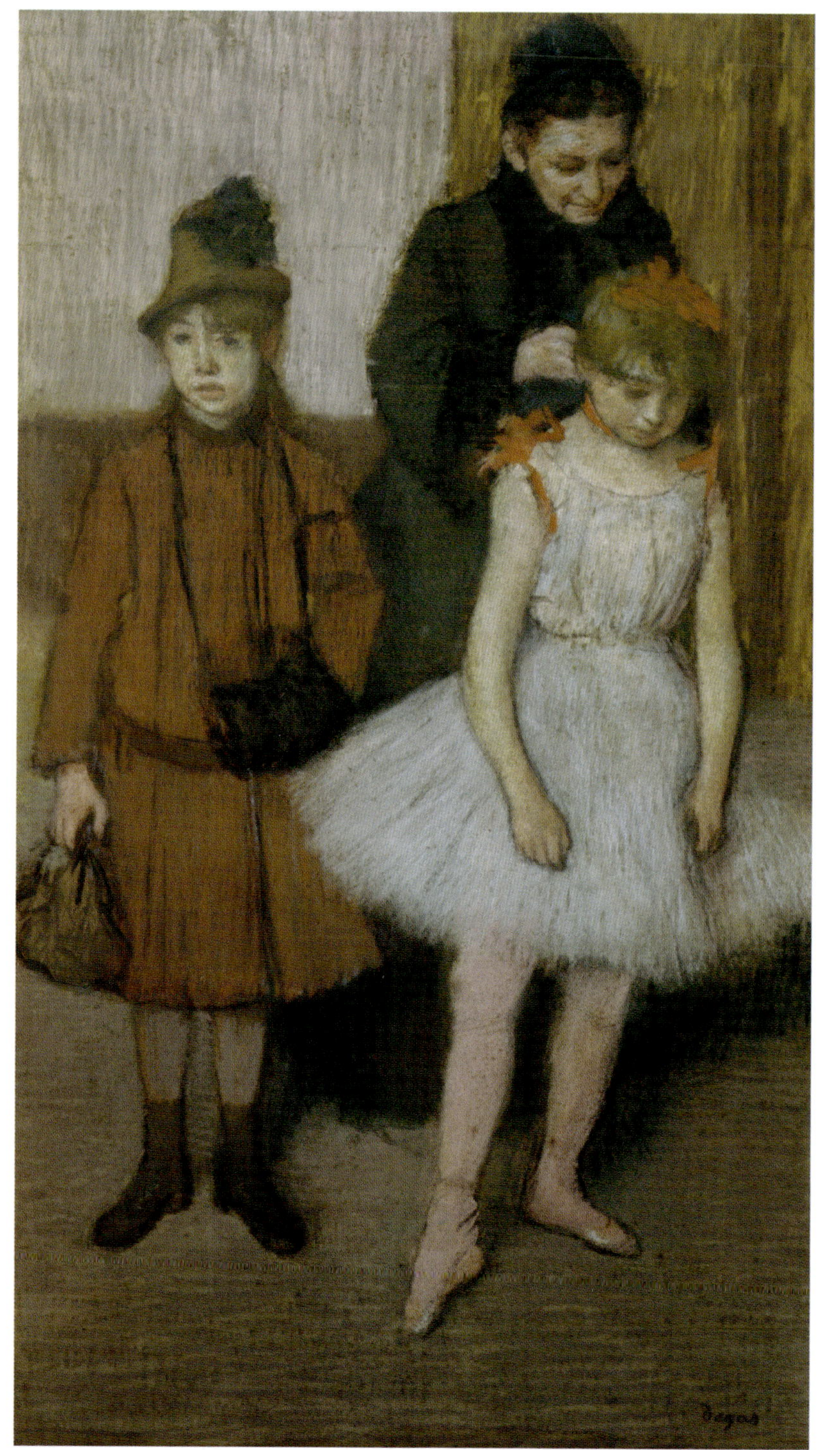

The Mante Family, _c._ 1889
Pastel on paper, 90 x 50 cm (30$^{1}/_{2}$ x 19$^{2}/_{3}$ in)
• Suzuki Collection, Tokyo, Japan

Mme Mante is shown adjusting the hair of her daughter Suzanne as she prepares for her ballet lesson or examination. Her older sister Blanche, dressed in daywear, seems indifferent to the situation.

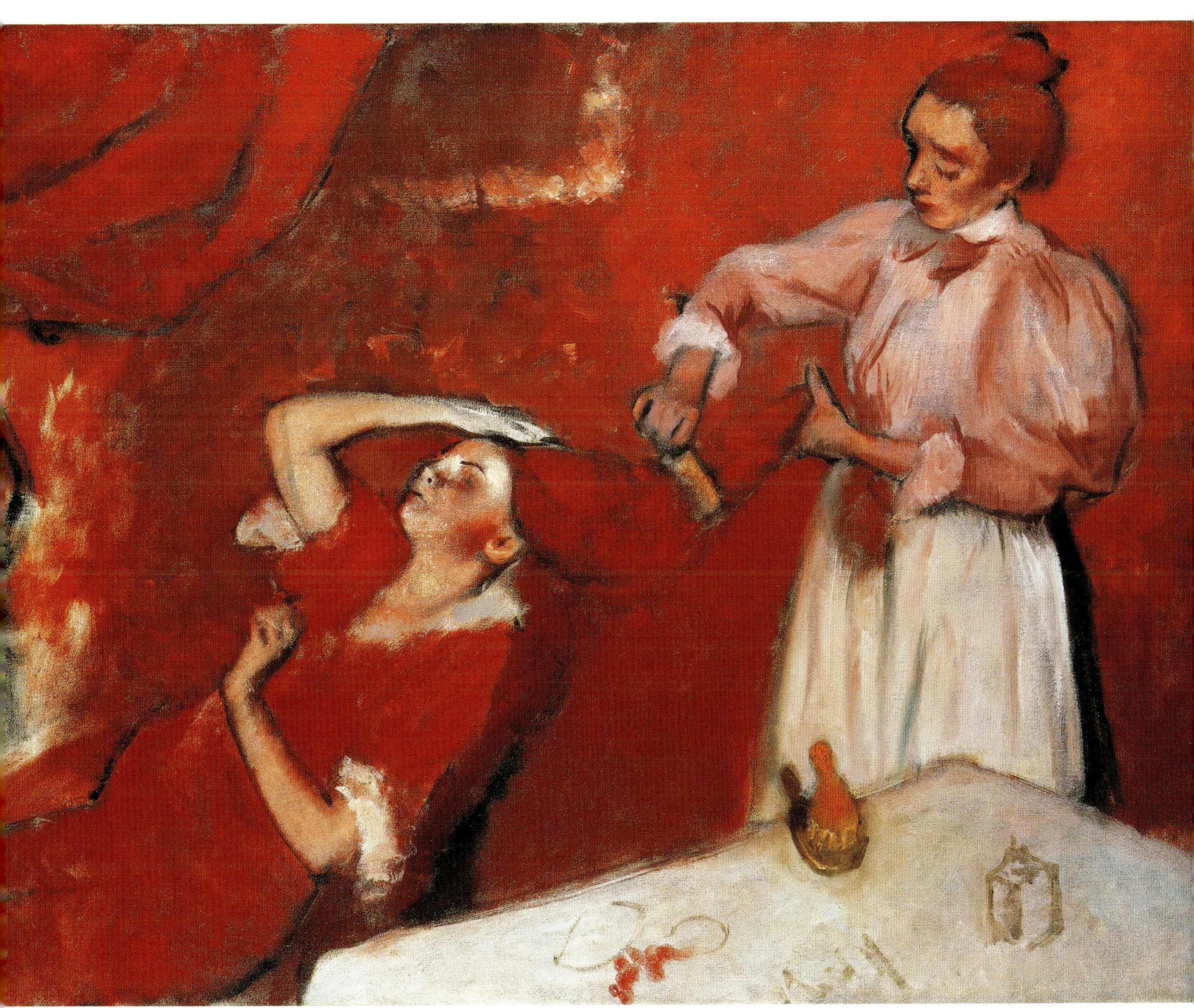

Combing the Hair (La Coiffure), c. 1896
Oil on canvas, 114.3 x 146.7 cm (45 x 57¾ in)
• National Gallery, London

The powerful colours used liberally by Degas at this time in his career are a result of his degenerative eye complaint that eventually left him blind. Henri Matisse (1869–1954) owned this painting at one time.

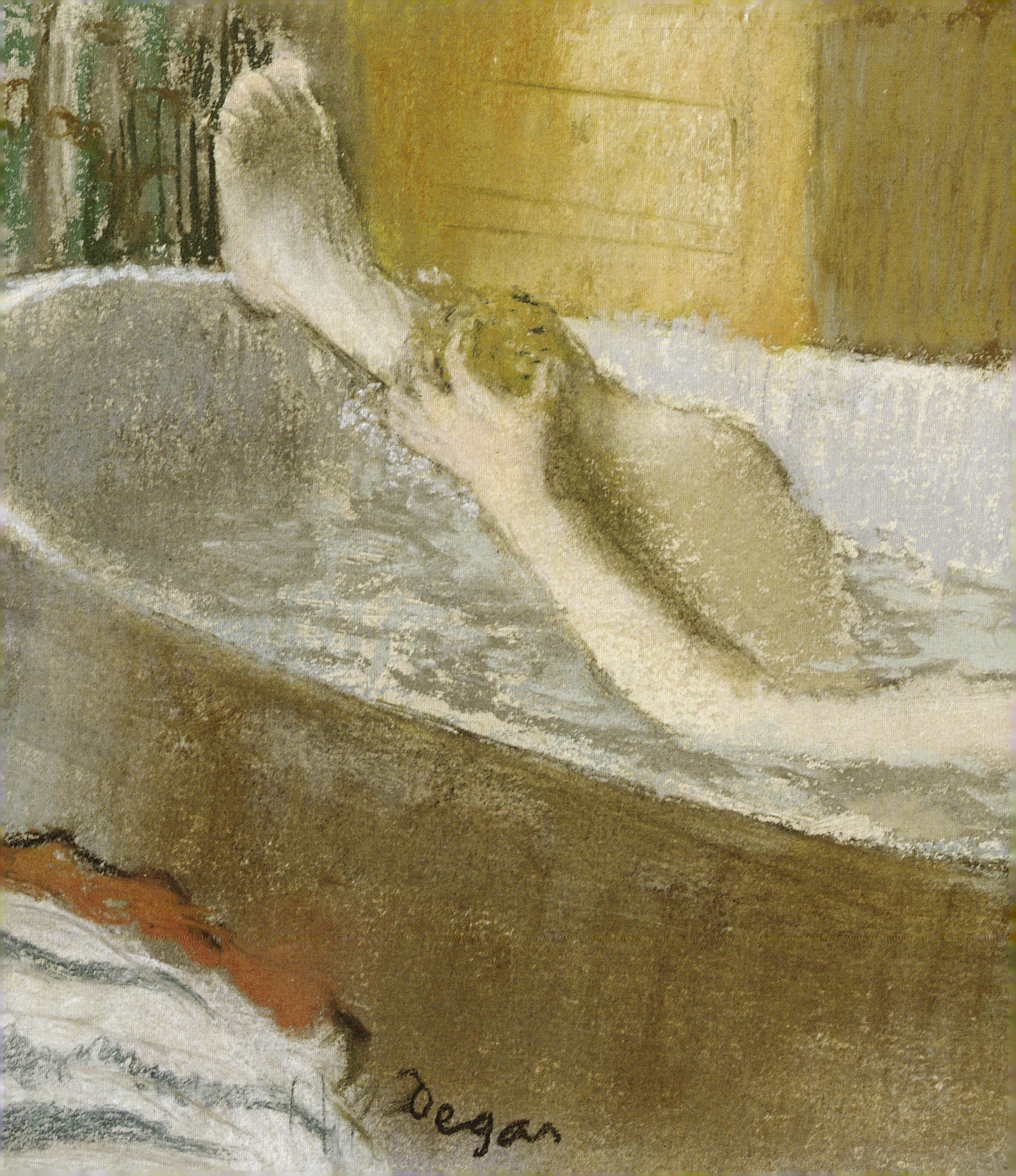
Degas

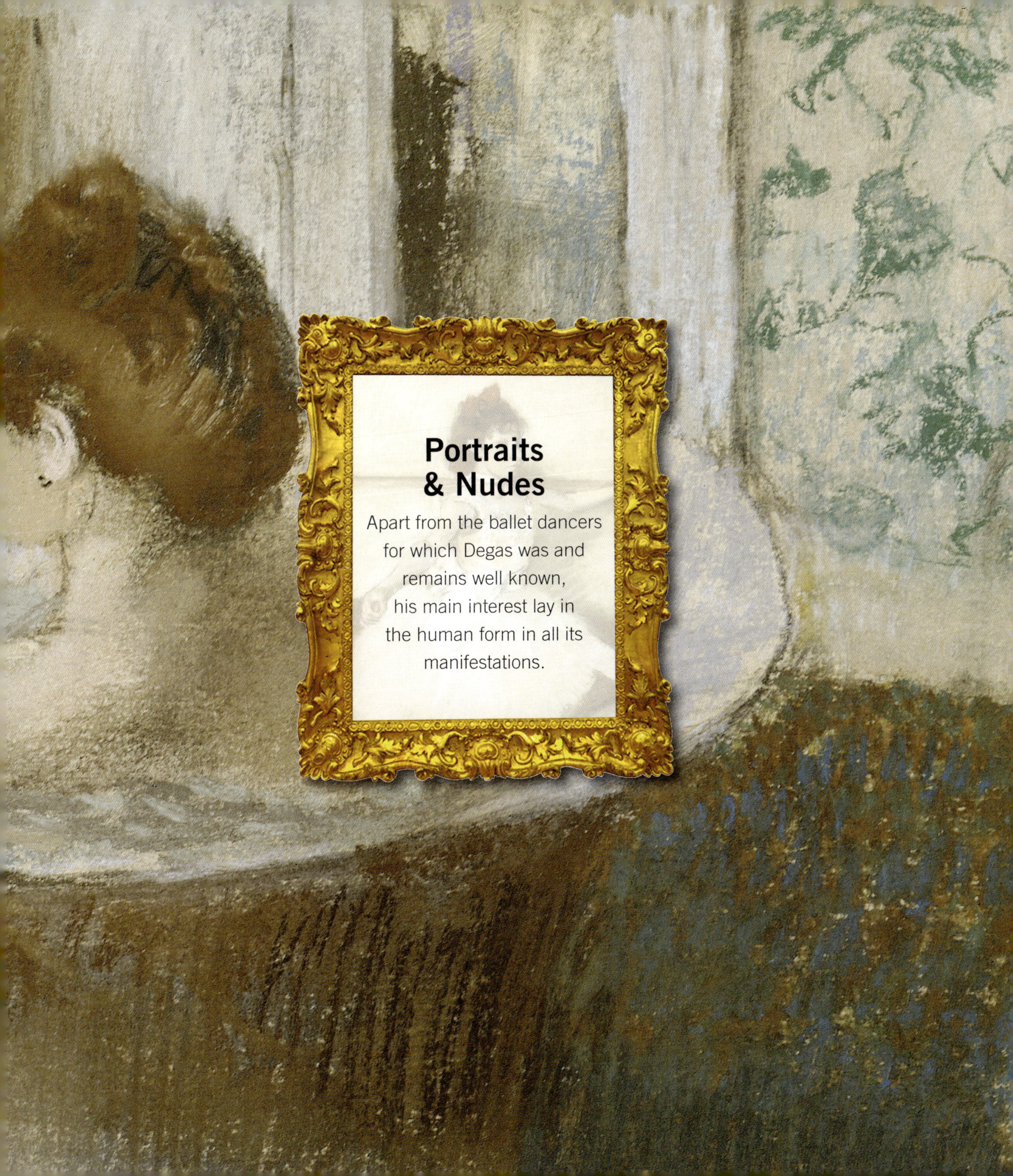

Portraits
& Nudes

Apart from the ballet dancers
for which Degas was and
remains well known,
his main interest lay in
the human form in all its
manifestations.

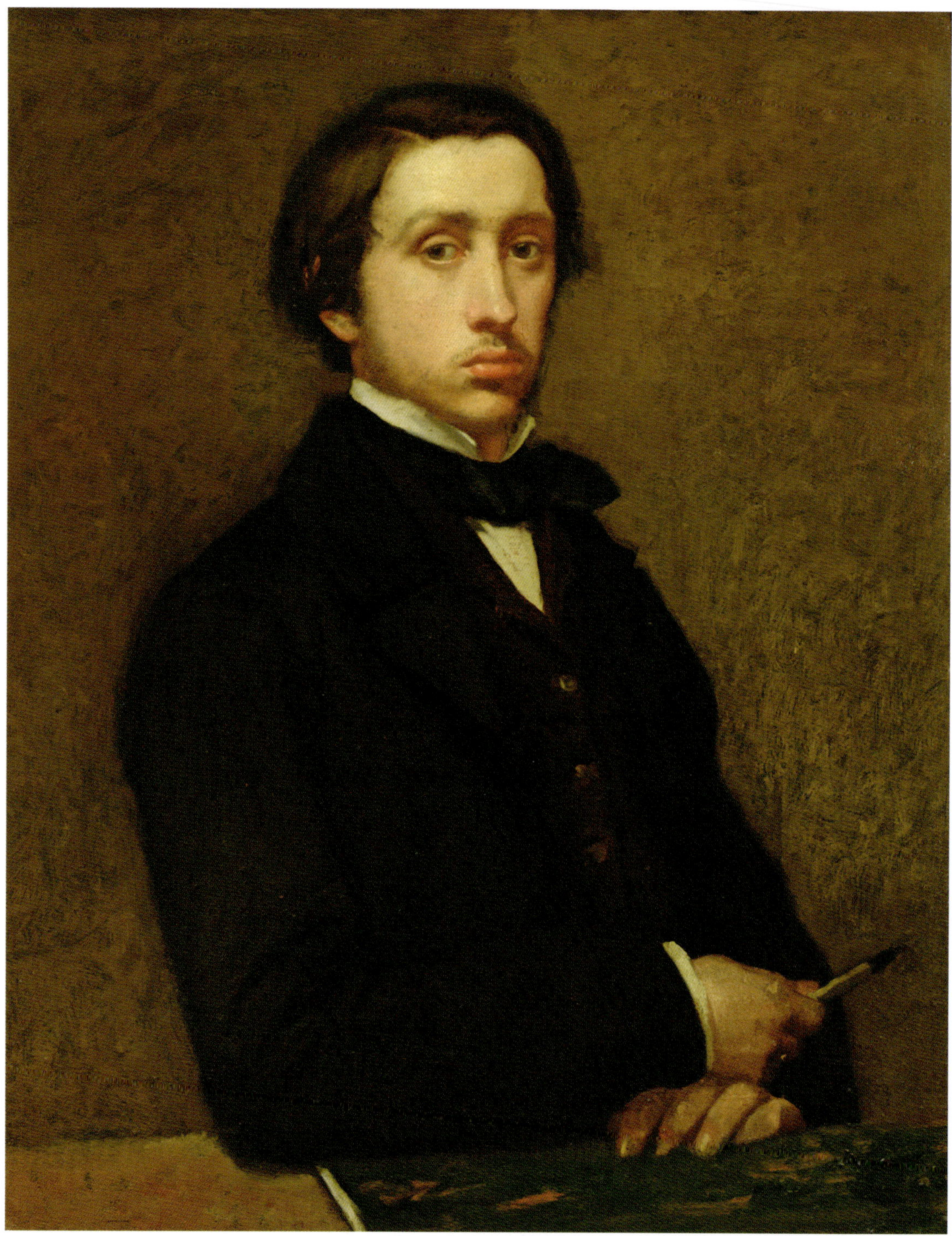

Self-portrait, 1855
Oil on canvas, 81 x 64.5 cm (31⁴/₅ x 25²/₅ in)
• Musée d'Orsay, Paris

A confident and ambitious 21-year-old Degas looks directly at his viewers.
At this stage in his career he has enrolled at the École des Beaux-Arts,
a student of art but already an accomplished artist.

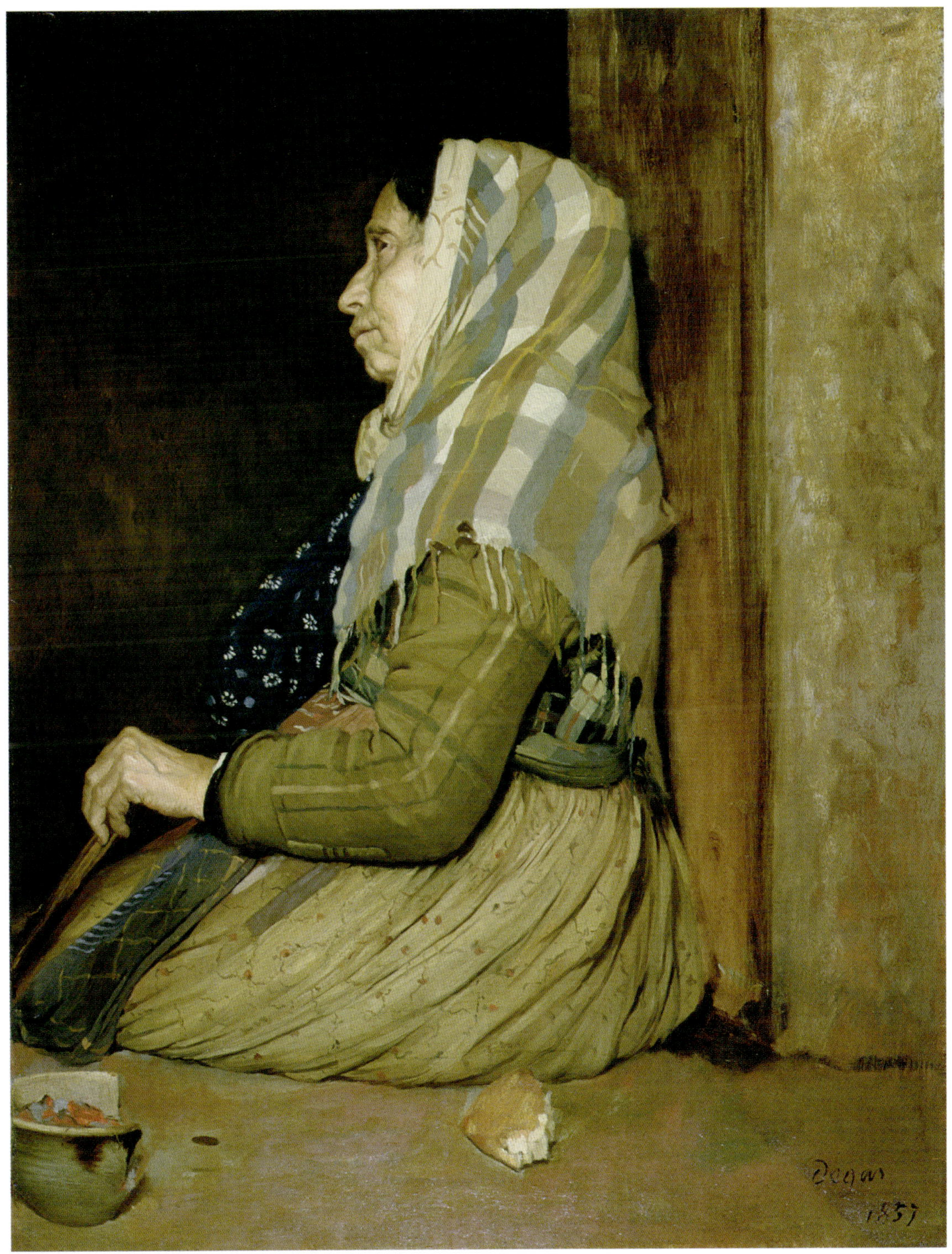

A Roman Beggar Woman, 1857
Oil on canvas, 100.3 x 75.2 cm (39$\frac{1}{2}$ x 29$\frac{2}{3}$ in)
• Birmingham Museums and Art Gallery, Birmingham

Executed while on his travels through Italy, this painting reveals one of the hallmarks of Degas' *oeuvre*: a view of a person unaware of the artist's presence. The draughtsmanship is clearly indebted to Degas' meeting with Ingres.

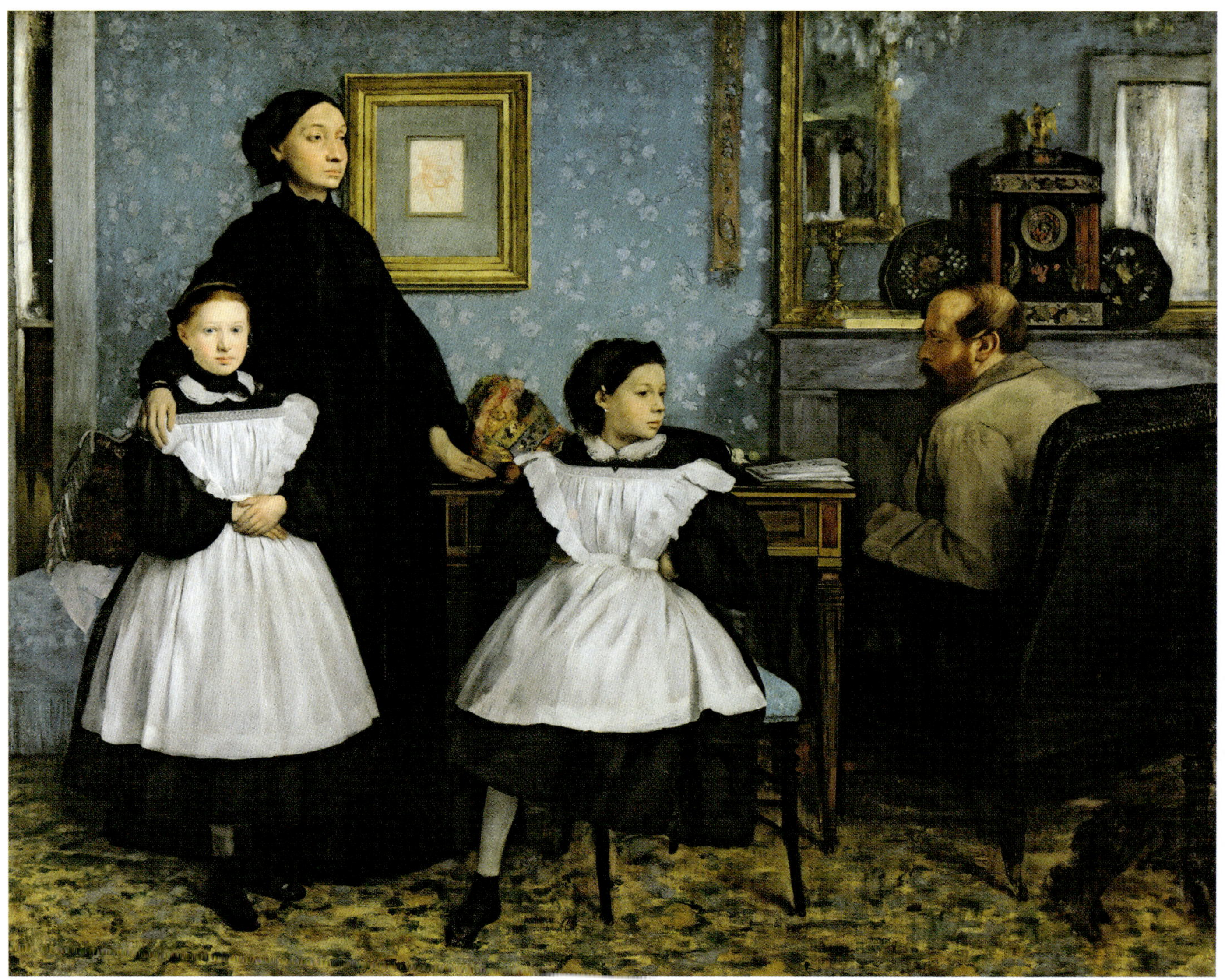

The Bellelli Family, 1858–67
Oil on canvas, 200 x 250 cm (78³/₄ x 98¹/₂ in)
• Musée d'Orsay, Paris

This ambitious painting was executed in Degas' studio after he made copious notes of his relatives during his stay with them in 1858–59. In it Degas has recorded the unhappy situation of his aunt's marriage.

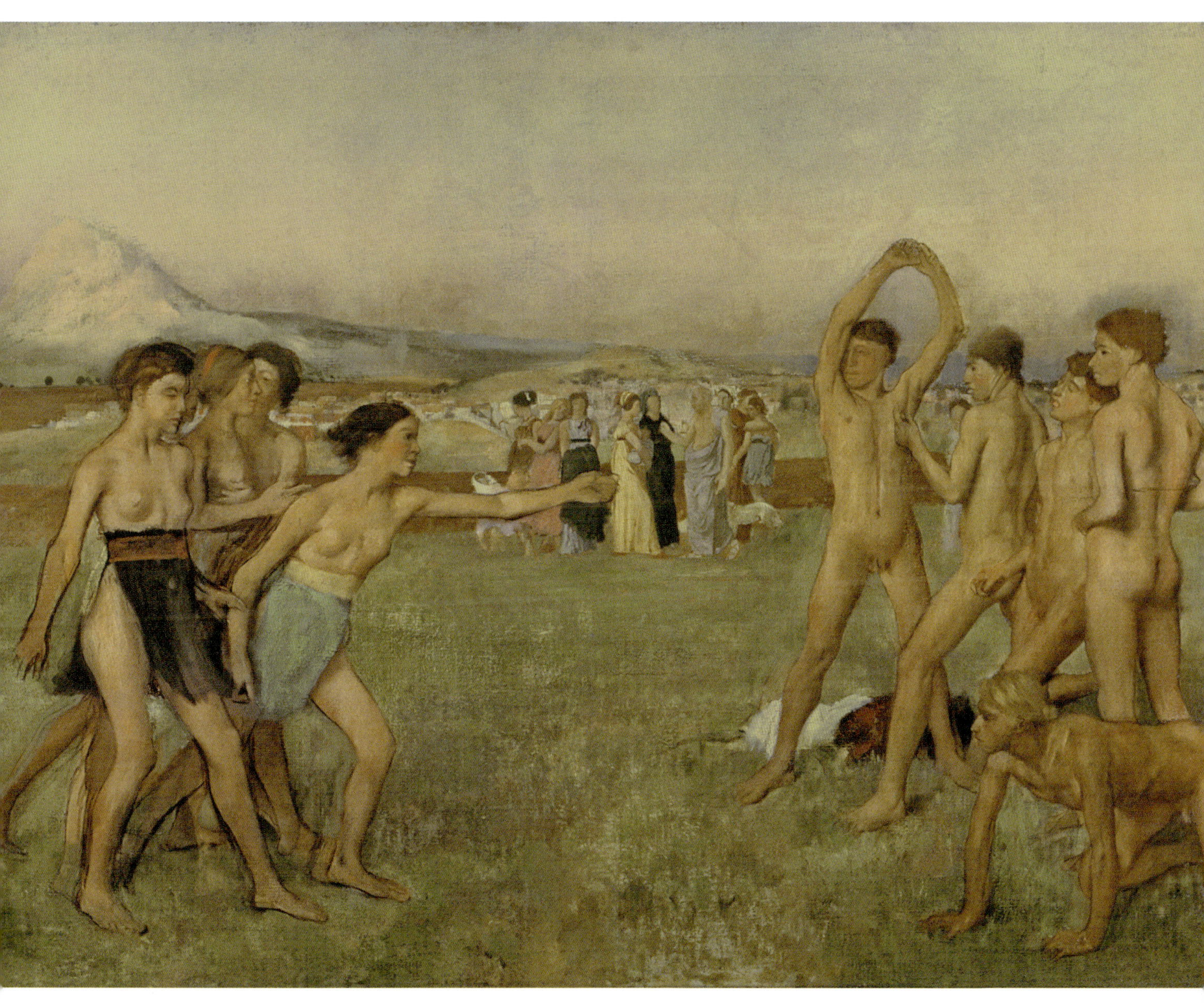

Young Spartans Exercising, *c.* 1860
Oil on canvas, 109.2 x 154.3 cm (43 x 60¾ in)
• National Gallery, London

On Degas' return to Paris in 1859, he was keen to prepare work for submission to the Salon in order to build his reputation as an artist. The historical narrative of the painting fulfils a criterion of that establishment.

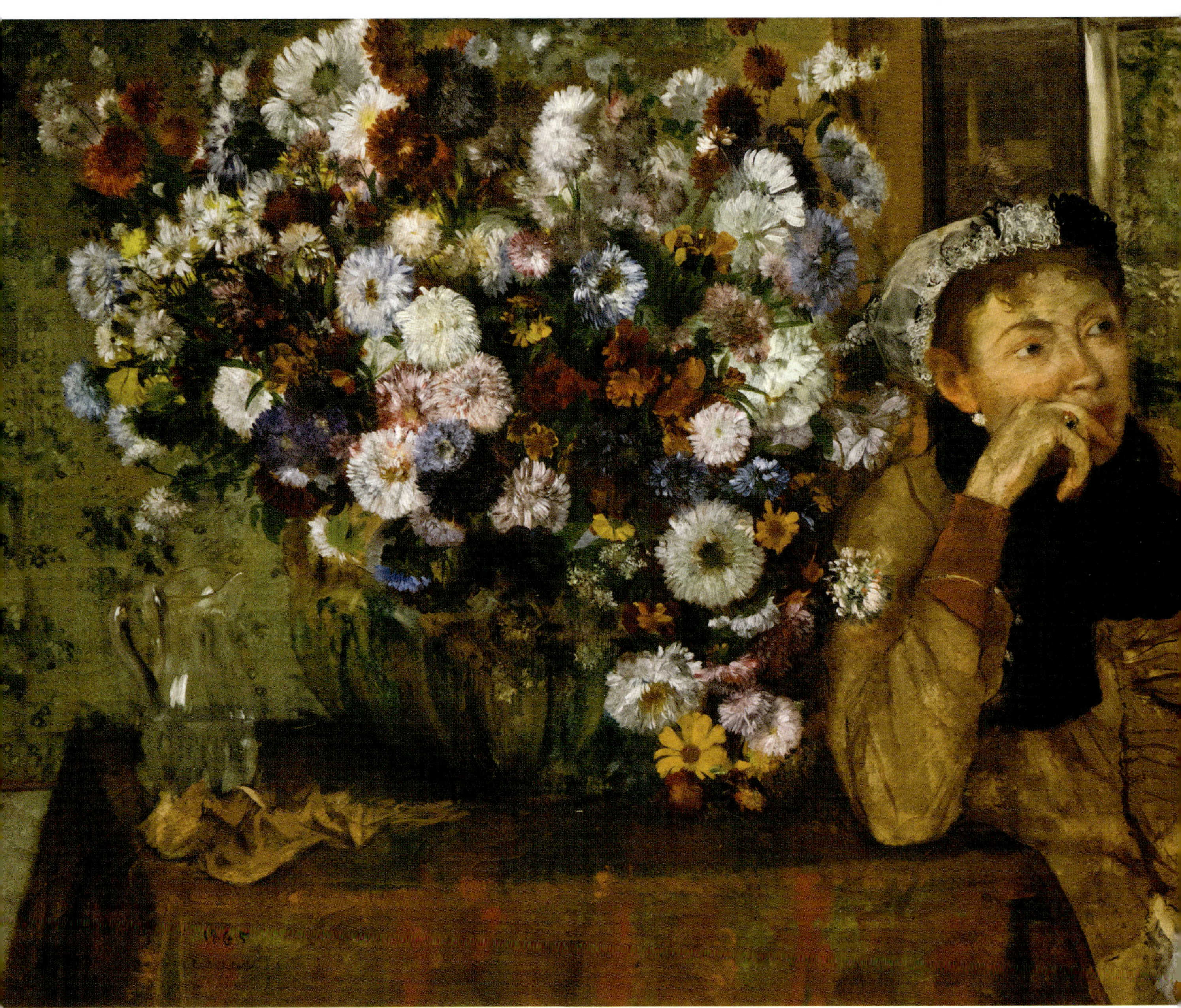

A Woman Seated Beside a Vase of Flowers, 1865
Oil on canvas, 74 x 92 cm (29 x 36¼ in)
• Metropolitan Museum of Art, New York

The sitter is Mme Valpinçon, a family friend with whom Degas was staying in Normandy.
Degas gives the sitter a similar air of elegance and refinement as that seen in Ingres'
portraits, some of which were hanging in the Valpinçon home.

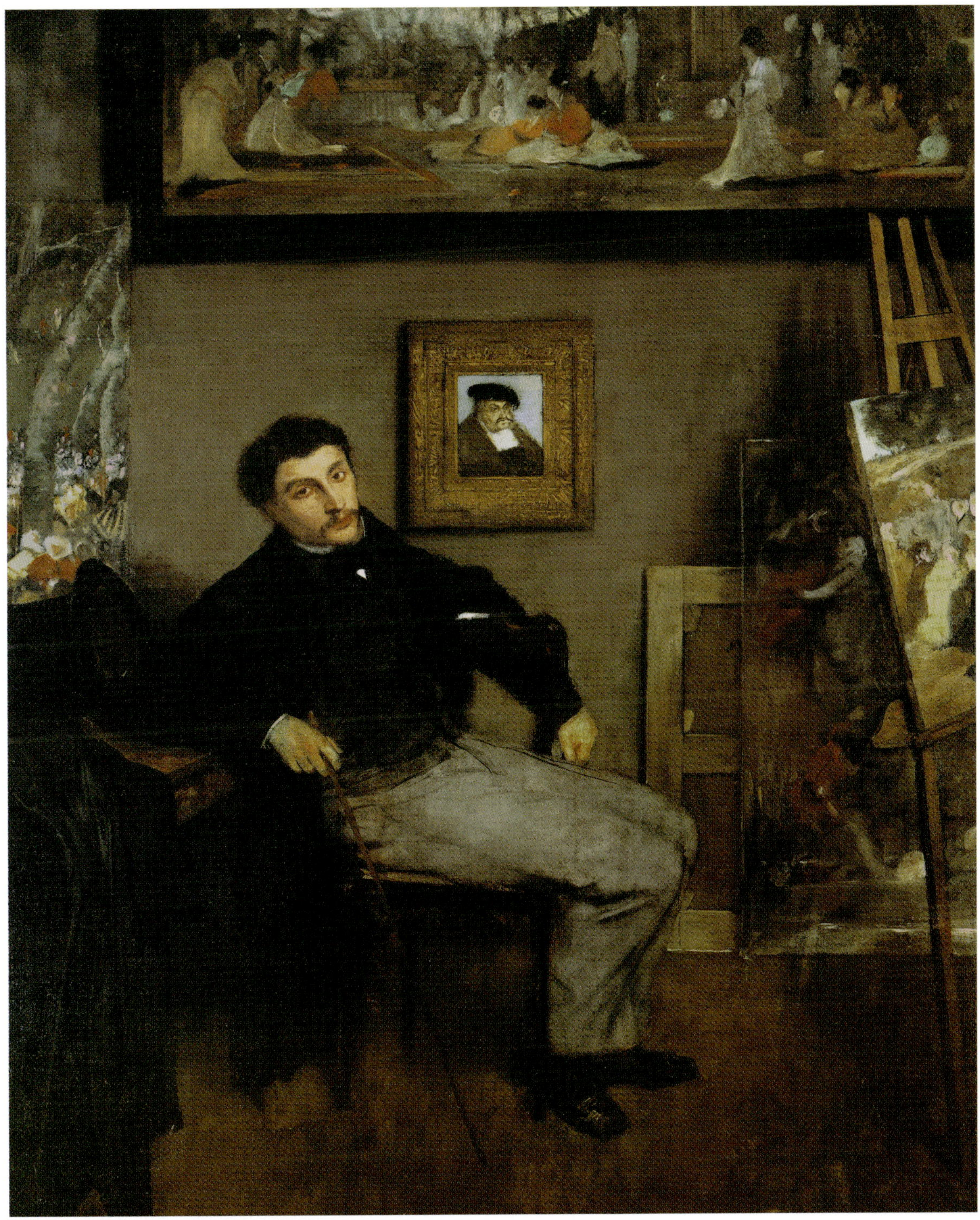

Portrait of Painter Tissot, 1867–68
Oil on canvas, 151.5 x 112 cm (59^{2}/3 x 44 in)
• Metropolitan Museum of Art, New York

Degas met Tissot at the studio of Louis Lamothe, their tutor. This portrait shows the artist surrounded by artworks in which Degas and Tissot had a shared interest, from *Japonisme* to the Renaissance.

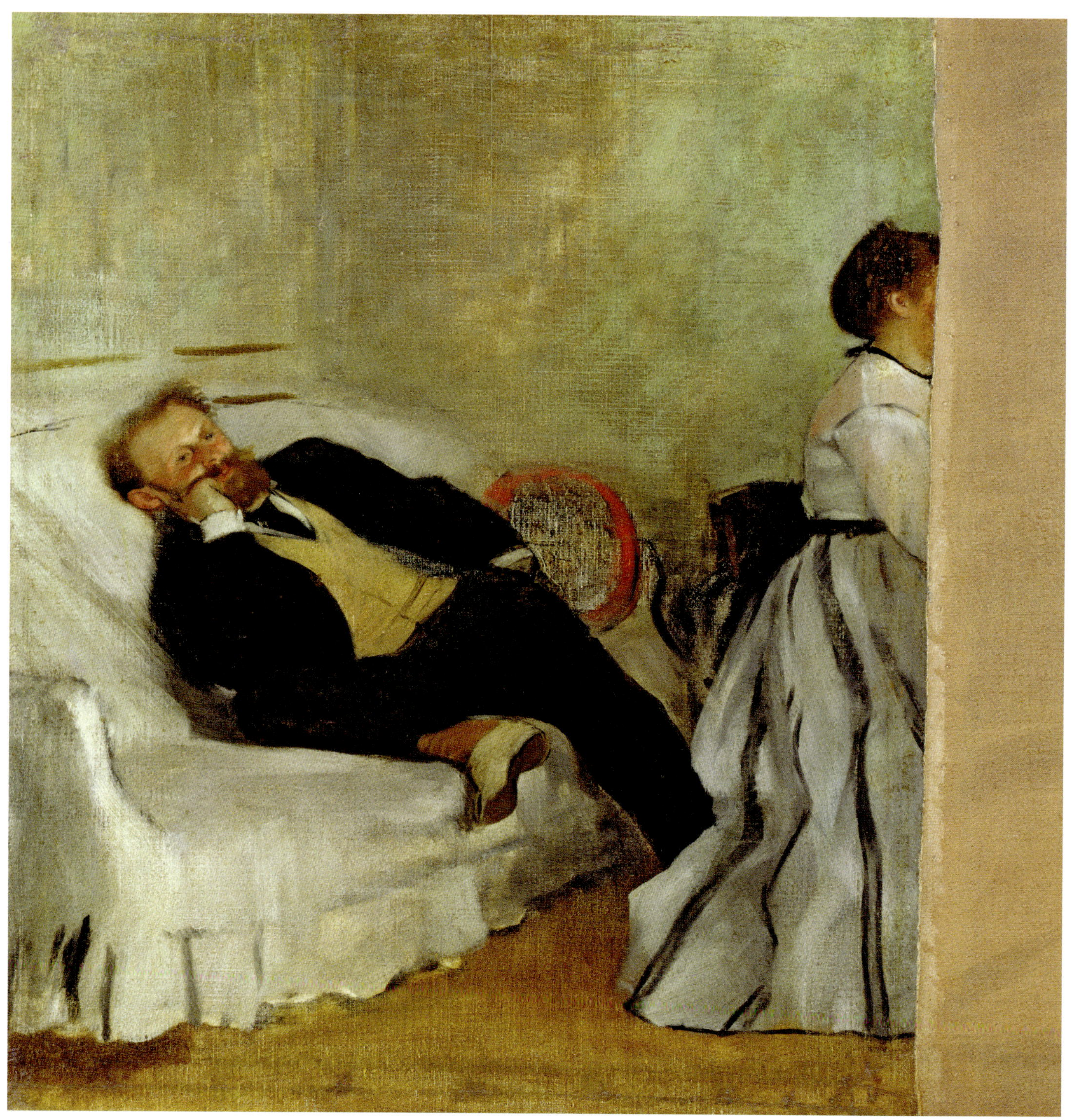

Monsieur and Madame Edouard Manet, 1868–69
Oil on canvas, 65.2 x 71.1 cm ($25\frac{2}{3}$ x 28 in)
• Municipal Museum of Art, Kitakyushu

Originally the portrait featured Mme Manet playing the piano. Degas gave the painting to Manet, who was upset about the rendition of his wife's face and cut that section off the canvas.

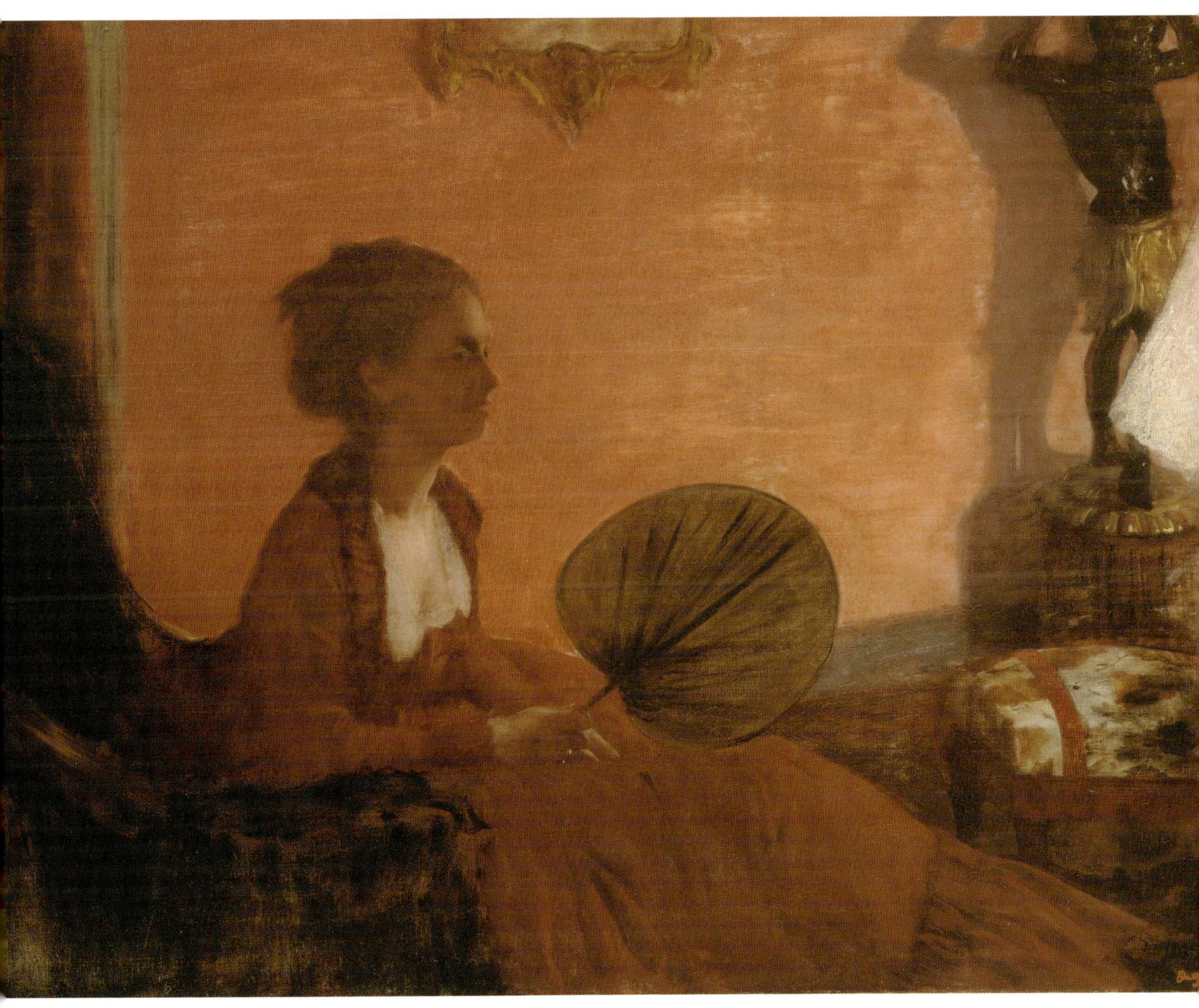

Madame Camus, 1869–70
Oil on canvas, 72.7 x 92.1 cm (28³/₄ x 36¹/₄ in)
• National Gallery of Art, Washington D.C.

This painting was submitted and accepted for exhibition at the official Salon of 1870, and was also included in the second Impressionist show in 1876 as *Portrait Ce Soir*. Mme Camus was a doctor's wife and skilled pianist.

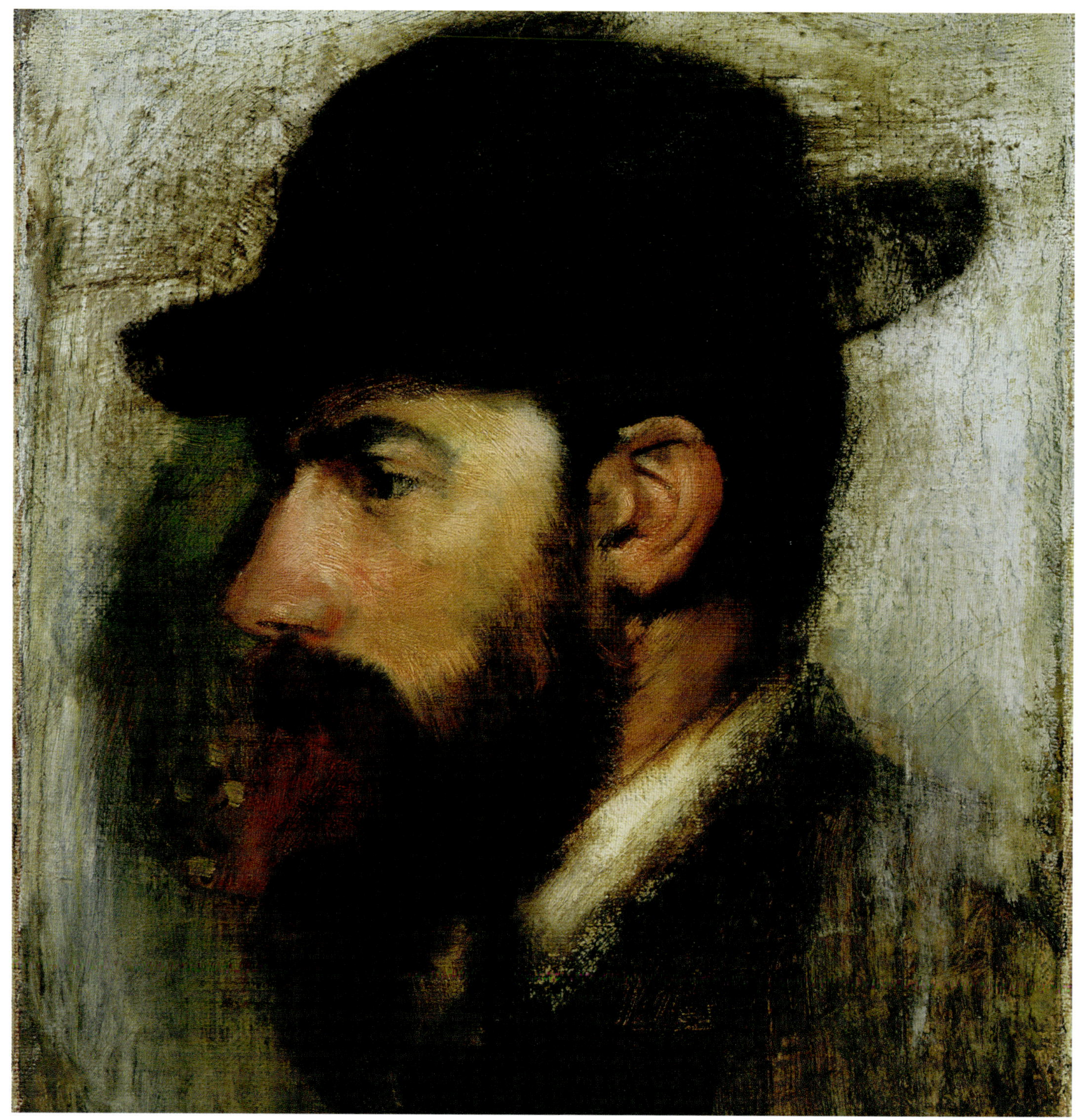

Portrait of Henri Rouart, 1871
Oil on canvas, 27 x 22 cm (10²/₃ x 8²/₃ in)
• Musée Marmottan Monet, Paris

This is a small oil study of Degas' friend Rouart for a much larger painting depicting the industrialist in front of his factory. This was painted shortly after the Franco-Prussian War, during which Rouart was Degas' commanding officer.

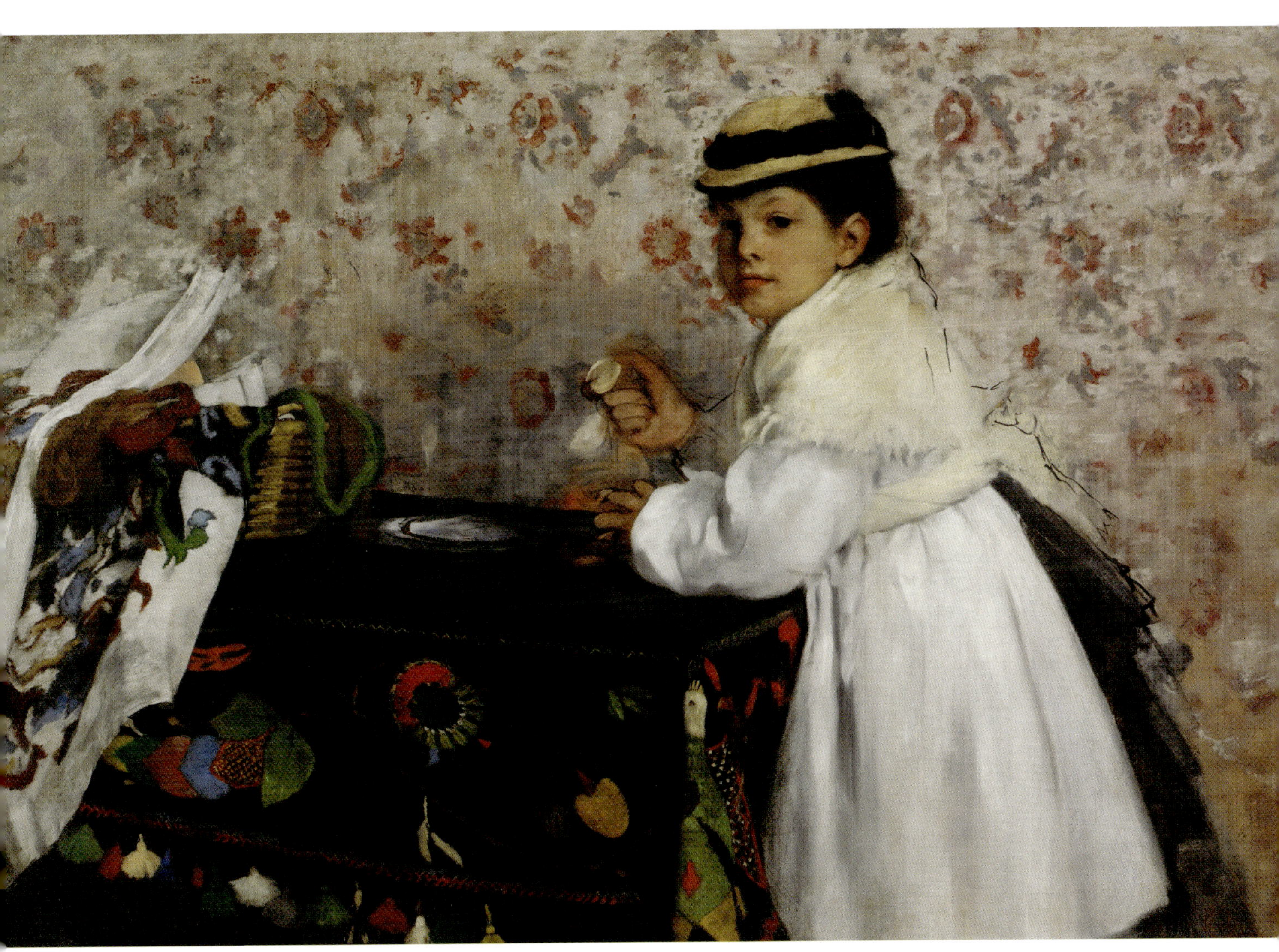

Portrait of Mlle Hortense Valpinçon, *c.* 1871
Oil on mattress ticking, 75.5 x 113.6 cm (30 x 44¾ in)
• The Minneapolis Institute of Arts, Minnesota

During the Paris Commune of 1871, Degas stayed with the Valpinçon family. This portrait
of their daughter makes overt reference to the artist's love for *Japonisme*, which was
popular at this time.

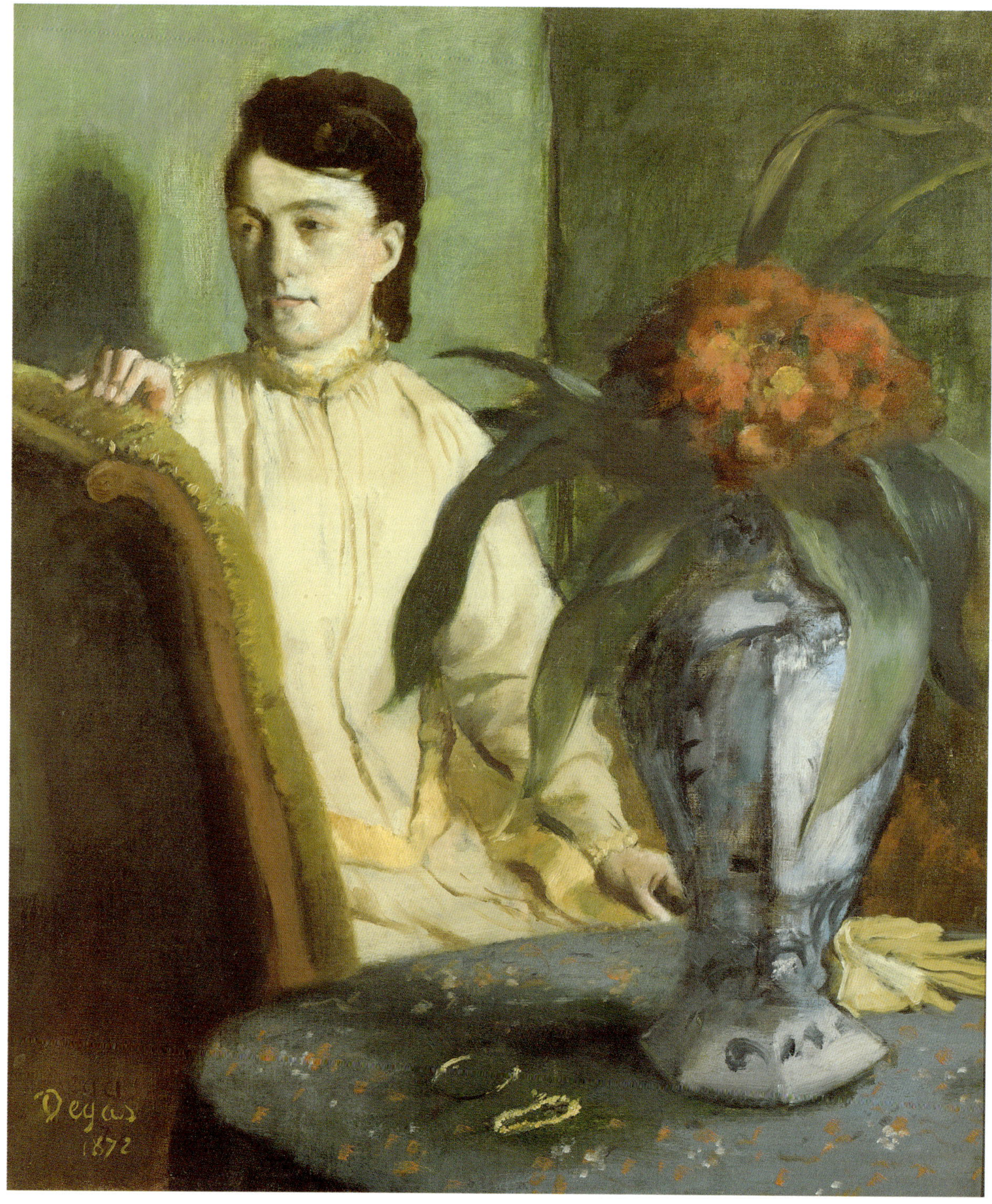

Woman with the Oriental Vase, 1872
Oil on canvas, 65 x 54 cm (25$^{1}/_{4}$ x 21$^{1}/_{4}$ in)
• Musée d'Orsay, Paris

This portrait is of Estelle Musson De Gas, the wife of Degas' brother René. She was blind and posed for Degas on three occasions while they were away in New Orleans.

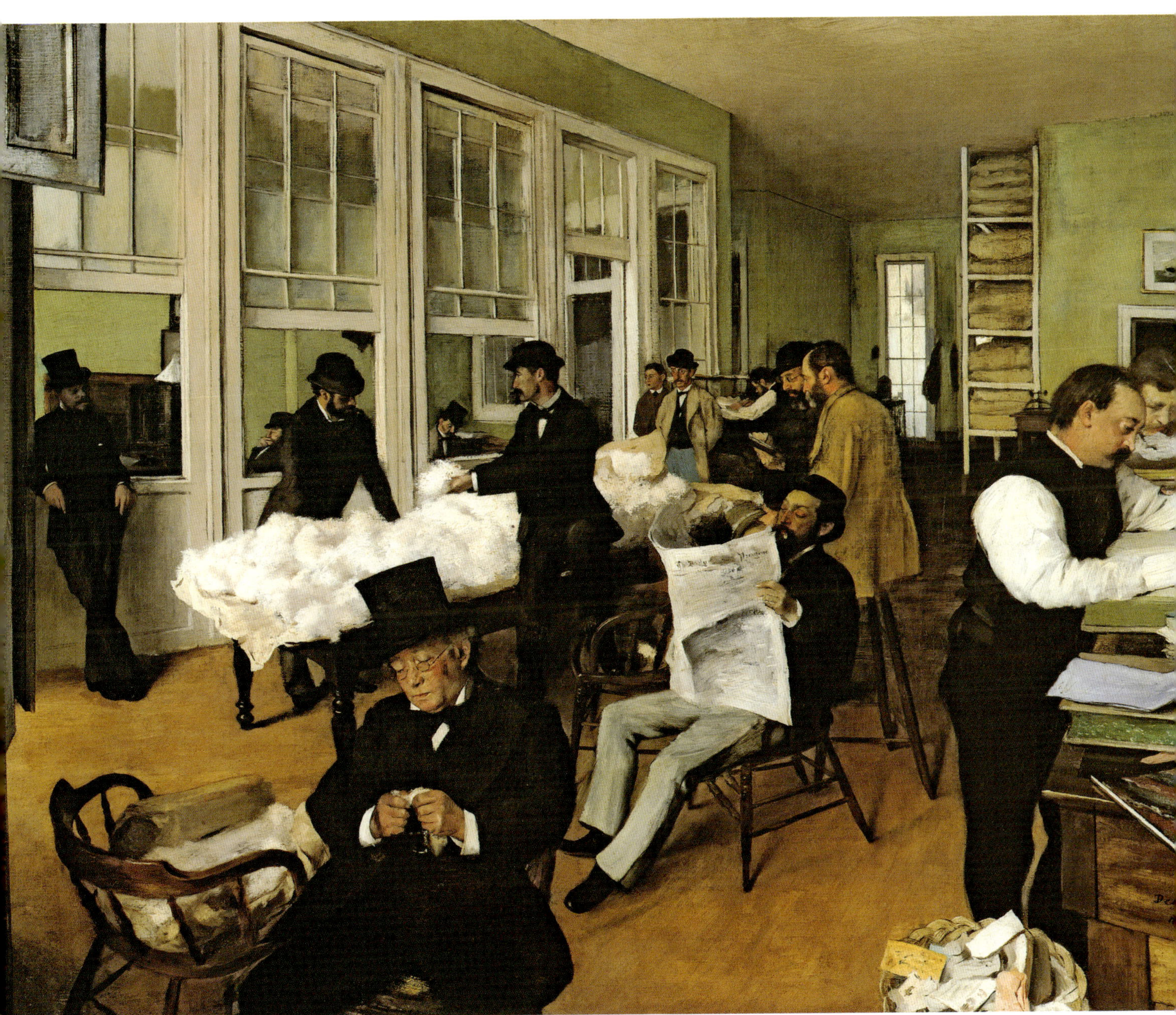

The Cotton Exchange, New Orleans, 1873
Oil on canvas, 73 x 92 cm (28¾ x 36¼ in)
• Musée des Beaux-Arts, Pau

Degas' brother René posed for this portrait reading a newspaper, the central figure disinterested in the hive of activity around him. Their uncle is seen in the foreground checking the quality of the cotton.

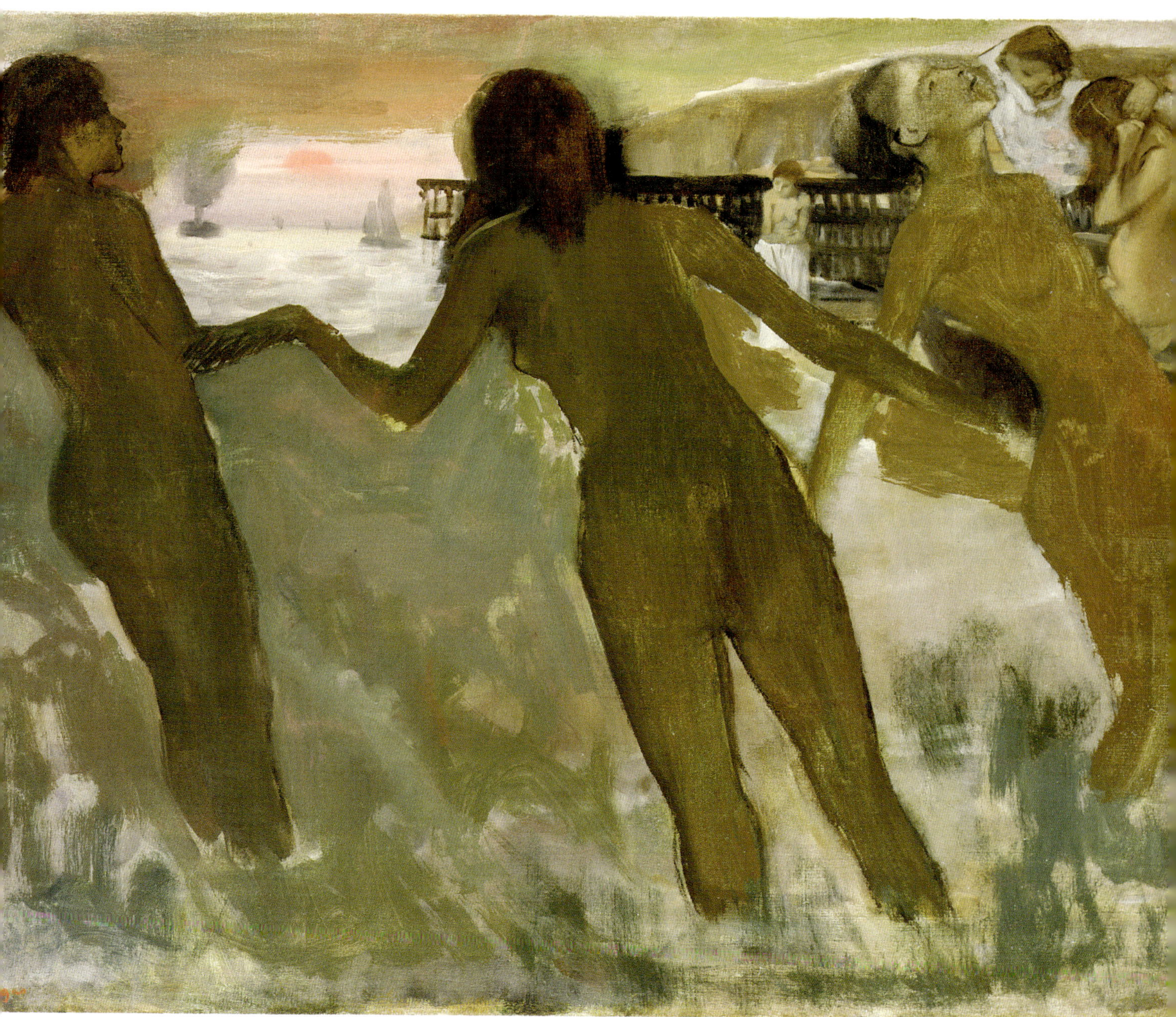

Peasant Girls Bathing in the Sea at Dusk, *c.* 1875–76
Oil on canvas, 65 × 84 cm (25²/₃ × 33¹/₄ in)
• Private Collection

Degas subverts the academic protocols for this painting by not clearly delineating the detailed forms of the girls for male consumption. In essence, the figures are almost abstracted from the human form.

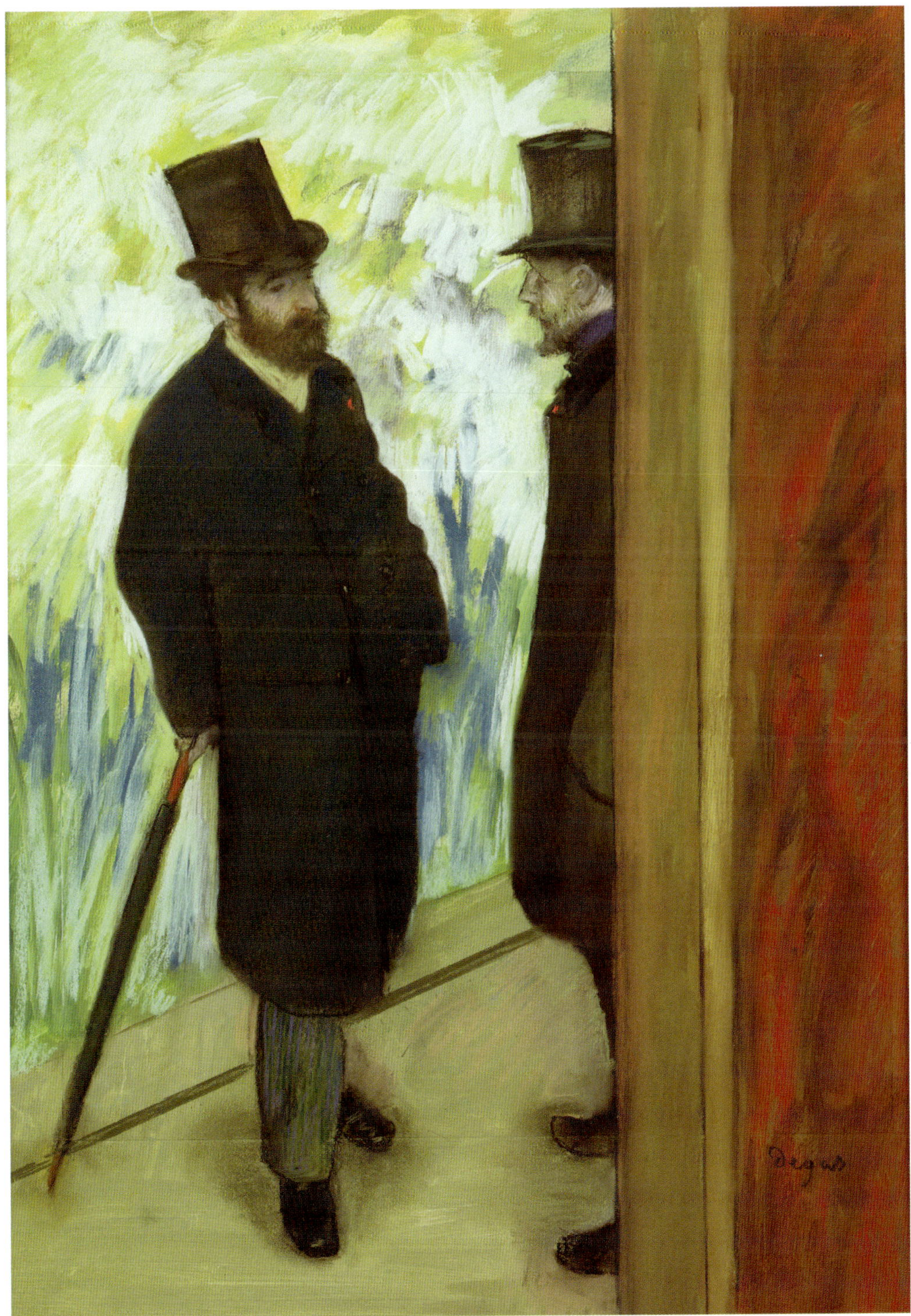

Friends at the Theatre, 1878–79
Pastel on paper, 79 x 55 cm (31 x 21²/₃ in)
• Musée d'Orsay, Paris

The writer Ludovic Halévy, one of the protagonists in this scene, purchased this picture in 1882. He is seen conversing with his friend Albert Cavé at the opera. It was shown at the fourth Impressionist exhibition in 1879.

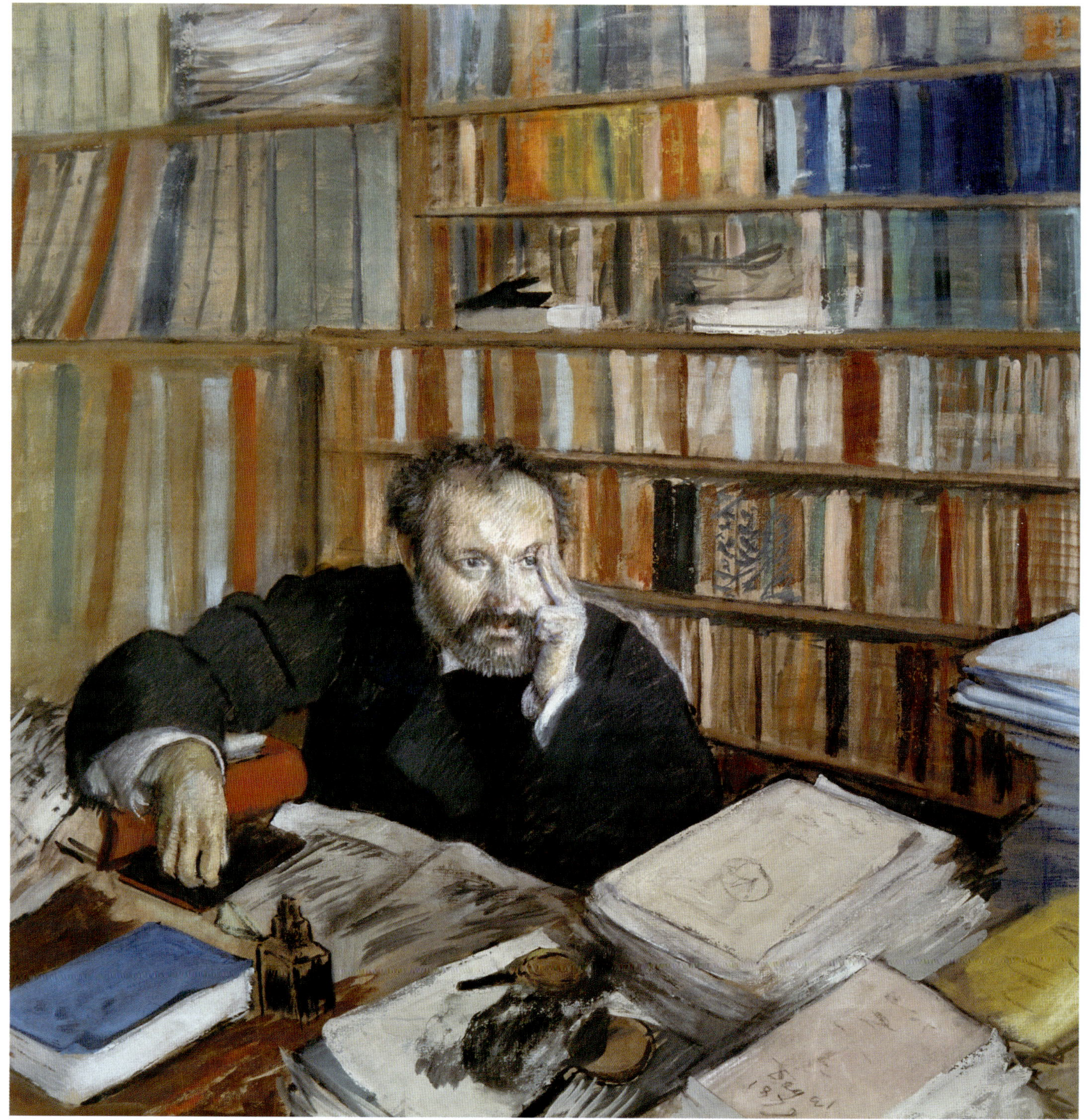

Edmond Duranty, 1879
Gouache and pastel on canvas, 100 x 100 cm (39$\frac{1}{3}$ x 39$\frac{1}{3}$ in)
• Glasgow Art Gallery and Museum, Glasgow

Degas perfectly captures the restless intelligence of his friend in this portrait, who is deep in thought and indifferent to the artist's presence. The writer and critic Duranty was influential to Degas' early success.

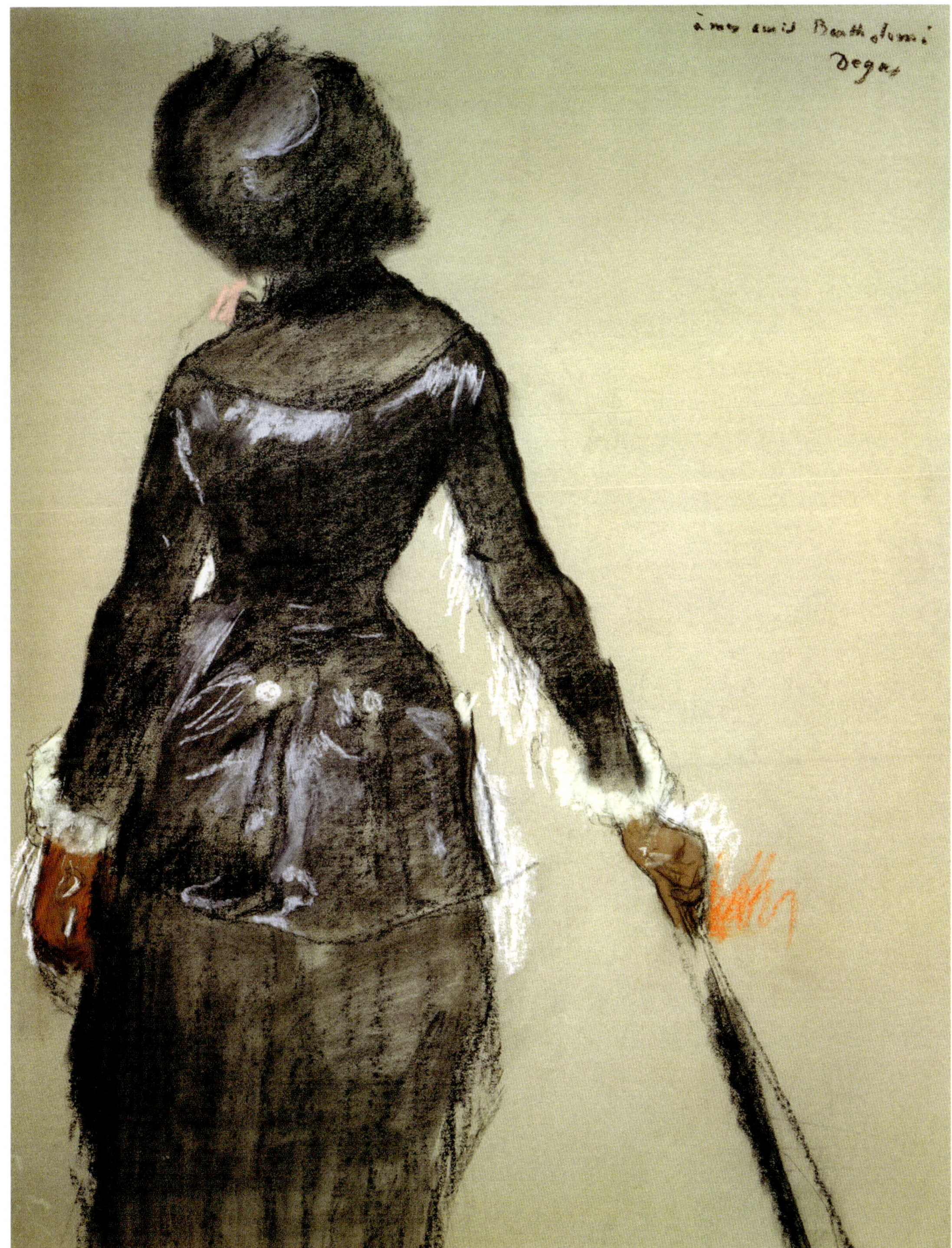

Mary Cassatt at the Louvre, *c.* 1880
Pastel on paper, 64 x 48 cm (25$^{1}/_{4}$ x 19 in)
• Private Collection

Degas' friend and fellow artist Mary Cassatt is captured perfectly, her elegant poise reflecting her upper-middle class background. Degas accompanied Cassatt and her sister on several trips to the Louvre.

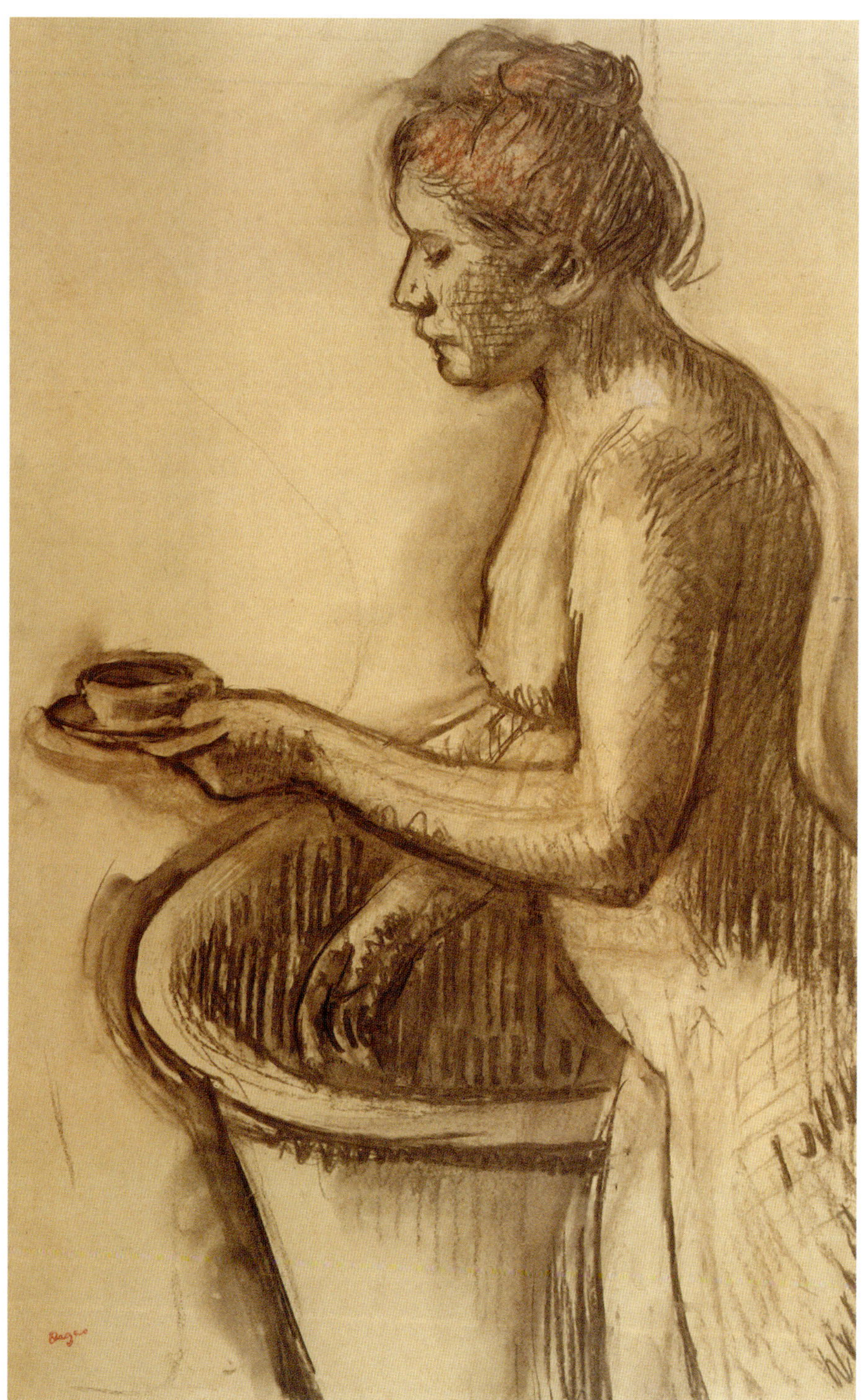

Female Nude, *c.* 1882–83

Charcoal on paper, • Private Collection

This is possibly a preliminary sketch for the work entitled *Breakfast After a Bath* (*see* page 119). The female nude shown here becomes the maid in the larger work, although in that picture she is fully dressed.

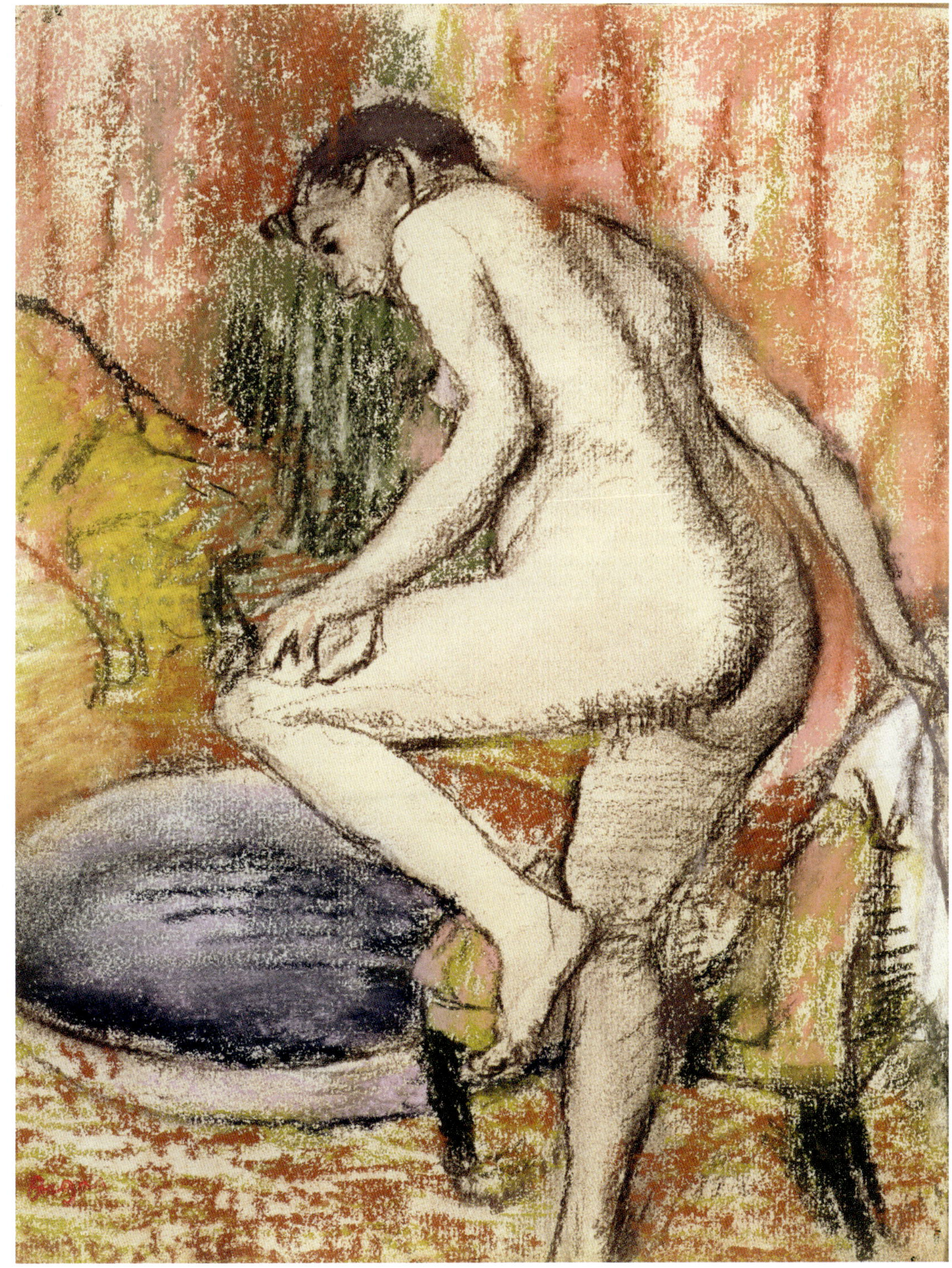

The Toilet, 1883
Pastel and chalk on paper, 30.5 x 24 cm (12 x 9$\frac{1}{3}$ in)
• Private Collection

Most of Degas' pictures in this genre are of naked women with their backs to the viewer, suggesting that we are voyeurs intruding on a private moment. These drawings were sometimes for personal consumption and not intended for exhibition.

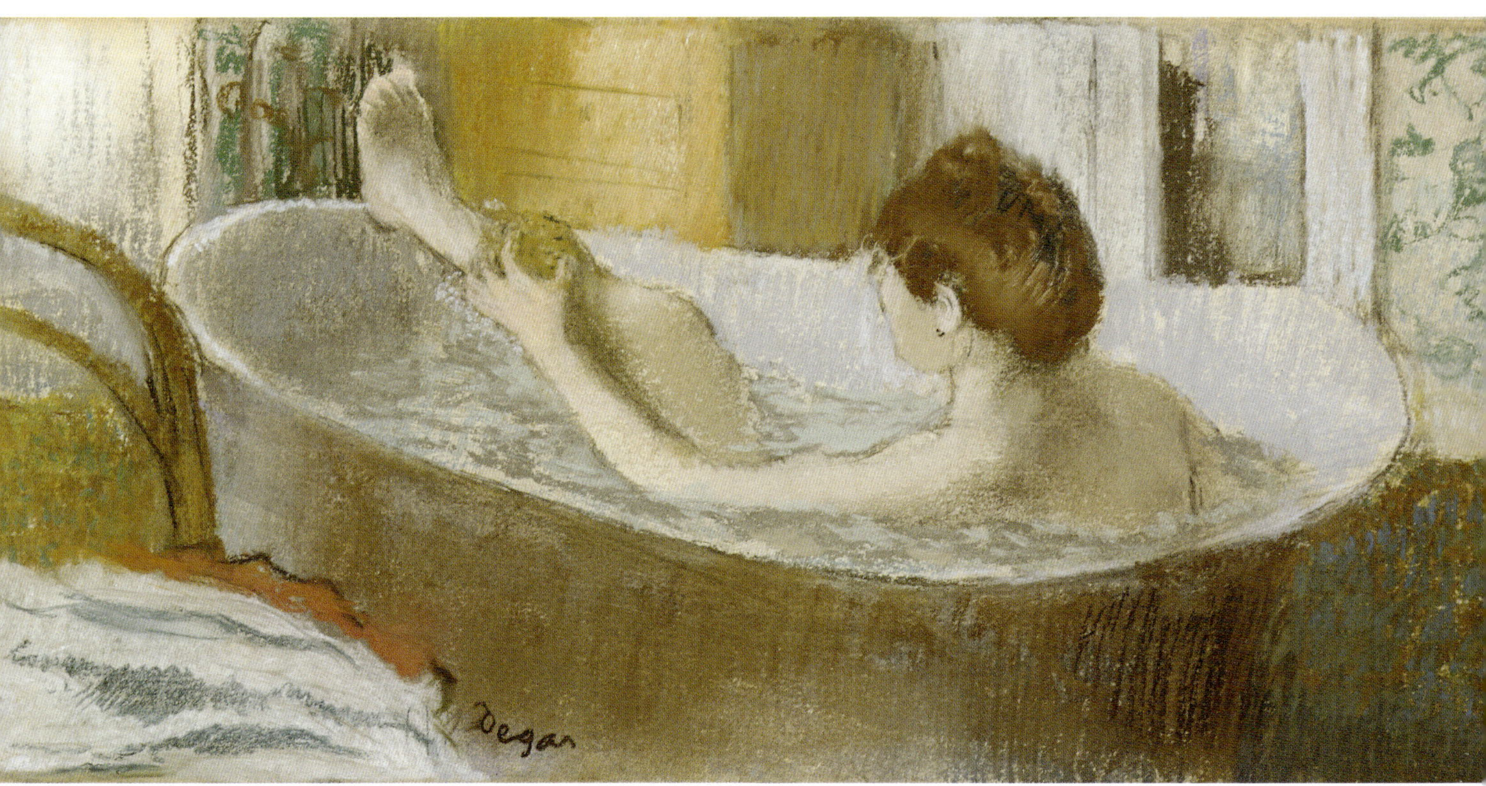

Woman in Her Bath, Sponging Her Leg, *c.* **1883**
Pastel on paper 19.7 x 41 cm (7⁴/₅ x 16 in)
• Musée d'Orsay, Paris

This picture was exhibited at the last Impressionist exhibition in 1886, a sensitive portrait of a woman bathing. The sensitivity is enhanced by the delicate use of pastel.

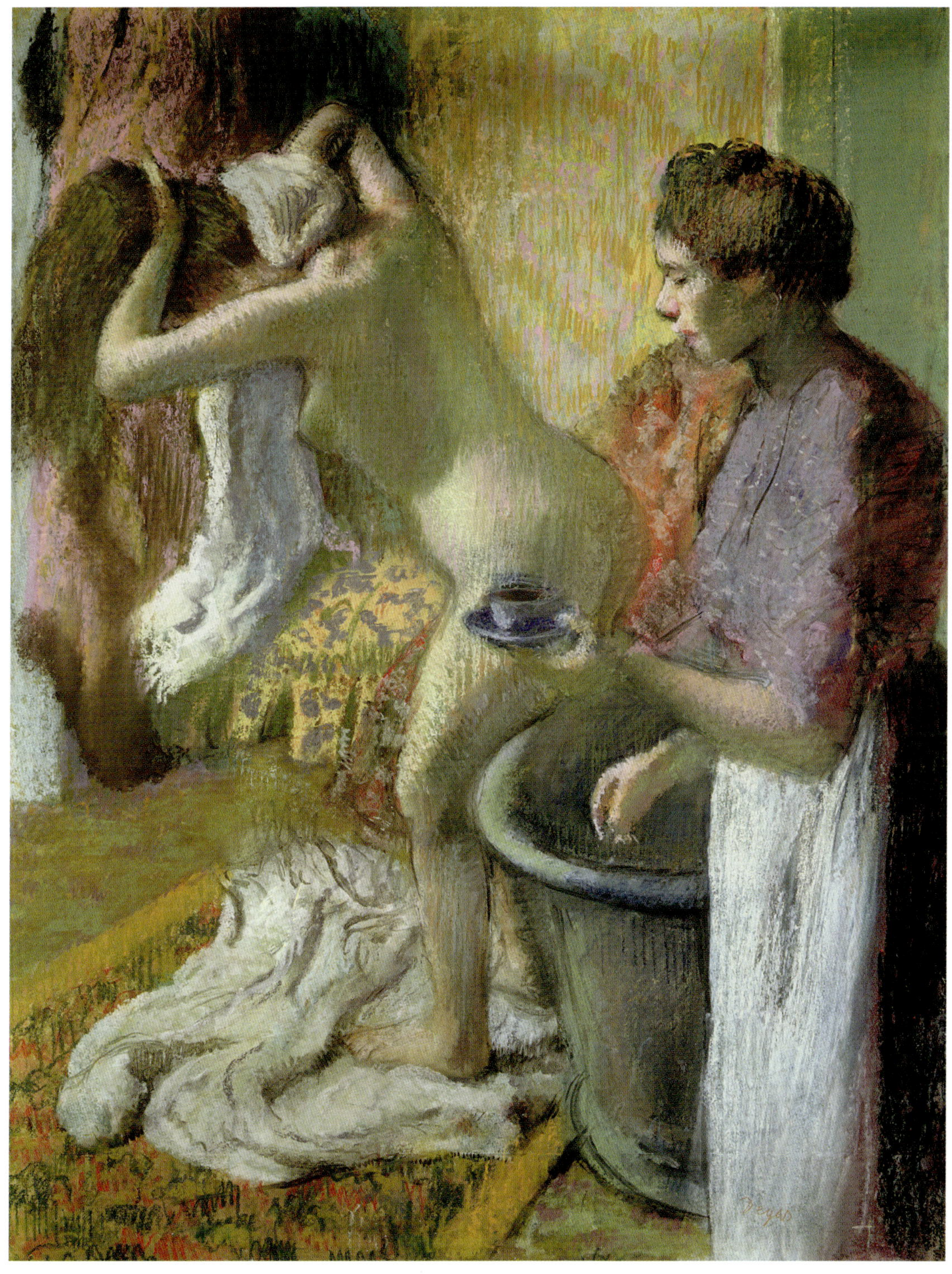

Breakfast After a Bath, 1883
Pastel on paper, 121 x 93 cm (47^2/$_3$ x 36^2/$_3$ in)
• Private Collection

This is a larger-than-normal format for a pastel drawing, but the space is well used by Degas, who fills every part of the composition using broad strokes of the pastel sticks.

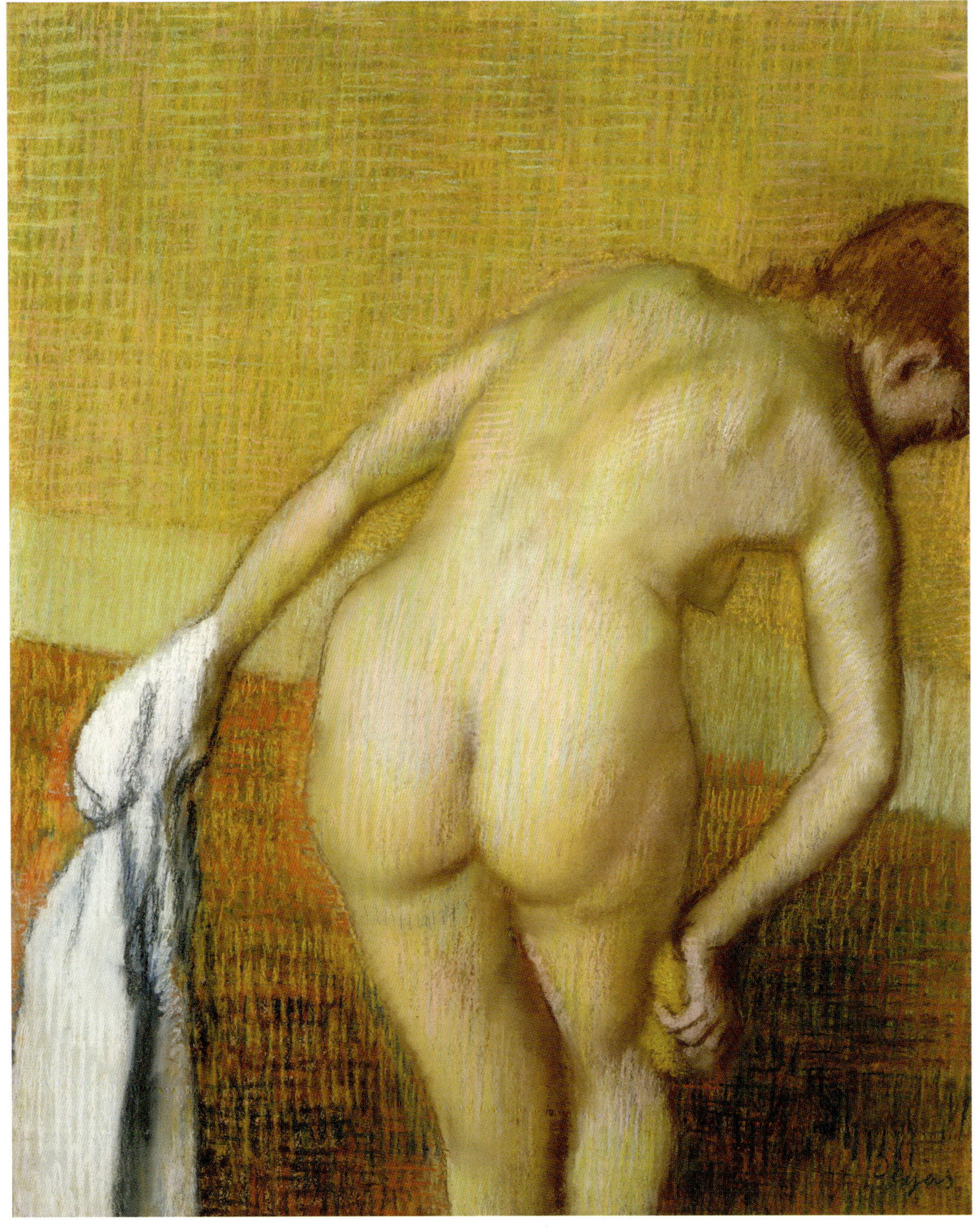

Woman Taking a Bath, 1886
Pastel on paper, 72 x 56 cm (28$\frac{1}{3}$ x 22 in)
• Private Collection

Though the artwork is titled *Woman Taking a Bath*, the subject shown here is not immersed in one. It was, however, customary to stand in a shallow tub of water and wash the body down.

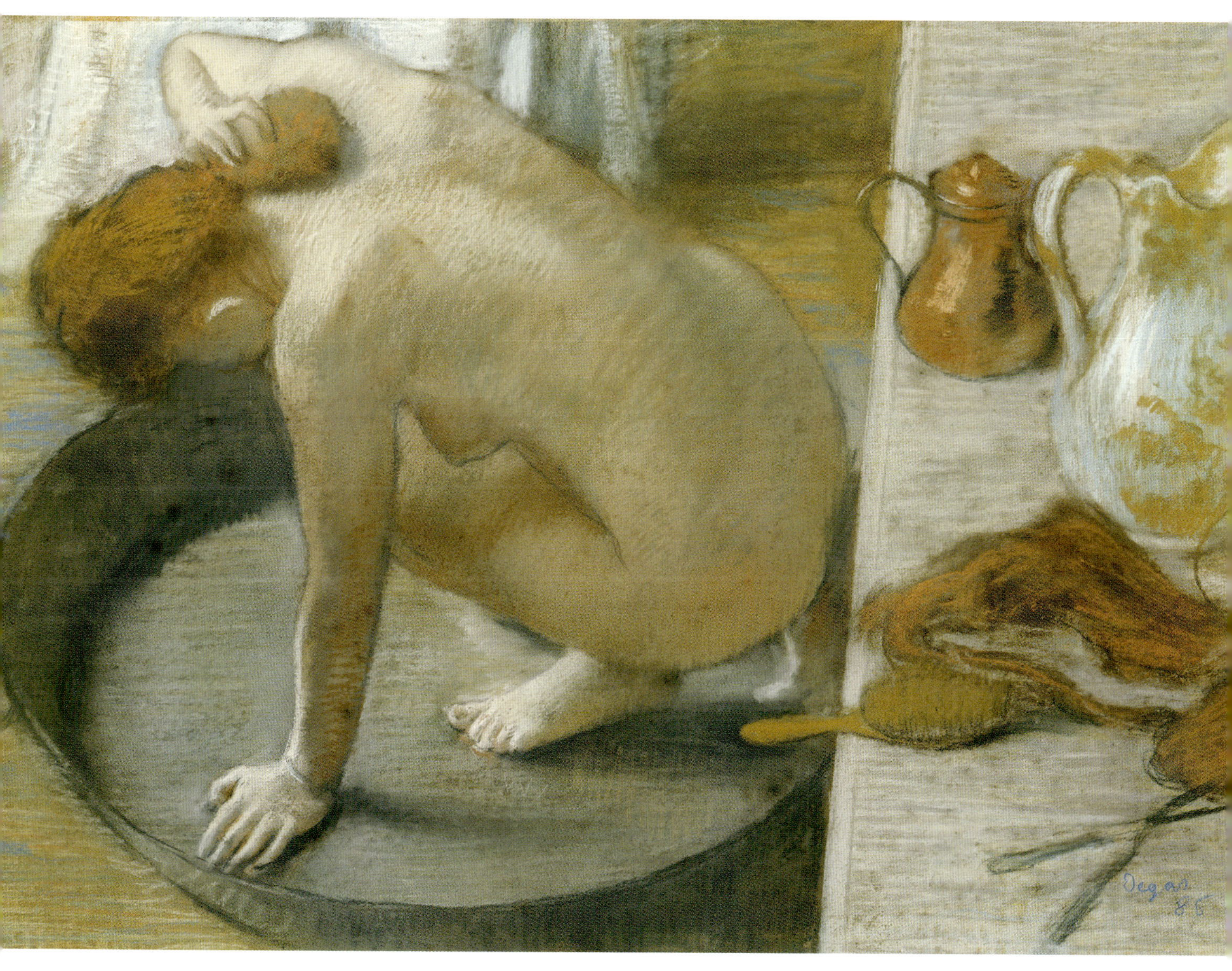

The Tub, 1886
Pastel on card, 60 x 83 cm (23²/₃ x 32²/₃ in)
• Musée d'Orsay, Paris

This picture was one of eight on the subject of the female nude that Degas submitted to the eighth and final Impressionist exhibition in 1886. The critics derided them as resembling 'animals'.

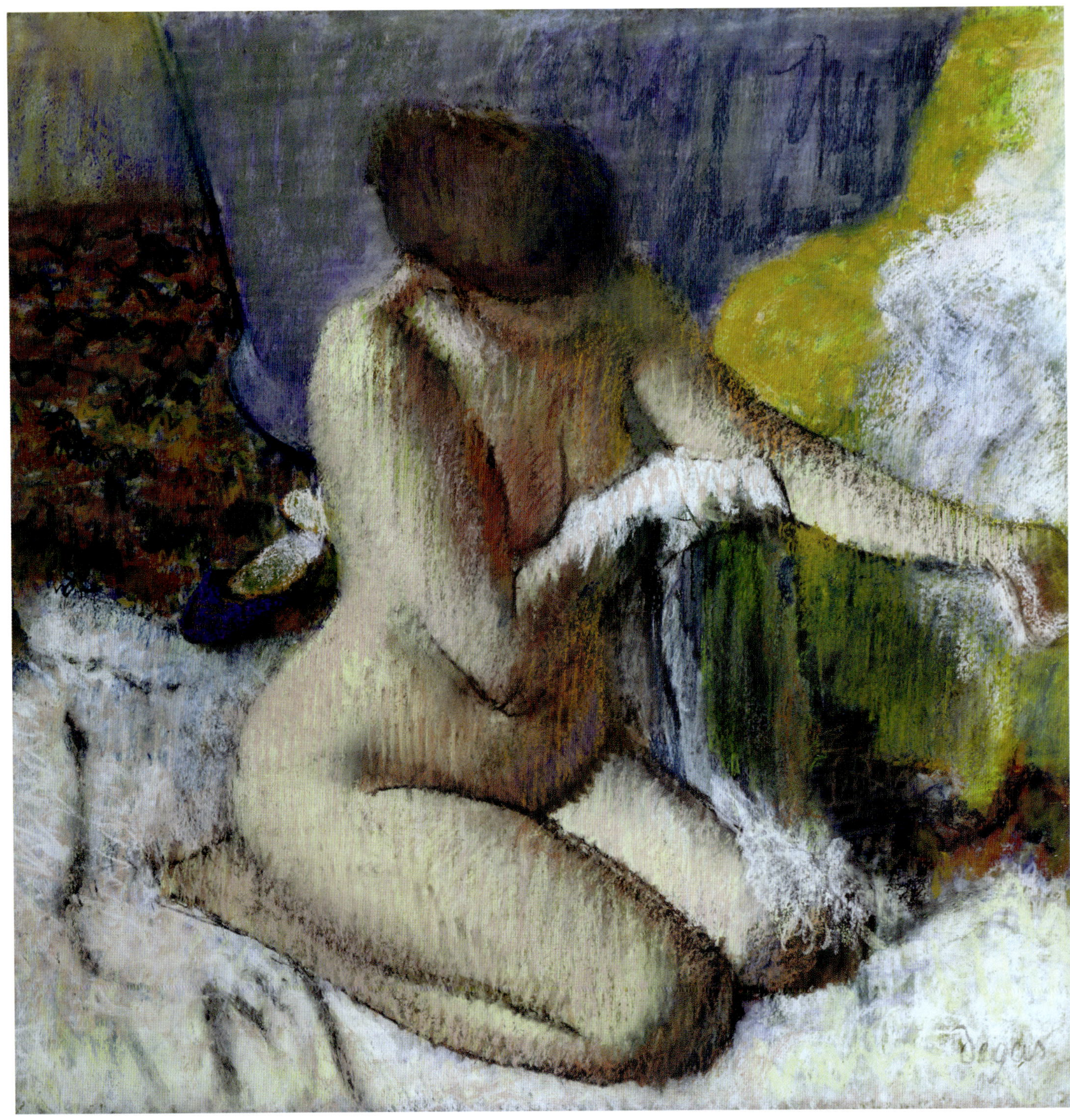

After the Bath, 1895
Pastel on mounted paper, 70 x 70 cm (27$^1/_2$ x 27$^1/_2$ in)
• Musée d'Orsay, Paris

Unusually for Degas, the nude is portrayed from the front. However, there is no coquettish glance towards the viewer. This is a private moment, but the intimate parts of her body are well concealed in the composition.

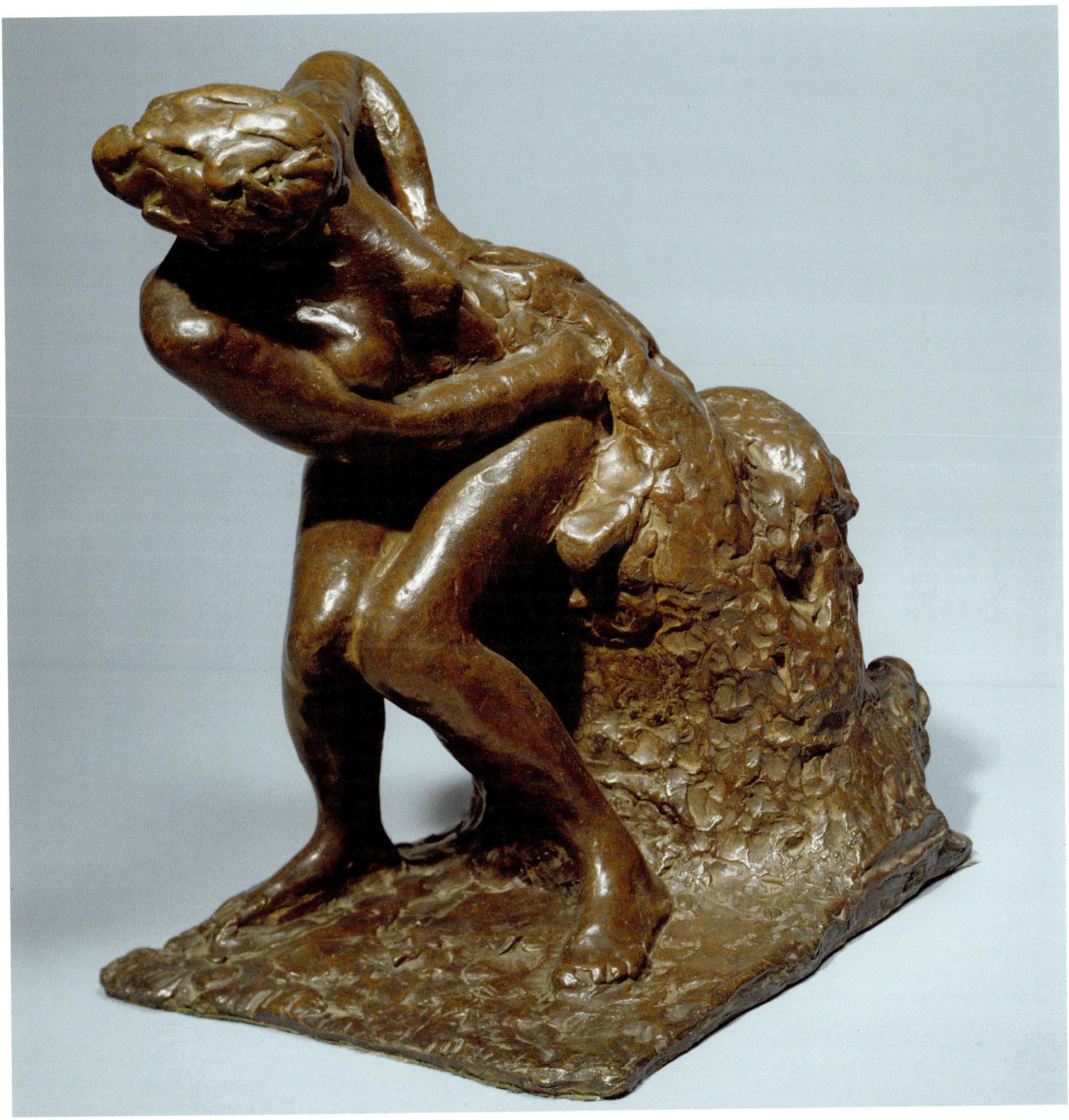

Woman Seated Drying her Left Side, *c.* 1896–1911
Bronze, height 33.5 cm (13¼ in)
• Private Collection

Degas was interested in the movements of the human body, the twists, turns and awkward poses, seeking to render them in two-dimensional works and sculpture. Like all of his sculptures, this was not intended for exhibition.

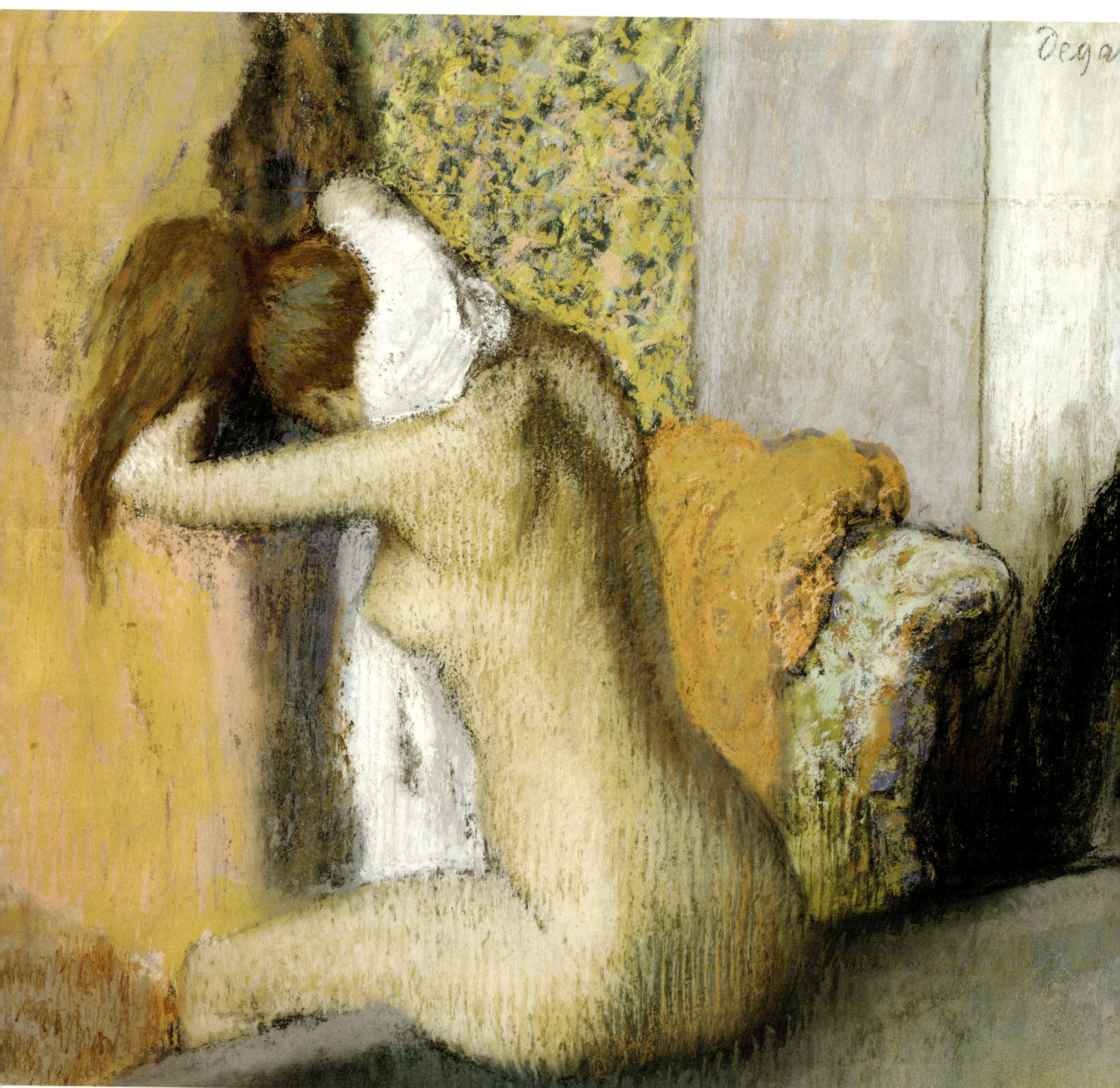

After the Bath, Woman Drying Her Neck, 1898
Pastel on mounted paper, 62.2 x 65 cm (24$\frac{1}{2}$ x 25$\frac{2}{3}$ in)
• Musée d'Orsay, Paris

Not exhibited in Degas' lifetime, the picture was for many years in the collection of the Durand-Ruel gallery before it came into state hands in 1914, being first held at the Louvre before its transfer to the Musée d'Orsay.

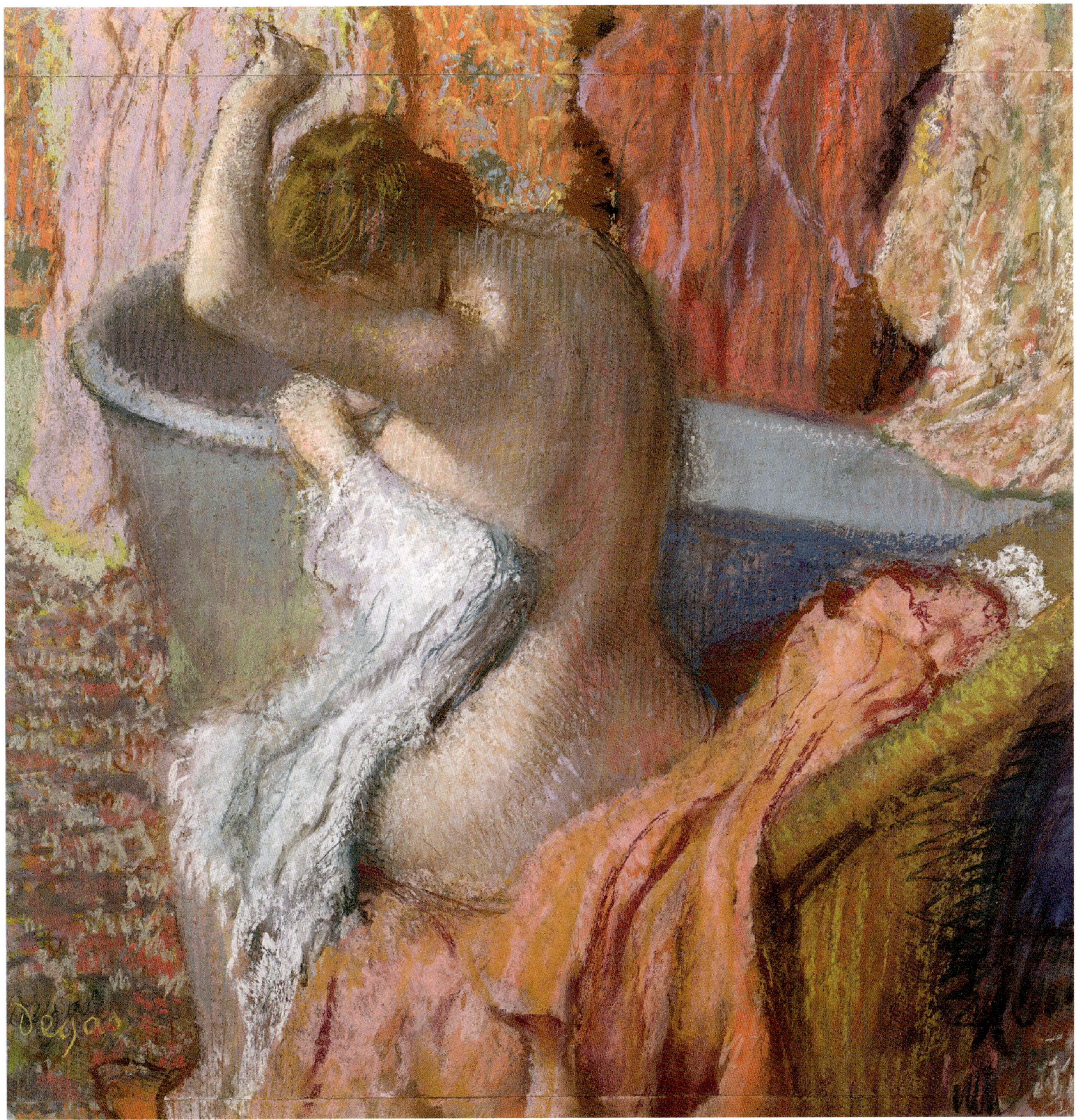

Seated Bather, 1899
Pastel on paper, 51 x 51 cm (20 x 20 in)
• Private Collection

This has to be the most sumptuous and decorative of all Degas' bathing scenes. The sinuous lines are redolent of the whiplash curves used in Art Nouveau design at this time.

Indexes

Index of Works

Page numbers in *italics* refer to
illustration captions.

General Index

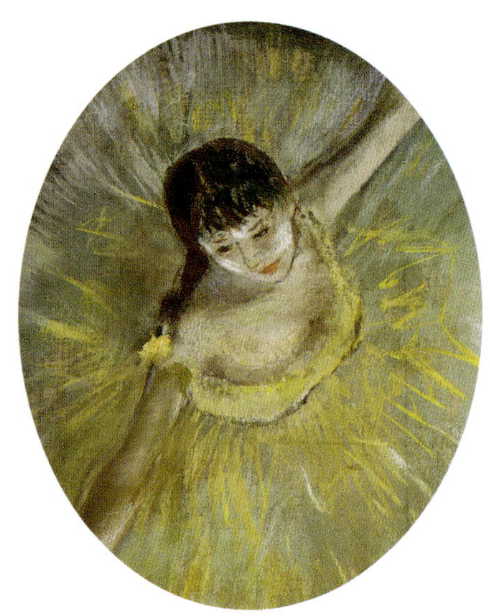

Masterpieces of Art
FLAME TREE PUBLISHING

A new series of carefully curated print and digital books covering the world's greatest art, artists and art movements.

If you enjoyed this book please sign up for updates, information and offers on further titles in this series at

blog.flametreepublishing.com/art-of-fine-gifts/